Love & Salt

A Spiritual Friendship Shared in Letters

AMY ANDREWS
JESSICA MESMAN GRIFFITH

LOYOLA PRESS.
A JESUIT MINISTRY
Chicago

LOYOLA PRESS.
A JESUIT MINISTRY

3441 N. Ashland Avenue
Chicago, Illinois 60657
(800) 621-1008
www.loyolapress.com

Portions of these letters have appeared in "It's a Wonderful Life," *Image* No. 50, and on Good Letters, the Image Blog.

Cover art credits: ©iStockphoto.com/diane555, ©iStockphoto.com/CSA_Images, Keattikorn/Veer, Leigh Prather/Veer

Library of Congress Cataloging-in-Publication Data
Andrews, Amy.
  Love & salt : a spiritual friendship shared in letters / Amy Andrews, Jessica Mesman Griffith.
       p. cm.
  Includes bibliographical references.
  ISBN-13: 978-0-8294-3831-4
  ISBN-10: 0-8294-3831-9
1. Andrews, Amy--Correspondence. 2. Griffith, Jessica Mesman--Correspondence.
3. Andrews, Amy--Religion. 4. Griffith, Jessica Mesman--Religion. 5. Female friendship--Religious aspects--Christianity. I. Griffith, Jessica Mesman. II. Title. III. Title: Love and salt.
  BR1713.A63 2013
  277.3'0830922—dc23
  [B]
                                                    2012037646

Printed in the United States of America.
13 14 15 16 17 18 Versa 10 9 8 7 6 5 4 3 2 1

A Letter is a Joy of Earth

It is denied the Gods.

—Emily Dickinson

Contents

for Clare and Carolyn

Prelude

In 2005, when we first began writing letters, we barely knew each other. We had no idea where this antiquated practice would lead, or what we would write. We only knew that we were both seeking God, that we both struggled with persistent doubt, and that somehow it would be better to seek and struggle together.

We had met several months earlier in Pittsburgh, at the end of graduate school, at that crucial last moment before everything changes—before jobs, marriages, houses, and children pin life down. We were away from home, jobless, and single. Jess arrived in Pittsburgh with a truck full of all her worldly possessions. For the first time in her life, she'd left Louisiana. Amy, on the other hand, had arrived already exhausted from a long line of moves, Pittsburgh being her fifth city, her eighteenth apartment since leaving her childhood home in rural Pennsylvania.

We met in a creative writing workshop. On the first day, all of us were enduring one of those awkward introductions, going around the table, describing our projects. We both confessed to writing about God—Jess about her Catholic and evangelical upbringing, Amy about growing up naturally religious in an agnostic household. We were both careful to conceal any current conviction, sensing we wouldn't be taken seriously if we admitted to belief. But for a second our eyes met across the table: *What, you too?*

When our workshop took an end-of-the-year trip to New York, we decided to stay on an extra day, just the two of us, crashing in the empty apartment of a friend. We'd been waiting for this chance to walk through the world alone and share our thoughts.

And that's what we did: we walked and talked, from one end of Manhattan to the other. It seemed unimportant where we went or what we did. There are vague memories of a bizarre black-and-white art flick, a play (something to do with angels), and a hot sandwich we bought from a street vendor and passed back and forth as we walked. We covered miles, pouring out our stories.

The day ended with what seems to us now almost a miracle. We walked into a bookstore for a few brief moments, just long enough for Amy to pull off the shelf a small pocket edition of the Old Testament Book of Ruth. What led us to that book? We can't remember. It's almost as if we walked in and someone said, "Oh, yes, here it is—the book you have come for."

That night, we sat shivering on the rooftop of our friend's apartment. The meatpacking district hummed below, but we felt cloistered from the world. We read the book aloud, passing it back and forth, alternately reading and listening with almost breathless attention. When Ruth, a widowed Moabite woman, is joined to the Israelites by proclaiming her undying loyalty to her mother-in-law, Naomi, we were electrified by the power of her ancient promise:

Whither thou goest, I will go.
Thy God shall be my God.

We were praying together for the first time, though we hardly realized it. In these two women—removed from us by centuries and cultures—we received a vision of friendship, a way of walking with each other toward God. But we could never have imagined the path we were starting down together.

A few weeks later, we left Pittsburgh: Jess for South Bend, Indiana, where she took a job at Notre Dame writing thank you letters to high-ticket donors; and Amy for Chicago, to return to teaching mathematics at DePaul. In a few months, we would both be married, Amy to a philosophy grad student, Jess to another writer. Our friendship was so new, and we both had such bad track records of keeping up with long-distance friends, that it seemed our connection would dim as quickly as it had flared.

Then Amy declared that she was converting, a decision that seemed somehow traceable to our long walk through New York. She asked Jess to be her sponsor.

How could we go down this path together, across a distance, in the midst of establishing new marriages and new careers? We decided to write letters—one letter for each day of Lent that would culminate in Amy entering the Church at Easter. But what began as a Lenten discipline soon became a habit, and we continued to write for years.

We wrote to preserve and make sense of our daily lives; we wrote to confess and console, to rant and grieve. But more than anything else, we wrote because it was the only way we knew how to pray. After a pause in our correspondence, the old alienation would creep back in, the sinking sense that there is no God, that it's all a big ruse of biology or history, and that we are fools. In our letters, we wrote ourselves back to belief.

After five years, we had between us over a thousand pages of largely handwritten letters. We compiled and bound them, photocopying each page, as a Christmas gift for each other. Reading them for the first time in their entirety, we saw that they told a story of two young women walking together through the trials of daily life, trading back and forth the role of guide and pilgrim, doubter and believer. Again and again, if one of us stumbled in the darkness, the other lit the lantern that helped her to make out the path to God.

When we faced tragedy together, our letters became the fulfillment of the vow we had made, however unwittingly, that first night in New York: *Whither thou goest, I will go.*

I

Conversion

Sir, more than kisses, letters mingle souls;
for, thus friends absent speak.
—John Donne

Lent 2005

Your letter made me think of all the little secret evasions I conduct every day, especially spiritual ones. I transpose the truth in my head, thinking that I pray, if I pray at all, for God's sake rather than my own. It's not as if God needs to be shored up by a decade or two of Hail Marys from the second floor of 1720 West Summerdale.

—Amy, February 12

• • • • • • •

I don't know that I've ever felt the presence of God in prayer. He seems to show up when we least expect him. But even if we don't feel that presence, should we pray anyway? We can't judge the fruits of any practice solely on the basis of our feelings. Prayer is either objectively worth something or it isn't.

—Jess, March 1

February 9, 2005
Ash Wednesday

Dear Amy,

Last night I made a solemn promise that each morning this Lent, I would get up at 5 a.m., pray the great Lenten prayer of St. Ephraim, and write a letter to you.

Day 1, and I've already blown it. The alarm went off at 5, and I hit snooze until 6:45, then turned it off altogether and went back to sleep until 7:15, at which point I tore from the bed to the shower and rinsed my bangs out instead of washing all my hair in an effort to make it to work on time. I was still fifteen minutes late, and I realized when I got there that I'd broken my Ash Wednesday fast by drinking coffee. Thankfully, I didn't have time to eat breakfast. I'm not a very good Catholic. Maybe it's ridiculous of me to even hope I could be a good sponsor.

At least I hoped that this Lent, by some daily sacrifice, I might be delivered from my sloth. Last week, I actually used prayer as an excuse to stay in bed an extra thirty minutes, pretending that I was praying the rosary when really I was just dozing.

And instead of writing to you last night, I fought with Dave about our future and then went with him to Corby's to watch the Notre Dame versus Boston College basketball game on the big screen and drink Miller Lite in plastic cups. The Irish won, and the beer helped us forget about our fight.

> How many times have I promised,
> Yet every time I failed to keep my word.
> But disregard this according to Thy Grace.

> —St. Ephraim

Tomorrow I will try again.

Love,

Jess

February 9, 2005

Dear Jess,

Today I received a rejection letter from one of the teaching jobs I applied for and immediately flew into a frenzy about my life. I stewed the afternoon away and then offered to pick up Mark from a lecture on Hegel he had attended down in Hyde Park. I think I did it just so that I could have him trapped in the car for half an hour to listen to my rantings, which were half directed at him, of course. I railed about the sad state of my life and how I am admirably ferocious and he too calm to realize the need for ferocity. "It will all work out," he managed to get in at one point. And I shot back, "Yes, *I* will make it work out and have a breakdown in the process." We arrived at home and didn't speak, staring at books in different rooms.

I've been reading the *Revelations of Divine Love*. Even in her bleakest hours Julian of Norwich begged God to come to her. I don't share her yearning for God, but I yearn to yearn for God. Hegel defines a human as the only creature who desires desire. Animals desire a particular end; their desires want simple satisfaction. We desire *desire* itself, always wanting to want more, or to want something else. Right now, though, even this does not seem to be the reason I am converting.

Actually, the reason is a bit of a mystery to me. I feel compelled to convert, the way I felt compelled to marry Mark. I didn't even try to drum up the doubts so that I could reason past them; I just knew that I should marry him and discover the reasons later. But some days my lack of desire for God astonishes me, and I think that

I should pray for desire, but I shy away from even that. What would God strike me with if I asked for such a desire? Might I shave my head or give away all my things?

So here is my first Lenten resolution: every day for the next forty days I will write to you and try to confess the state of my soul and some of the story that has brought me to conversion. Maybe by telling you I will begin to make sense of it.

I'm enclosing a little gift, an icon of Ruth and Naomi. Ruth was a gleaner, so she is shown offering a sheaf of grain to Naomi. Instead of sheaves, I will send you letters. Actually I'm not sure which of us plays which role. I am older so that suggests Naomi, but you are already Catholic, so it is I who must say, "And thy God my God."

Love,
Amy

February 10, 2005

Dear Amy,
Today is my boss's birthday, and we all went to Starbucks this morning and sat in a circle and told stories about our most memorable birthdays.

Here's mine: Moments before my eighth birthday party—Ms. Pac-Man cake on the table, streamers and balloons hanging from the ceiling—my mom was arrested. It turned out to be a case of mistaken identity. But it was my first hint of what it would feel like when something took her from me for good. I remember sitting next door at the Carusos' house, staring out their bay window at the police cruiser in our driveway, panic gripping my heart.

Only in telling the story did I realize that the women I work with might find it weird and morbid, so I tried instead to be funny about it. Of course, others had happier stories to tell: Libby remembered the cutest boys on her block making her a lopsided cake for her twelfth birthday; Teri remembered her twentieth, walking with a boy she didn't yet know would be her husband, the electric and awkward feeling of his arm around her waist. Sitting there, drinking coffee with a group of women, hearing their fondest memories and seeing the looks of joy on their faces, it was actually a beautiful way to spend thirty minutes. I almost forgot how much I hate my job.

But I wanted to write about the Ash Wednesday Mass. Dave and I went to the basilica in the evening, and it was packed. We were thirty minutes early and lucky to get a seat. It was beautiful, as it always is here. The Brothers of the Holy Cross flooded the aisle with their purple robes. I love that even the president of Notre Dame is just one of these men—he disappears into the Mass with the rest of them, all mouthing the words behind the celebrant, all raising their hands and saying, "This is my body; this is the cup of my blood."

And yet I was still homesick for Sacred Heart in Pittsburgh. It felt like an Ingmar Bergman movie in there: dark, cavernous, eternally winter. It always seemed to be just me, the cantor with the Peter Brady crack in his voice, and the old foggy priest with the great sweep of silver hair and booming voice. When he said, "Remember! You are dust, and to dust you shall return!" it sounded like the very voice of God. He'd grip my skull as he ground the sign of the cross on my forehead, working in the ashes with the proper gravity. Last night, the priest who gave me my ashes was the sculptor who drank whiskey with me and Dave at the ethics conference.

Now I've got to go sing "Happy Birthday" in the break room.

Love,

Jess

February 10, 2005

Dear Jess,

Well, today I desire God, or at least the sad God of Ash Wednesday. As I walked into the church yesterday, everything seemed draped with mystery, and I wasn't sure how to act or what would happen. I have never experienced anything quite like it before. After the long, initial hush, a single handbell tolled and the procession walked down the central aisle. The chant choir sang, "Lord have mercy, Christ have mercy, Lord have mercy," again and again, as the solo *Kyries* rang out over the top. And then later, when the priest crossed my forehead with ashes, I felt overwhelmed with gratitude. Isn't that strange? I felt grateful right as someone was telling me I was going to die. Well, I think about death all the time anyway, but here I saw death being confronted as I think it should—a tragedy, but not the final word.

I am struggling right now with one of Julian of Norwich's revelations of divine love. God places in her hand a little thing, the size of a hazelnut and round as a ball. She thinks, *What can this be?* And then it comes to her that the hazelnut is all that is made. She looks upon the little ball and knows she must see the world as insignificant in order to love God.

For Julian, seeing all of existence made small was somehow an aid to reaching God. So she interpreted this vision as a divine revelation. I hope if I'm ever granted such a vision it will be of an almost opposite nature—all of the world, or at least my part in it, handed back to me. Instead of the world being small as a hazelnut, it would be as large as it is yet still capable of being grasped. I can't bear how life is constantly slipping away, falling into the past and out of mind.

I'm hoping that through Lent, being drawn for the first time through the life of Christ—not reading it in one sitting or watching it dramatized, but moving through the story—might show me how to get beyond this tragic view of life. For the story of Christ is the story of how something unimaginably large and all-encompassing is contained and revealed by a single life.

One of the great surprises to me about Mass is how it tells a story, over and over, on every Sunday and through every year. And it doesn't just tell the story (as one might be told in a didactic sermon) but plays it out, letting us enter it ourselves. In his homily tonight, Father Brian said that Christ is the beginning, the end, and the plot of every story; if we want to know the meaning, we must keep our eyes fixed on him. It makes me think of something Tolkien wrote in his essay on fairy stories:

> This story [the Christian story] begins and ends in joy. It has pre-eminently the inner consistency of reality. There is no tale ever told that men would rather find was true, and none which so many skeptical men have accepted as true on its own merits. For the Art of it has the supremely convincing tone of Primary Art, that is of Creation. To reject it leads either to sadness or to wrath.

He doesn't rest his faith on history or logic or testimony but on the merits of the story itself. Tolkien believes that the truest things are necessarily in story form. And he doesn't seem to restrict truth to the Christian story, for he even goes so far as to say that *all* good tales may eventually come true (though in radically different forms than we might imagine). But only by entering a story can one really see it for what it is (only by marrying can one know marriage). This is another way to explain why I'm converting: I want to enter the story.

—Amy

February 11, 2005

Dear Amy,

I've been thinking a lot about last year's Lent. You and I had just met, and we were still circling each other, wondering if we would be great friends or archrivals.

I'd walk to Sacred Heart on Fridays at 3 p.m. for the stations of the cross. I'd sit in the last pew and watch the schoolchildren file in behind their teachers, and feel so grateful for the unchanged rhythm of the "Stabat Mater," the heads dipping in formation, the touching of scabby knees to kneelers. I remembered my younger self in Catholic-school dress doing the same, unwittingly preparing for my own passion and the pain that was bound to come—it did come, when my mother died. We've been dipping, touching, singing this same refrain for centuries, and will be for centuries to come.

Last year it all seemed so magical to me, but now, I feel depleted. Last night, I sat on the sofa and read a book I want to review, a new interpretation of the way of the cross, while I stared at Dave's back as he sat working away on his book in the other room. The house was very quiet, and I began to feel that I might have something important to say about it all, but then I picked up the pen, and it just floated away. I determined that I'd get up early this morning and read it all again, try to get it back.

But of course, the alarm sounded, and I hit the snooze button. I think I'd better pray and write to you at night instead.

—Jess

February 11, 2005

Dear Jess,

When I was little, God lived in the trees and the animals and the sky. But when I grew old enough to be aware of myself in the world, the natural world seemed to draw back, and so did God. I remember kneeling by my bed to pray. These were the first of my awkward prayers, usually offered when I was upset. "Please God, I promise to be good, if only . . ." I would listen to the silent room and wonder.

For a long time then, God seemed distant and fleeting, something to be grasped in only brief glimpses. This is the God of James Joyce's delicate and evanescent moments. This is Sylvia Plath's angel, flaring suddenly at the elbow. I remember one time in particular when I stepped out, alone, onto the deck of a boat and saw the moon shining across the lake. Suddenly, inexplicably, I felt a deep peace. I remember thinking that I could die right then and there and feel satisfied. But usually God was hidden.

Then in college, during my brief stint as a born-again, God was the leader of the campus fellowship. He was one of those fervent believers who tries to look like an apostle, with a shaggy beard and head. I felt his legalistic gaze on me wherever I went. I felt as if I lived in a box. Every thought was scrutinized for its potential evil and its potential spiritual significance. I felt a tremendous pressure for something to happen, but instead of lightning bolts I just felt the walls of the box narrowing around my head.

After I left the fellowship, God oscillated between being the box and being hidden. I guess there were a few times he showed himself—once when I was on a train across Scotland, once in the middle of the night. But again these were just fleeting sensations of peace or joy—inklings, nothing more.

I have long wanted God to live closer to my mind and more continuously in it. I'm sure he does (if he's there at all), but I don't see him. Now, I think, God lives at St. Gregory's. When I go out for walks, sometimes I peer up the block and see the ruddy bricks of the church in the distance. I picture God inside, in the ashes, draped on the high wooden cross, in the faint smell of incense, or shining from the windows. And sometimes I walk past, just to be closer, just a wall of bricks away from God. You wouldn't think it would be too much to ask, only four blocks away, to come for a visit, but he seems to keep his distance. I know the problem is really me, and that is why I am trying to pray.

I need to pick a patron saint. I am thinking of Teresa of Ávila. She struggled with many of the same things I do: distraction and discomfort during prayer, intense love for her friends, and vanity. I plan to follow in her footsteps. She kept her friends by founding a new convent and bringing them with her. But instead of a convent of many, I will found a hermitage. I like to imagine that this is what we are doing with our letters, creating a little cell, a place for our conversation apart from the world.

Love,
Amy

February 12, 2005

Dear Amy,
I love the icon of Ruth and Naomi. I think that as your sponsor I'm supposed to be giving you gifts, not the other way around. See—you're already a better Catholic than I am.

I may have been baptized Catholic as a baby, but the church I'm coming to know as an adult sometimes bears little resemblance to the church of my childhood, and I'm beginning to wonder how much of that existed only in my imagination.

As a child, I never heard the word *catechism*. I couldn't have told you the first thing about dogma or doctrine. I didn't know who Thomas Aquinas was until I met Dave. The church I knew really was the church of New Orleans, a cultural church full of folk tradition and apocryphal belief.

Most people we knew were Catholic, and everyone we knew was Christian; there were no clear lines between our school years at Our Lady of Lourdes and summers at Vacation Bible School at the Baptist church, or marking an X on the windshield when a black cat crossed in front of our car and praying to St. Anthony for a lost earring. All seemed to coexist peacefully with a highly attentive, personal God sitting sovereign, as real as the sun or the moon, responsive to the most minute details of our daily comings and goings, ready to dispatch a colorfully robed saint at a moment's notice. I've always imagined God and the saints as extravagantly adorned as the figures that decorate Mardi Gras floats, which probably also explains my tendency to conflate Scripture with Greek and Roman mythology and to conceive of God as a deity who can be placated, hidden from, bargained with, and sometimes even outsmarted.

Much of this is what my dad rejected as superstitious, nonessential, and downright blasphemous according to his Bible-alone way. I haven't completely escaped his influence—I still can't pray the rosary without wondering whether Jesus really approves.

Today at the museum, I saw a painting of the Black Madonna of Częstochowa, given to Notre Dame by some Polish Carmelite sisters. The placard said that Black Madonnas symbolize cultural perspectives not emphasized in traditional doctrine. In other words, they belong not to the realm of theology but to that of lived faith. Some people (and maybe some of those Carmelite sisters) believed that the Black Madonnas had been miraculously darkened. But there is a theory that they date from pre-Christian history, from days of nature worship, and were merely baptized by the early Church like so many other pagan traditions. I love the idea that the pagan reverence for Mother Earth was realized in Mary, the new Ceres or Demeter, and that Christianity is the realization of all those old, searching myths, the truths held close by generations.

All this would leave my dad apoplectic. But the church of my childhood brought religion to life in a way theology never could.

—Jess

February 12, 2005

Dearest Jess,

It was so thrilling to see your first letter sitting there in my box. I don't know, but I would hate to lose that thrill by switching to e-mail. At first we thought we would be alternating in the standard way, but the demand of a letter a day will make that impossible. I think our correspondence will be different, more like an ongoing conversation, which draws upon the whole body of things we have said.

I loved your confession of sloth, of waking up in the morning and washing your bangs in the sink. I do that so often—once I was trying to move so fast that I even gouged my forehead on the spigot. Your letter made me think of all the little secret evasions I conduct every day, especially spiritual ones. I transpose the truth in my head, thinking that I pray, if I pray at all, for God's sake rather than my own. It's not as if God needs to be shored up by a decade or two of Hail Marys from the second floor of 1720 West Summerdale.

Speaking of evasions, I just realized that I've already forgotten my solemn promise to tell you the state of my soul on a daily basis. Well, this is one of those days, like so many others, that has gone by, at least until now, without even as much as a bow toward God. I feel so harried, so overwhelmed by life, that I can't seem to find time to think about, to pray, to contemplate God.

Lately, I've been trying to think of spiritual truths more like the laws of physics than like human laws. If we are selfish, it is not that God will punish us or that we would be just fine if God eased up the rules a bit. It's that being selfish chips away at our happiness the way a river washes away rock. Coveting our neighbor's book deal eats away at our own souls with the same certainty and inevitability as the tendency of bodies in motion to stay in motion. It's physics, not punishment. If we really believed this—that the Ten Commandments, the Beatitudes, et cetera, are true not because God enforces them like some sort of noble dictator, but because they were woven into the fabric of creation—how would we behave then?

I suppose instead we could just believe that all our constraints and laws, all our happiness is purely this-worldly, with no divine origin. But in the end, the secular interpretation offers no satisfactory answers to the questions of suffering and death.

Have I told you my two-stage theory yet? We live on a human stage clearly marked by death. So we are all tragic characters. But if the Resurrection did in fact happen, then we have the chance to live with a different sort of knowledge, that death is not really the end. The Resurrection turns the tragedy into a comedy, in the sense of reconciliation and a return to harmony (the Greek and Shakespearean comedies always end with a return, a marriage, a celebration, which I guess makes the story of the prodigal son a comedy). So then, with this knowledge, we become comic characters on a tragic stage. We become like Hugo Rahner's grave-merry men. This is the only way I have ever been able to make death square with the intuitive human tendency to hope and to love as if love would never end.

In any case, forgive this tangent (another evasion). I think the original point was my failure to pray. That is why this letter practice is so good for me. I want to do whatever I can to trick myself into faith, because it sure ain't gonna come natural.

—Amy

February 13, 2005

Dear Amy,

When my mother got sick, I lost her and my religion too. When it became clear that medicine wasn't going to cure her cancer, both she and my dad fled Catholicism in search of a bona fide faith healing. My childhood parish wasn't that kind of place, but they found what they thought they were looking for at the First Assembly of God off the I-10 service road, and my sister and I were rebaptized in a Jacuzzi in front of the whole church. I remember I was wearing my gym shorts.

They didn't get the healing, obviously. But my dad did meet his second wife, my stepmother, there. Maybe this is why I so strongly link our flight from Catholicism with the end of my childhood. My stepmother was the first person I'd ever met who was openly anti-Catholic. There would be no more Mardi Gras in our home. No more Greeks, Romans, saints, or throwing of salt over the shoulder. No more magic.

I couldn't bear my dad's remarriage, or this new vision of the world as sick and evil, the province not of a benevolent, if inscrutable, God but of a malicious and powerful Satan. I spent the next ten years wandering, homeless in every sense of the word. I lived on friends' sofas, in my car, and with my grandmother, when we could stand each other. And I wandered in and out of churches of all kinds.

But when my homesickness became unbearable, I always went back to Our Lady of Lourdes, to lie in a lacquered pew and smell the burned wicks of the candles in the cry room. Something about those candles, each flickering light a plea to heaven, brought the surety of childhood faith back to me.

So I've always hidden out in Catholic churches and proudly considered myself culturally Catholic. But with my childhood vision of the Mardi-Gras God—that seamless garment that seemed to include faith in anything supernatural—I've found it difficult to commit to the actual practice of Catholicism. In many ways the church is as new to me as it is to you, and there's so much to be uncertain about. (In fact, I'm certain that your knowledge of theology and apologetics far exceeds my own. Did I have the humility to admit that I didn't know who G. K. Chesterton was until you recommended him to me?) I sometimes worry that my faith is nothing more than nostalgia for my childhood, or rebellion against my father.

But I don't want to believe only in the power of my own imagination. It's got to be more than a symbol or, as Flannery O'Connor famously said, to hell with it.

When I first began to go to Mass again, about two years ago, I found it difficult to accept its subtlety. The church of my imagination (and occasionally, as in New Orleans, in practice) is full of great drama, procession, color, spiritual pyrotechnics, apparitions, and mysticism. But a typical Sunday Mass in the average American parish offers little in the way of pageantry. When I first began to go again, the embrace of nostalgia, the feeling of being home again, was enough to bring me back for several weeks, but soon I was as bored and restless as a child.

I found myself disappointed that I didn't seem to *feel* anything during Mass. After years of my dad's now-preferred style of worship, which includes Marshall stack amplifiers and the occasional random bugle call from an exceptionally vocal, tongues-speaking congregation (admittedly pretty exciting), I was convinced that just showing up wasn't good enough; you had to emote, fall on your knees, weep, shout, run laps around the congregation. If it wasn't for Dave, I'm not sure I would have continued to attend Mass. I probably would have kept wandering in and out of churches of all sects, denominations, and persuasions, and leaving feeling jilted, offended, and unsatisfied.

But with Dave, I kept going. Slogging it out. Showing up. Standing, sitting, kneeling. Thinking about anything else. But there came a point, I'm not sure exactly when, when I was no longer slogging or just showing up. I began to desire it. Not just because it felt familiar, like home. That was certainly part of it, but it wasn't the whole story. The Mass was steady and unchanging and familiar, but at some point I decided that it was also true. And I think, now, that it was precisely because the Mass didn't depend on me to feel anything at all. It wasn't up to me, or how I felt on a certain day, how much emotion I could gin up. Neither did it depend on the rhetorical flourishes of a preacher or the set list of the worship team. It wasn't up to any of us. The self had receded, and God was there.

—Jess

February 13, 2005

Dear Jess,

I got a phone call this morning from a close friend, and when I hung up I realized I hadn't told her that I am converting. If I had just forgotten to mention it, that would be one thing, but I avoided it. "What's going on in your life?" she said. "Oh, nothing much, nothing new," I said.

This happens to me all the time. The other day I ran into an old poet friend in a coffee shop. "So I hear you're converting?" he said in his typically awkward way. "Uh . . . yes," I stammered, and left it at that. Then we just stood there, saying nothing, his hands stuffed into his pockets, me biting my nails, both waiting for our coffees.

The thing that stops me is the skepticism and even resentment I imagine they'll feel. The problem boils down to the creed—"I believe in one God"—the declaration that one thing is true above all others. And I shouldn't blame other people, for it is really my own skepticism that I project. It is so easy for me to imagine standing in the nonbeliever's shoes; I've stood there so recently and still do many days. It is even so easy to imagine choosing an entirely different spiritual path. The plausibility, and even appeal, of so many other ways of looking at life has always been, for me, one of the greatest barriers to conversion.

I felt this acutely a few weeks ago when Mark and I were still in India. In the evenings, I would take a break from my Ramanujan research, and we'd go out, trying to pretend we were on the honeymoon we never took. One night we found ourselves in the audience at a Carnatic music concert.

Carnatic music is a South Indian classical form that supposedly is descended from the gods. Its lyrics are Vedic hymns. On this particular night the singer was a woman. She sat in the center of a semicircle of instrumentalists, her feet bare, her eyes closed. Her voice seemed to start somewhere mid-chest, a deep, resonant moan, and then rise up through her body, until it ended in a high-pitched cry. I had no idea what she was saying, but it seemed obvious she was calling out to God. It was not just sorrowful, but sorrow calling out in the hopes of being heard (like the groaning voice of the psalms). She seemed alone, even though seated before hundreds, as her arms rose up above her head, accompanying her voice in an open-palmed gesture of supplication.

As I listened, I felt the old crisis of faith coming on: How could I convert if conversion means shutting this out? Or believing that this woman is somehow farther away from God than I am? Or that she is simply wrong? At such times I feel the temptation to remain outside it all. But I've tried that too, and it staves off my restlessness only for a time.

I once heard a story about Joseph Campbell. I have looked for the reference many times and have never been able to find it, but I feel sure it was him. Campbell said that sometimes he feels envious of the believer, for as a person who stays perpetually outside all faiths in order to observe and compare, he will never know what the believer knows. This comforts me to some extent. In a world in which so many lives are sympathetic, so many ways plausible, we are all—believers and nonbelievers alike—in the same boat. We don't avoid exclusion or alienation by refusing to choose, for then we are still cut off from those who have chosen and from what they know.

In reading more about Teresa of Ávila, I recently came across a piece of advice she once gave her sisters: "There is no reason why we should expect everyone else to travel by our own road, and we should not attempt to point them to the spiritual path when perhaps we do not know what it is. . . . It is better to do what our Rule tells us—to try to live ever in silence and in hope, and the Lord will take care of His own."

So maybe my tendency to say nothing at all is not entirely misplaced.

—Amy

February 14, 2005

Dear Amy,

Dave and I are in separate rooms now, pretending not to be hurt and angry and homesick, because it's Valentine's Day, and I've ruined it. I want to blame him for how miserable I am here, how much I hate my job, how much I miss our duplex on Kirtland Street, the sound of our friends laughing on the front porch, the neighbors' children playing in the street, the long walk to work through the cemetery. I want to blame anyone. But in the end I'm left with the terrible knowledge that it was all me—my restlessness, my impulsiveness, my job, my decision.

I spent most of today panicking about my story, which was due yesterday. I was staring at my blank computer screen, willing words to appear, when the new-message indicator pinged. It was an e-mail from a childhood friend, Tammi.

I haven't seen her in at least ten years. We kept in touch throughout adolescence with regular letters and occasional visits. But when I left Louisiana, I wanted to obliterate all ties to my past.

Tammi had always been strange, even as a kid. She was quiet, arty, and obsessively neat. She was blind in one eye and wore enormous glasses. My sister and her friends would have been more natural playmates (Tammi was their age, four years older than me) for her. But for whatever reason she was more comfortable with me, and even at that young age we had a strong bond. After she moved, I spent many afternoons on our front porch, staring longingly at her house at the end of our street. Even at age seven I could conjure melancholy. My mom called it having a Tammi-attack.

Months and then years passed. I'd forget her for a while, and then a letter would arrive. And every so often, I'd hear a knock at the door, and there she'd be, suitcase in hand, parents already driving away and leaving her behind. She never called first. We never knew how long she'd stay. She didn't seem to have a life of her own or a family of her own. She'd simply materialize out of thin air and then disappear again after a few days.

I don't know that I ever even asked her much about her life; I was so young, I never imagined her existence beyond her relationship to me.

Like I said, it's been at least ten years since I've seen her, but she never forgets me. After a few years of silence she always tracks me down. And so I walked into my office today, and there was the yellow Post-it on my computer screen: "Tammi called." My heart jumped like I'd seen a ghost.

I couldn't bring myself to call her. But when she e-mailed, I wrote back with many apologies. She responded almost immediately, deflected all my guilty apologies for losing touch, saying in her sympathetic and mystifyingly patient way that of course she understood. Since we last talked, her dad (we all knew him as Mr. Rock) and her older sister had both died of cancer. Tammi is now raising her four-year-old nephew. She wrote it all as if not a day had passed, as if we were still as close as we had been at ages seven and eleven.

I sat staring at her e-mail for a while. I'm ashamed to say that I thought first about what a fabulous letter writer she has always been. I was surprised to see her mirroring my own attempts at style back to me—only more naturally, effortlessly; I must have unconsciously imitated her all my life. Only then did I contemplate the heartache her message revealed and the revelation that she still thought me her dearest and closest friend. I haven't yet responded.

I'm not sure how to end this story, or why I told it. In fact, I hadn't planned to tell you any of this at all. I planned to write about your rite of election, and how good it felt to stand with you before the crowd and make the sign of the cross on your forehead. But there you go. That is the serendipitous nature of our project.

If we're meant to see God in each other, what has Tammi shown me about God, in the quiet and thankless way she shaped my life, in the way I so easily forget her, and in the consistency of her love, despite my negligence? And even with this revelation, how is it that I can't bring myself to reform? I will continue to hide, and she will continue to find me.

Now, I must go apologize to my husband.

—Jess

February 14, 2005

Dear Jess,

Last night at the rite of election, when I was standing at the back of that crowd of catechumens on the altar, I started thinking about what brings a person to God. What's odd about my story is that when I was born my father was a committed atheist and my mother an agnostic. I always tell people I am a second-generation *not*, a not-anything. I wasn't even baptized just in case.

And yet I recall many religious gestures: scratching my desire to have a dog on a small stone and burying it under the willow tree, or kneeling by my bed to beg God to help me and promising to be good in exchange. Although I'm not sure where it came from, it seems I have always at least suspected that God was there.

Did I ever tell you I went through an Ayn Rand phase in college (and along with it a try at atheism)? It all seems so silly now, but back then I was quite enamored. I even tried to dress the part. I still have a shot of me in a black, jaunty hat with a dramatic feather curling up, long lace gloves, and a short, tight black dress. I don't recall why I thought this would be an appropriate costume for a gorgeous, hopelessly rational and unbelievably intelligent "objectivist woman" (the odd name for Rand's followers), but there I was suited up and trying as hard as I could to be devastating on all fronts. But despite all the fervent debates and the arguments I finally assented to, I would still lie in bed at night, and when my mind calmed, there it was, my belief in God, as undeniable as daylight. This was the first time I realized there were certain things true of my mind that were not under my conscious control, that I could be misled as to my actual nature.

I then tried religion, but my stint with the campus Christians didn't end much better. At a gathering one night I looked up and saw a bright felt banner hanging from the loft of the campus center, proclaiming in large glitter letters: "Jesus is Lord." I had one of those moments of radical disconnect between the physical location of my body and my inner being. *How did I get here?* I thought. Soon after this, I left the group, just as I had the objectivists. Neither belief nor unbelief seemed to alter or fit my stubborn orientation toward God.

Part of my problem in understanding my story is how different it is from most conversion stories, or at least the ones that make the press. A voice coming from the clouds, Paul on the road to Tarsus—now that is something to report. These are the dramatic tales that begin with an epiphany. For me, the way to conversion has been more like a long crescendo, a long accumulation of experience, tries at this and that, false starts, and only now, looking back, am I trying to make sense of it.

I've actually thought a lot about this—the way truth is more likely to come to light in this slow way rather than in a firestorm. I've always been fascinated by Marguerite Duras's book *The Lover* for exactly this reason. She has a mental image of herself as a girl: about to cross a river, in a certain flat-brimmed hat, a certain pair of gold lamé shoes. She writes, "It is always there, in that same silence, amazing." The image was not frozen in a photo, so it continued on in her imagination and Duras eventually perceived the reach of it. *The Lover* is the story of an image that gained meaning through time. The girl who stood there about to cross the river was not the one with insight; it was the older woman looking back who was amazed.

If I could collapse all my experience into an instant, that gradual unfurling of belief that has brought me to this Lent, it would likely be as loud as a thunderclap, bright as a burning bush. But as it is, I squint my eyes and strain my ears and try to discern God.

Love,
Amy

P.S. I guess I betrayed myself by referring to the rite of election as "last night." Yes, I confess, I wrote the letter this morning. Hopefully, another will be produced tonight.

February 15, 2005

Dear Amy,
I read today that the purpose of Lent is to bring us to compunction. The word *compunction* is etymologically related to the verb *puncture* and suggests a deflation of the ego, a challenge to self-deceit:

> By hitting us again and again with demands which we not only fail to obey, but which we come to recognize as being quite beyond us . . . [Lent's]purpose is not to confirm us in our sense of virtue but to bring home to us our radical need of salvation.
>
> —Mark Searle, "The Spirit of Lent"

Well, my ego can't take much more deflation today. It's 2:51 p.m., and I haven't yet heard from my editor. I'm afraid that means that he's formulating a tactful way to tell me he hates the story. I did, however, get an e-mail from another editor asking for three pages of revisions on something I wrote two months ago.

At Mass today the readings were all about prayer, and I meant to pay attention so that I could write to you about them, but I quickly lost concentration and found myself thinking instead about what I should pack for the trip to Pittsburgh this weekend.

It was uncharacteristically warm today, and after Mass I sat on a bench in front of the Golden Dome, where Mary stands, queen of all she surveys. I like to imagine her up there keeping an eye on everything; it helps with that panicked feeling that I'm living in a bad dream, that if I shake my head I'll wake up in my bed on Kirtland Street, hear the wheezing of the screen door closing as Dave leaves for the bus stop in the early-morning darkness.

An ancient retired chemistry professor joined me for a bit. I see him at Mass every day. He told me that nobody hated it here more than he did when he first arrived fifty-five years ago. He seemed to see something in me, some loneliness or misery that reminded him of those early days. And yet now, every day, he comes to this campus and sits on this same bench. He calls it his satellite office. I felt embarrassed by how pathetic I must have seemed, wallowing on my bench. Normally, my pride would surge and I would put on a brave face and pretend that I was perfectly happy. But not today. I accepted his words as the comfort he intended, and I was grateful.

I feel exhausted. I need a retreat from Lent. I long to be in familiar territory.

—Jess

February 15, 2005

Dear Jess,

I was so disappointed yesterday when I discovered that I won't be baptized at Easter. It's hard for me to see my college conversion as the real deal since I didn't stick with it, and after I left the fellowship I spent years keeping my distance from Christians and reading Eastern thinkers. I've always regarded that time as inauthentic. But Father Brian looked at my certificate of baptism and determined it was legitimate.

"Are you *sure*?" I asked him, still holding the paper in front of his face. He was sure.

So my entry into the church will consist of just confirmation and first communion.

I had wanted to write it off, that biblical dunking in the Connecticut River, along with so much other college foolishness, but I guess God doesn't see it that way. And I should probably take this as yet another sign that I don't understand myself, or the events of my life, as well as I like to think I do.

I left out something important from this morning's letter, what happened between my objectivist and Christian stages. In short, I had an existential crisis. I don't remember exactly when it started, but suddenly I was overcome with the thought that I didn't know myself, that I wasn't anyone in particular. All the hype of high school was past, and it then seemed to me that I had substituted that trumped-up, small-world glamour for a real personality. For maybe several weeks, I walked around like someone recovering from a shock—slightly dazed, on the verge of tears, not able to articulate anything clearly. I felt that the world was peopled with interesting creatures and I was a shell with some small-town decorations.

But soon another fear began to edge that one out. *I am dying*, I thought. First I believed it was the disease Stephen Hawking has. I studied my hands, sure that they were becoming weaker. I thought of those books—*A Thousand Paper Swans* and *Too Young to Die*—and remembered a scene where a girl was standing in her kitchen using some appliance. Suddenly her sickness caused her arms to go limp and the electric mixer, or whatever it was, flew across the kitchen, flinging batter on the walls. It's funny now, but then I was living in a state of horror, my own body the site of horror.

I took three showers a day. Only under the stream of hot water would I finally begin to lose some of the panic. I would just stand there leaning against the tiles of the dorm stall and bow my head under the stream. Nothing would occur to me—just the roar in my ears and the rush of water over my scalp and down my face and back. Maybe it was life I sought in the shower, but as soon as I was out, I could feel my hands maybe beginning to shake or have trouble balling up a fist or feel an odd tingle crawling up my scalp.

I started failing exams. I remember a physics test in particular: I stared at the piece of paper, blurring the words with an unfocused, unblinking gaze, and couldn't drum up an iota of concern for the demands of my actual life. I went to the doctor, and, trying to be helpful, he said, "Well, nothing seems to be wrong but sometimes people have a sixth sense about these things." *He knows I am dying, too*, I thought. My life narrowed until I would walk out of movies unable to bear sitting still for two hours, until I was almost solely and maniacally aware of my hands and forearms.

After several torturous months, I remember one afternoon walking out into the light, the first day I had really looked at in months. Spring was almost on the air, everything muddy and wet, rain falling from a few passing clouds even as the sun shone, and I ran. As I ran I began to notice my legs and my heart beating hard in my chest. I made my way across campus to the huge graveyard on the far side. I stayed there all afternoon, sitting alone by the pillared monuments, looking down the craggy hillside through a forest of tombs.

There was a strange comfort that day in having death confirmed, not unlike how I felt on Ash Wednesday. But what played the role of the church back then, what countered death? Looking back now, I think what helped me was my latent belief in God suddenly rising to the surface as I sat among so many sure markers of death. Over the following few weeks, I emerged from that strange haze, and it was in this state of recovery that I first began to take religion seriously. It might sound as if I am saying I sought God as an antidote to fear (the proverbial crutch), but that's not it at all. In going through such a sustained meditation on death (my death), I finally realized that in some sense I didn't fully believe in death.

Remembering this helps me see my college baptism as an authentic beginning. It wasn't the beginning of my faith in God, but it's when I began to seek out God in churches.

Love,

Amy

February 16, 2005

Dear Amy,

I've gone to Mass and am now at lunch. The priest was so homely—tall and gangly, stoop shouldered, his shiny bald skull wreathed with brown hair, his demeanor at the altar so businesslike, as if he were counting out singles at the bank window—that I was shocked by his beautiful singing voice.

I now recognize most of the faces at the 11:30 Mass. Sometimes I pretend that Notre Dame is an isolated Old World Catholic village, especially when I'm leaving the basilica feeling refreshed and the bells are ringing as I walk to get lunch and a newspaper. Living here is like being cloistered, removed from the world.

Thomas Merton said that a monk should want to be irrelevant. Monks should have no real purpose. They should be useless, so that they can be, exclusively, men of God. From this perspective, they should have a critical sense of the world's failure to provide people with "lives that are fully sane and human." They must be in creative tension with the world, removed from the world and yet obsessed with its problems and hopes. It gave me a way to think of living here that I might be able to bear. I've always been attracted to the stance of the contrarian.

Most days I have very little contact with anyone besides Dave. I wonder, *how will it change us?* I'm more anxious than ever about the state of our lives. Will Dave go back to school? Write his book? Will I have to write letters for the president of Notre Dame all the rest of my days? It's easy here to feel completely irrelevant. But maybe this irrelevance will bring about a new perspective.

I'm still looking forward to our weekend away, and taking a little break from the cloister.

With love,

Jess

February 17, 2005

(a day late, and also I broke my Lenten resolve with an M&M cookie—am I five?)

Dear Jess,

Do you talk to God every day? Somehow I think you might. I don't. Prayer has always been so hard for me. I still have the books on prayer I read in college instead of actually praying. I remember the sense of walking into my bedroom and feeling absolute emptiness around me. The unself-consciousness of early childhood that makes it so easy to imagine a presence outside the self disappears when self-awareness kicks in. The space around you in an empty room becomes filled with your own self-perception. Everywhere you look, your own image is ricocheting off the walls. You can barely think a thought, before you hear loudly echoing back: *I am thinking this thought. How do I pray?* you think. *How do I pray?* your voice returns. You see yourself standing there, an expression suddenly stiff on your face, your hands unsure how they should best accompany these words, and worst of all, the sight of yourself utterly alone in the room.

Anyway, ever since then, prayer has been like that for me. I feel more distant from God when I am actually trying to pray. Now I am thankful for those ancient mantras such as the rosary and the Jesus prayer. St. Augustine in a letter to Proba (who he describes as a "devoted handmaid of God") talks of arrow prayers, or the brief prayers of the Coptic monks. These were simple phrases like

"Lord, make haste to help me" or "Lord Jesus, have mercy" or simply "Lord," repeated again and again, as your fingers count the beads, in an attempt to still the heart.

It makes me think of when you gave me that rosary shortly after we met. I can still picture you rustling around in your giant purse and bringing out your hands cupped together as if you were holding something secret and fragile. "I hope you won't think this is too weird," you said with your hands still closed. "It's a rosary. I had it blessed by a priest." You finally opened your hands. "It was made by nuns out of rose petals." Now whenever I take it down from its nail, that rosary always makes me think of how you looked when you gave it to me—embarrassed and tender, as if you thought you held either a great hoax or a piece of holiness in your hands, and you weren't sure if you should get me mixed up in it.

Last night I said a full circle of the Jesus prayer (by the way, the beads still smell of roses). I can't say yet that I feel God's presence or that my prayer life is particularly committed or sincere, but at least participating in these ancient mantras makes me feel connected to the centuries of people who sat alone like me, trying to reach God.

Love,

Amy

P.S. Isn't it beautiful to imagine St. Augustine writing spiritual letters? We are in good company. I think I will address you henceforth as a devoted handmaid of God. Do you think our friends in Pittsburgh would find that odd? Maybe I'll try it this weekend.

February 20, 2005

Dear Amy,

Last night, when I went to bed, I was inexplicably afraid. I lay there, going over the events of the weekend in my head, until my anxiety reached such a pitch that it felt electric, like the low-grade buzz of being shocked by a small appliance. I would have left Dave's sleeping form and gone downstairs to watch television, but I was too afraid to face the darkened house. I was like a child, huddling under the covers, perfectly still, almost afraid to open my eyes.

I used to work myself into these states in high school. When my dad remarried, I spent many nights at the house of my best friend, Erika. Her family was Norwegian, and they collected troll figurines—apparently trolls are kind of a Norwegian mascot. Trolls peered out at me from the fireplace mantle, the bathroom counter; trolls propped open doors and kept the newspapers in a neat stack near the fireplace for kindling. My dad couldn't understand why anyone would decorate with little demons, as he called them. "Why would you invite the devil into your house?" he'd say, and I'd laugh at his paranoia. Who could fear a little grumpy doll in a floppy hat? But late in the night at Erika's, his words would echo in my head as I listened to the ticking of the cuckoo clock in the hallway, and I'd shut my eyes against visions of those awful trolls encircling my bed.

As I hid under the covers last night, I thought of the trolls again and of a vision my mother had, of a man in flowing robes swishing into the hospital room where she was receiving chemotherapy. At first she thought it was our Uncle Jack, a priest who lived in Texas near the cancer hospital. He sat on the edge of her bed. She felt the pressure of his weight shifting her own. She could hear my dad rustling the pages of the newspaper he was reading in the chair next to her; she wondered why he didn't say hello. The man took her hand, and when he opened his mouth to speak, she felt his breath, cold on her face, smelling like something dead. He asked, so sweetly, "And what's the matter with this little girl?" and she, instinctively, she said, pulled his hand to her mouth to tear her teeth through his skin. "But there wasn't any skin," she told me. "It was just hard and cold. Like a hoof."

As unlikely as it all seems in the light of day, when I'm alone in the dark, I remember all that childhood fear, every story my parents ever told me about the devil, the adversary, the enemy, the troll, until I feel a menacing energy all around me. Sometimes, my mom told me, even after he's gone, you feel his presence, like the lingering of a woman's perfume.

It started this weekend in Pittsburgh. I had been so excited to visit our grad-school friends and my former coworkers at the journal, thinking we'd all pick up right where we left off. Instead I had to face the insult that life had of course gone on without me and that all I'd left behind was thriving in my absence. I don't know if I expected them to celebrate our return, but I certainly didn't expect to feel so trivialized and dismissed. Worse, when Elaine sang out our arrival at Kristen's apartment: "It's our favorite Catholic girls!" I was convinced they'd been making fun of us. I sat there in Kristen's apartment, sinking deeper into the dark conviction that I had made the wrong choice—that my whole life was here and I'd thrown it away to go to Notre Dame based on some religious fervor and my desire for a paycheck.

You were there. Was I only imagining it? There were no trolls or bogeymen in black robes, but there was the look on Gwen's face. For much of the night she lay on the sofa in what I thought was a wine-induced torpor. But at some point she sat up and stared right at me, as if she knew how badly I needed to feel important. I keep hearing her voice: "But you're so beautiful, Jess." She was probably just being Gwen, playfully fawning over me. But there was nothing playful in her face or her tone. I heard it as mockery, and I felt my blood run cold. I heard the cooing of my mother's terrible vision, "And what's the matter with this little girl?"

Later, at Kathy's, I let it overtake me, and I ranted and laughed until my stomach hurt. Every ugly thing in me seemed to pour forth until her apartment was full of it and we were both afraid. When I called her today, she told me she'd slept with the light on, which she hasn't done since she was little.

I'm a little embarrassed to have written this. It's ridiculous to think I'm responsible for your conversion in any way, but I do take my sponsorship seriously, and I worry all the time that I'll reveal something that will make you decide that it's all hocus-pocus and you'll turn away. The truth is I'm often tempted to hide my eyes.

My family always wrestled with the devil. I felt tempted to soften that by writing "the presence of evil," but no—for us the man with the pitchfork was a reality: the devil, bringing sickness to my mother and mocking her fear; the devil, inspiring all my teenage rebellion; the devil, driving my dad to drink. I don't want to believe it, or at least I don't want to admit in polite company that I believe it. But a return to the faith of my childhood inevitably means facing down that darkness, too, the cruel specter swishing into the room in his cloaks.

—Jess

February 21, 2005

Dear Jess,

When we got off the phone last night, I felt terrible. I wish I had been able to think of something helpful to say. It's actually hard for me to understand how you could think you are a poor sponsor, but

I guess you have been worrying about that and telling me as much ever since we met. Do you remember the trip to see the relics last summer, soon after we met? That day reminds me of how you are feeling now—your fears of turning me away from God, our different orientations (you the mystic, me the rationalist).

It's funny, but I vainly remember what I wore on that pilgrimage to St. Anthony's, but not what you wore. Yet I don't think this is just a sign of my vanity. I put on my prettiest sundress hoping, as on a first date, to impress you. I can still feel the thrill of walking up that hill toward the doors of the church, full of anticipation.

And we were definitely in the throes of some kind of love as we walked toward the doors, our bare arms brushing now and then. Were we both dizzy? It seems so looking back. And there was something forbidden about that trip, even if it wasn't our friendship. We were there not as tourists but as pilgrims. We wanted to walk through those doors and be part of what we saw. We wanted not to pass it off as a curiosity or some bizarre sight, a tidbit of quirky religion to drop into a poem or conversation; we wanted to believe in it. I think we went together because we knew that either of us alone would never be up to the task. We opened the doors to that cavern of bones and blood and enshrined bits of withered skin, and we entered.

From a distance, it looked like thousands of tiny picture frames hung in vast galleries on the walls, but up close the horrors, as you called them, took shape. The crossed femurs, the skulls barely visible through their veils of lace, the chips of bone, the molars, incisors, and shards of nail. I think it made it worse that these bits of bodies were pinned against velvet in gold casings, sealed in wax. It seemed decadent, depraved almost, as if we were there for a peep show. I stood back in the pews and watched you circle the front. You told me you thought you might throw up.

Watching you reel in front of those bones gave me the feeling of vicarious vertigo, of watching someone else stand on the edge of a cliff. You might have felt the question looming of whether or not you should stay in the church, but I was wondering if I should even enter. The bones and vials of blood were the riddle at the bridge. Would we solve the riddle differently and find ourselves crossing paths or running in opposite directions?

But I think we both sensed that what the other did, we ourselves would do. *Whither thou goest.* Some things seem to come to life only when shared. It makes me think of the line "wherever two or three are gathered together in my name, there am I in the midst of them." The gathering is what reveals the presence of Christ. The gathering is not optional.

So did we walk up the path to St. Anthony's in the name of Christ? At the time, I doubt either one of us would have admitted that as our motive. But then why did we choose St. Anthony's as our destiny? In truth, I think we went to St. Anthony's because we both hoped to find holiness there.

I think it was the very strangeness of that place that appealed to me. It was so far outside any image of holiness that I could have dreamed up. It was gory and dark, and yet those bones and skulls were there because of the great saints who had carried them within their living flesh. These were the scattered, carved-up remains of holiness, and now it was upon us to see past the horror to God. And it wasn't just the horror that presented the challenge but also the superstition and potential hoax of it all. Were they really the bones of saints, or just the bones of a gravedigger's cat? And even if they were the bones of saints, isn't it idolatry, or just plain foolishness, to treat them with such reverence? But doesn't the cross (and all of our lives for that matter) present the same challenge—to see through the apparent absurdity, to see past the carnage to Julian Norwich's "all shall be well, and all shall be well, all manner of thing shall be well"?

And what showed it to me, that glimmer of holiness beyond the bones, was your presence there. At the time it took the form of a dare: *I'll stay if you stay. If you can believe despite all this, then so can I.* We stood there, amid the skulls, in awe of our shared desire to still believe, the desire our unspoken dare seemed to reveal. It was the thrill I imagine extreme skiers might feel, to witness themselves alive despite every indication that they should die. *Life is strong enough to withstand this*, they must think, and they push it farther. How about this? It is the desire for the eternal, something unbreakable and fixed. We wanted to look on tempests (or gaudy bones) and not be shaken.

Throughout our visit I wasn't sure if we were amid holiness or horror. But isn't that how people feel in the presence of angels—in love, in horror, in awe? Your presence—the presence of us together at St. Anthony's—was the first sign to me that I could enter the church. If you could stand there, swaying before the bones but still standing, then so could I, or at least I could stand there with you.

So there. You are my sponsor, like it or not.

Love,
Amy

February 21, 2005

Dear Amy,
Today I jumped at my own reflection in the mirror. I know it's absurd when I get in these states, but I just can't help it. I lived for years in a house where exorcisms were performed as a matter of course. If you had a cold, my dad and stepmother would pray for the devil to release his grip on your nose. If you talked back, they'd call

out, "Demon, be gone!" and clap their hands in front of your face. I usually laughed it off in defiance. But they scared me all the same. Did I really have a devil inside? Do I still?

My dad may have sworn off Catholicism as superstition, but he certainly believes in the supernatural. When my mom got sick, he spent all his time looking for some secret combination of things to cure her: the right church, the right faith healer, the right placement of hands, the right kind of prayer. I felt I was the rationalist then. But it wasn't that I lost my faith. I never stopped believing in God, even a God who could heal. But I felt certain that, this time, he wouldn't—that she would die. And that conviction tore me away from my father.

When we got back from Pittsburgh Sunday night, all I wanted to do was call my dad. I confess I was at least a little bit pleased to have something spiritual to confide in him, some common ground we might occupy for at least a few moments.

Once, during a particularly low point in my life with my dad and stepmother, I told them over breakfast that I thought I'd had a vision. I had awakened in the early morning to find a very tall man—at least seven feet tall—with golden hair to his waist, standing in the corner of my bedroom. He was stark naked, and yet I hadn't seen a penis.

"Well, you know, Jess," my stepmother said, "angels don't have genitalia."

This was at a time in my life when I was sure they despised me for all the trouble I was causing at home. But when they heard this story, they gathered around me as if I were a celebrity, talking excitedly, giving me more pancakes and coffee, and I lapped up the attention, embellishing the story and pretending to be more shaken than I was.

But the feeling didn't last. I guess that's the problem with frenzied spiritual experience. It's fleeting. You have to keep trying to ascend to higher heights—do the altar call one more time.

The excitement, that tingling fear, subsides, and what it leaves behind is real and lasting: despair. Maybe that's why I would become so enraged when my dad tried to exorcise my teen angst. What I was enduring might have been evil—puberty, grief, the loss of my mother, of my entire life as I'd known it. But it wasn't something he could cast out with the right combination of Bible verses, the right placement of his hands. And neither was my mom's cancer. There was no quick fix. Only a long, slow process that began with lying on the church pews and lighting candles, enduring the absence of her, the absence of God, returning to Mass week after week, feeling nothing long before I began to feel the stirrings of something true.

No, not a quick fix. Only lifelong conversion.

—Jess

February 23, 2005

Dear Jess,

I have been thinking about our drive home from Pittsburgh and the question of evil, or rather of any spiritual presence. It wasn't just your imagination; I felt everything that you felt this weekend visiting our grad-school friends, the almost-palpable gloom and envy (theirs, ours). And then how it all overtook us on the way home and we actually had to pull over to the side of the road to steady ourselves in order to keep driving. At the time I was mildly horrified that I had let myself get so worked up. Mark reminded me of how Hegel characterizes American religion: "the extremes of insanity," "the transports of enthusiasm," which seem to him ridiculous, self-indulgent attempts at worship. It makes me remember how uncomfortable I felt trying to enter the worship-session ecstasies in college. I felt like a sham when I raised my hands and tried to look overcome.

On the one hand, my explanations tend to domesticate evil (and good). They tend to say, "Yes, but what is really going on is . . ." My explanations tend to take God and the entire spiritual realm out of the picture. Your terror of evil (which did become my terror, at least at some foggy point on I-76) is probably much closer to the way we should respond. Evil should never be regarded as tame or merely thus and so—or *mere* at all. Evil (which I like to think of as anything that brings us to a point of despair) is powerful and real. But on the other hand, if we run around in a state of fear, worrying that someone's head might start to spin around, we will fail to see how evil is working its way into our hearts and becoming part of us, not just an external presence.

My overly rationalistic approach is also my problem with providence, or seeing any sort of spiritual influence whatsoever. I talked to Mark about all of this, and I thought that he would immediately come down on the side of dismissive reason. But instead he told me about a little thought experiment. Bear with me for a minute, because this is hard to explain, and I might flounder a bit to get it down.

Imagine this: There is a basketball competition with a million contestants. Everyone is given ten half-court shots. Statistics will predict a certain random possibility that a single contestant will make all ten shots. But now imagine that you are one of the contestants. You make the first shot. Luck? Then the second. Double luck. Then the third, the fourth, and the fifth. A charm? The sixth, the seventh, the eighth. Now you begin to suspect some sort of intervention, some sort of gift. The ninth, and then, inconceivably, the tenth. You walk away from the court in a daze, feeling that you

were momentarily lifted beyond human limitation. Without thinking, you whisper a prayer of thanksgiving and wonder what this
miracle of sorts means. But in the aftermath of the competition,
commentators talk about luck and statistics. You read these explanations and begin to wonder if this event was just a statistic. The
experience of being there, shocked by the steadiness and uncanny
regularity of your aim, is fading. You question the whole thing and
decide to chalk it up to chance.

There are always two ways to look at apparently serendipitous
events. From the perspective of the world, of statistics, everything
can be explained away. We can always say that this or that particular
configuration of happenings was bound to occur at some point in
someone's life. But the second perspective is that of the individual.
From the position of the witness, statistical explanations never seem
compelling (at least at first). As you stand there on the court knowing the usual limitations of your body and your poor record with
half-court shots and the way your palms are sweating, it can seem
like only grace when you start to make shot after shot after shot. So
the question is, which is the right perspective?

Mark suggested that the statistical explanation, which may be
appropriate in the case of basketball, can mislead us about our most
meaningful experiences. It suggests that we can all look at our lives as
if they are infinitely repeatable (as if we could try life out again and
again until any occurrence seems possible or even likely in our millions or billions of lives). But instead, we have only one life. When
events of our lives conspire in such a way that the most obvious
interpretation is that some sort of intention or purpose or meaning
is behind them, rather than chance or coincidence, it's not crazy to
take this seriously.

Divine intervention, if it does indeed happen, will always look like the random statistic, a single instance of a highly unlikely event. It will seem like winning the lottery or getting a rare disease. So if God (or the devil) does speak to us, how will we know we've been spoken to if we interpret automatically all uncanny events or series of coincidences in these scientific terms?

I think our weekend opened my eyes to a spiritual reality. I don't mean that I look back and think that the devil had taken hold of one of us or that some *Exorcist*-like atmosphere overcame our car in the middle of Ohio. But whatever did happen, good and evil should never be taken lightly. It might be best to work on our imaginations—or rather, *my* imagination, yours is on overtime already—and think of angels and demons pacing about while we work and drive and sleep, swooping, spreading, descending upon us. Maybe then we will treat evil and good with the proper degree of fear and trembling.

Hopefully our two approaches will complement each other. I'll keep you steady, and you'll keep me honest.

—Amy

February 23, 2005

Dear Amy,

Yesterday I went to confession. I wasn't really planning on it, but I went to the 11:30 Mass at the basilica and noticed that the little green light was on above the confessional, and so I went in. It was unbearably hot in there, dry heat hissing from an unseen radiator, and I wondered if they piped it in especially, just to heighten the feeling of judgment. I chose to sit in front of the priest, Father Ayo. He looks like Santa Claus: a round face, red cheeks, bushy white beard—grandfatherly, gentle.

I told him, inarticulately, of your conversion and my role as your sponsor, and of my odd contortions of pride and envy and the persistent buzz of evil in my guts and head, and my irrational (it is irrational, isn't it?) fear of the devil.

He began by saying, "Satan's not a little man with horns and a pitchfork waiting for you around every corner."

Sure he isn't, I thought to myself. *But go on.*

He went on: "To believe so is to underestimate the nature of the struggle we face."

Then he told me this story. A woman carried two pots of water to the temple every day, not knowing that one of the pots was cracked. When she reached the temple, she was always horrified to discover that the pot was empty, and she felt useless and foolish. But what she didn't know was that every day, she left a trail of water all the way from the village to the temple, and along that trail, wildflowers had begun to grow.

My penance was this: "Be hopeful." Since when do they give Hallmark cards instead of penances?

At Mass, the gospel was the one about St. Peter, when Jesus tells him he's the rock upon which he will build the church. The homily was all about human weakness and frailty. We'll be forgiven everything, even denying Jesus three times. Why is it so hard to accept that we might be loved so completely?

—Jess

February 24, 2005

Dear Jess,

All this talk of my rationalism and your mysticism has got me thinking. I've lived much of my life with the ridiculous assumption that I will eventually get to the bottom of things—the bottom of housework, the bottom of bad habits, the bottom of God. At some point I will have cleared all the mess away and left my home and myself and the world clean and articulate. Like Iris Gaines says in the movie *The Natural*, "I believe we have two lives . . . the life we learn with and the life we live with after that." I sometimes live with the apparent headlong intent of getting to that second life. I launch new campaigns to organize my house. I pursue conversation with an almost desperate intensity, as if each one might be leading to a conclusion that will finally settle it all. It feels as if I am perpetually trying to clear a path so that I can get to some assumed destination, which "was there from the very beginning, a measured distance away, standing in the ordinary light like some plain house."* It makes me think of the first few lines of J. M. Coetzee's *Elizabeth Costello*:

> There is first of all the problem of the opening, namely, how to get us from where we are, which is, as yet, nowhere, to the far bank. It is a simple bridging problem, a problem of knocking together a bridge.

That is what I'm always trying to do: knock together a bridge.

Earlier today Mark and I had a conversation about the story of Jesus going to the home of Mary and Martha. Martha busied herself with work, trying to earn the right to sit down with her guest. Like me, Martha was a bridge builder. "We're smart people," Mark said. "We could spend our lives erecting problems, which would then have to be reasoned through. It is wrong to assume there would ever be an end." Mary, instead, sat at the feet of Jesus and listened; Mary was on the far bank. At some point, in order to have faith at all, we have to act as if we are already there. Coetzee goes on to say:

---

* Marilynne Robinson, *Housekeeping* (New York: Picador, 2004), 9–10.

Let us assume that, however it may have been done, it is done. Let us take it that the bridge is built and crossed, that we can put it out of our mind. We have left behind the territory in which we were. We are in the far country, where we want to be.

I'm not really trying to say that you have to be done with reason. I'm glad I've spent some time fretting with Martha in the kitchen; it's helped me. But I no longer think that faith can be acquired by reason alone. At some point I'll just have to take a step into the far country, or stop imagining that I'm not there already.

Love,
Amy

February 24, 2005

Dear Amy,

Dave is sitting at the computer, blogging away about the Abu Ghraib prison photos, and I am sitting at the dinner table, staring at his back, trying not to drink the last two beers that are in the refrigerator because then I will want to smoke the cigarettes that are hidden in the junk drawer.

I'm listening to Neil Young's song, "Old Man," and thinking of my dad. He once told me that yawning is a sign of demon possession—that whenever they cast out demons at church, people yawn (and sometimes laugh) uncontrollably. Now, each time I yawn, I think of the devil and then inwardly roll my eyes. My self-created spiritual dramas are really very tiresome. I'm a wannabe mystic. Or maybe just a hysteric. Or maybe just pathetic. I'm worried that religion is just too much cosmic fun, and that I'm my father's daughter, after all, with a propensity for misguided zeal and a gene for fanaticism. Have I ever told you that when he was young he wanted to be a Catholic priest? His father drove him to visit the seminary when he was fourteen. He ended up going to St. Paul's instead, the boys' school near my mother's all-girls school, St. Scholastica. He saw her standing under an oak tree one day and decided he wouldn't be a priest after all.

I worry over the undeniable thrill I feel when I think about a supernatural evil—is all this another desperate attempt to re-create the world of childhood? Is it driven by that same infantile pride in being special, the best, favored by God? Do I have the potential, like my dad, to feel spiritually superior when my soul is in turmoil ("the devil always goes after God's favorites," he'd tell me)?

Do I want to be a Christian at all if I can't be a writhing mystic?

In the confessional, the priest told me that evil was nothing more than giving in to despair. At first I thought he was minimizing the existence of evil, but I think I understand what he meant when he said that I shouldn't underestimate the struggle we face. It's no less horrifying to take responsibility for the darkness we find within us. It may be self-created, but it's real.

I've been trying to pray the Liturgy of the Hours, and getting a little better at it, I think. I have to say it out loud. If I read the prayers silently, I'm soon distracted and making grocery lists in my head. But out loud, I get the poetry of the psalms, and I seem to be able to access that feeling of praying in community, as if in my voice, I hear someone else's. Maybe this is the beginning of getting outside of myself, which suddenly seems essential. All I'm finding inside is fear.

Dave and I have settled into an odd routine. I've never known him to be so focused. He works into the night and comes to bed hours after I've fallen asleep.

Last night I had the most terrible dreams, and I woke to find myself caressing the inside of my arm, comforting myself the way my mother used to when I was little. Such a little thing, but it brings on a fresh round of mourning, wondering at how I get through any days without her. I've been in a daze ever since.

I think I'll go ahead and drink that beer.

Love,
Jess

February 26, 2005

Dear Jess,

Last night not only did I read three of your letters, but I also went to the Our Lady of Sorrows vespers at St. Gregory's. So there is much to write about. But first I wanted to say something about sin.

You told me, laughing, that you recently heard someone say that God loves us more the more we sin. In some sense that seems absurd and exactly what we'd want to believe. But it is clearly true that if God loves us at all, he loves us even though we sin. Mark's problem with sin (or how sin is often approached) is that he doesn't believe one should identify a standard, separate from all one knows and all one is able to achieve, and then wrench one's life away from its course to meet the standards of this abstraction. This also seems right. So we must be careful how we understand sin.

One thing that does seem clear to me is that love comes before reformation. Loving God awakens in us a desire to love what is good. This is not external change, an artificial grasping after some sort of holiness we cannot see or understand; it is not self-flagellation but an internal change that happens slowly. The mechanism of change is love, not shame.

Anyway, as I said, last night at 7:00 we went to the vespers service. The church was dark inside except for the dim, red glow of the tabernacle candle ("the perpetual fire which shall never go out"), that same light Charles Ryder found "burning anew among the old stones" in *Brideshead Revisited*. It gave me this tremendous sense that God is always there, waiting. We forget and forget, and then there he is again, and we realize that he was always there. That is one of the values of having a church—it is a physical reminder of God's omnipresence. Unfortunately, we don't tend to have God attacks, like your Tammi attacks, to remind us.

The service began with a lecture by the artist-in-residence, Joe Malham (the one who used to be a monk). He talked about the scenes from Jesus' life that are most often portrayed in art: the Nativity, the Transfiguration, the Sermon on the Mount, the Last Supper, the Crucifixion, and the Resurrection. All of these, he said, are marked by symmetry and the centrality of the figure of Jesus. But the pietà, an image of suffering, is not only not biblical; it also doesn't have any of these artistic qualities—it is an improvisation on Scripture. In the parlance of jazz, he said, it is a spiritual riff.

The pietà is marked by asymmetry. It is shockingly asymmetrical, he said. It portrays a broken God, flung across the lap of a girlish, agonized mother. God is not at the center, the lines do not meet at him; the eye is not drawn first to his lifeless form. Instead, we look at the eyes of Mary. They look back as us; they show us that if she could suffer this and still have hope, there is nothing we can't suffer too. In his homily, Scott talked about how sorrow is evident at every stage of Mary's life, that joy and sorrow are never parted in her heart. It made me think of your wedding, of you and your sister placing roses at Mary's feet in honor of your mother.

We then sang three psalms. I wish I could sing them here (I always wish I could make sounds on the page). They were so longing and sad, so yearning after God, like that Carnatic singer I heard in India. And finally, the whole congregation processed to the pietà shrine, where we sang the "Salve Regina": "To thee do we cry, poor banished children of Eve; to thee do we send up our sighs, mourning and weeping in this valley of tears."

I almost forgot to mention what Father Bart said to open the service. He spoke of the many shrines in the church and how each one, over the years, has had clients. I love his idea of clients—people who regularly come to a shrine as if to a shop or a shrink, trying to reap some benefit. At various times in our lives, he said, we have the need to meditate on different aspects of God. These shrines offer physical reminders of these various facets of God. Sometimes, he said, we need to become clients of suffering, sometimes of joy, sometimes of obedience or humility or glory.

I went home and prayed my first full cycle of the rosary.

Love,
Amy

February 26, 2005

Dear Amy,

I'm sitting in South Bend's only coffee shop, supposedly writing my thank-you notes for the president. It's nearly empty here now. Miles Davis is on the PA, but the cooks are in the kitchen listening to the Beastie Boys, *License to Ill*. Only the owner is here, reading on a sofa in the corner. What does it say about me that it's the Beastie Boys that have inspired my reverie, and not Miles Davis?

Hearing those songs again, I slipped into a memory of my sophomore year of high school, driving with my best friend. We were always driving, because we never wanted to go home. Sometimes we drove all night. It was one of those nights that we ended up at St. Margaret Mary's, the parish across town. I'm not sure how I knew that the chapel was open all night—a few cars in the parking lot, maybe, or the stained-glass windows glowing with a warm, inviting light. They were having perpetual adoration, although I had no idea what that meant at the time, or that the Eucharist was there. I just liked that it was quiet and candlelit and safe. We signed our names in the little book at the back of the church, found seats in separate pews. I'm not sure if we prayed. I might have slept. The chapel was empty, quiet, dim. No music, the only noise coming from the air-conditioning rattling on and off, the only smoke rising from our spent matches. I couldn't believe our dumb luck at finding such a refuge, a place that was beautiful and safe, where the doors were always open. I remember that we were alone there, but maybe that's just a trick of memory. I know now that people sign up for every hour of the night so that the Host is never unwatched. Maybe that person noticed me, prayed for me.

Sometimes I wonder how I found the strength to survive that time of my life. It was either the worst case of dumb adolescent pride or divine grace. For God must have been there, not just in that chapel, but along all those dark roads I navigated, even if I was too blind to notice him. Grace operates whether we acknowledge it or not.

I also benefited from a very real fear of hell, which I'm convinced isn't always unhealthy for a child. At my lowest points, any half-hearted thoughts of suicide were immediately derailed by the thought that there was a place that could actually be worse. That fear probably saved my life.

As part of my renewed commitment to establishing some sort of prayer life beyond endlessly talking to myself, I think I will attempt an hour of adoration. There is a sign-up sheet hanging in the student center, with the call to action: "Could you not keep watch even for an hour?" that chills me every time I walk by it.

It's very hard to reconcile that with the song "Girls," which is now blasting from the kitchen.

—Jess

February 27, 2005

Dear Jess,

I am feeling terribly down today. The laundry in the bedroom is weighing on my mind, as are the towels in the bathroom, the dusty floors, and all my things. This would be a good day to torch the house if I had it in me. Can you imagine what it must have been like for some of those saints, those first violent steps toward total renunciation? I can imagine it, but imagining it and even imagining doing it are worlds away from actually doing it. It is like those times when you see a knife lying on the kitchen counter and the horrifying image of picking it up and stabbing yourself or someone else flashes through your mind. You think about it fiercely for a second: *Am I going to do it? Grab the knife and senselessly stab myself? Am I going to jump off the building? Turn the wheel into oncoming traffic?* We shudder with the knowledge that we really do have the power to act in radical ways—to take our own lives or the lives of others, to break ourselves away from all that came before. The fact of our free will terrifies us, but we are held back by some strong allegiance (to life? to one another? to God?). These allegiances, too, prevent us (or most of us) from giving away all our things, burning down the house, or adopting the life of a beggar.

Anyway, I don't know where that came from. Moving right along.

I have been thinking recently about how you and I seem to thrive on a certain type of irreverence. I actually think it helps us deal with all the moments of apparent absurdity and disbelief in the life of faith. Sometimes, in order to keep showing up, we have to be clients of God's laughter. But I used to be attracted to people who were terribly serious, priding myself in my ability to sustain marathon, intense conversations (often at the pitch of debate). That is probably part of the reason I was drawn to the Ayn Rand crowd and then to the fundamentalists in college. I am so far from that now. Don't laugh! Really, I am. I have come to feel that such extreme serious-ness not only is monotonous but actually hides truth. There seems to be little room for sympathy in entirely serious hearts, and by "sympathy" I mean an ability to see that life isn't easily articulated. Serious people articulate everything and live by these articulations; they follow a grammar of living. A sense of humor seems to work against that.

I'm not sure I'm getting it right. This idea of a God who is not wholly serious always makes me think of the long poem "On Heaven" by Ford Madox Ford (Ford said he wrote it for a friend who asked for a "working heaven"). Although there is nothing in the poem that explicitly addresses what I am saying, I still get the sense of it. The poem goes on for pages. Here is a little from the middle and end:

> We saw, coming down from the road that leads to the olives and
> Alpilles,
> A man of great stature,
> In a great cloak,
> With a great stride
> And a little joke
> For all and sundry, coming down with a hound at his side.

And he stood at the cross-roads, passing the time of day
In a great, kind voice, the voice of a man-and-a-half!—
With a great laugh, and a great clap on the back . . .

. . . That, that is God's nature,
For God's a good brother, and God is no blind man,
And God's a good mother and loves sons who're rovers,
And God is our father and loves all good lovers . . .
. . . And much he loves sweet joys in such as ever took
Sweet joys on earth.

Chesterton says it much more dramatically: "There was something that [Jesus] hid from all men when He went up a mountain to pray. There was something that He covered constantly by abrupt silence or impetuous isolation. There was some one thing that was too great for God to show us when He walked upon our earth; and I have sometimes fancied that it was his mirth."

I like to think of being in the company of God and angels, not only at the solemn times, at funerals and Mass and Vespers, but when we are doubled over, holding our stomachs, laughing.

Love,
Amy

March 1, 2005

Dear Amy,
Another storm is blowing in from Lake Michigan. Everything is dead, and South Bend looks like Poland in *The Decalogue*. At least I came home to a letter from you waiting on the steps, where Dave always leaves the mail.

I have now attempted to adore the Eucharist twice, although one time it was on TV and so I don't think it counts. I was flipping channels and the priest on EWTN said to just sit and be still before

God, and so I did. He quoted St. Gregory: "to adore means to raise a hymn of silence to God." He called it "sinking into the bottomless ocean of God." He quoted Psalm 37, verses 5–7: "Be still before the Lord."

I've been telling myself for a long time that as a writer I'm endlessly composing prayers in my head and on paper, as a way of justifying my inability to sustain any real practice of prayer. And it *is* a strange exercise to rearticulate those thoughts in what feels like a one-sided conversation, as you've described it. I don't know that I've ever felt the presence of God in prayer. He seems to show up when we least expect him. But even if we don't feel that presence, should we pray anyway? We can't judge the fruits of any practice solely on the basis of our feelings. Prayer is either objectively worth something or it isn't.

Why have I always put so much stock in what I have to say to God, anyway? Listening to that TV priest, I thought, *Yes, that's what I desperately need: stillness.* To stop my brain from spinning out horrible scenarios of what life might become, from giving in to despair, as I have done once more this evening, the wind banging the shutters like in some Gothic novel.

The hard part of eucharistic adoration is that we are truly supposed to believe that Jesus is there with us in the Host. The TV priest called it "hiding under the Eucharistic Species," which has to be the most bizarre thing I've ever heard. I try to believe. I really, truly do. But sometimes I am overwhelmed by the unlikeliness of it all.

I've noticed, though, that after sitting and staring at the communion wafer for an hour, it's surprisingly difficult to watch the priest remove it from the monstrance and place it in the tabernacle, where it will remain until we eat it in the Mass. It's horrifying—the way he touches it so gently, the tenderness I feel for it. I'm breathless that he'll handle it too roughly. And then, a voice in my head: *But this is only a cracker! How can you feel such tenderness for a scrap of bread?*

If I sat and meditated on some other object, any object—a glass, a strawberry, a ballpoint pen—would I grow in such fondness for it? Would I tense when the officiant handled it? Would I believe in the divinity of anything so lovingly wrapped in fine linens and smoked with incense, kept in a golden crypt?

I want to believe that those tender feelings are moments of grace and love for God. Meanwhile I remain as full of doubt as ever, and crushingly tired. Today is one of those days when I just want to sit in the passenger seat of the car and stare, stare, stare at the great, gray, vast deadness of the northern Indiana winter, saving the energy it would take to avert my eyes.

My penance was to be hopeful. I have failed spectacularly.

—Jess

March 1, 2005

Dear Jess,

This morning I spent two hours on the phone with health-insurance companies. Did you know it costs $400 a month for maternity insurance? And if you decide to wait and add it later, you can't get pregnant for another year (unless you want to pay for it yourself, which brings you back to square one). It's not that I am planning this second to get pregnant, but I want to be able to get pregnant. The whole thing sent me into a tailspin. I finally stumbled away from my desk, my ear hurting from have the receiver pressed into it for so long, and fell onto our disheveled little couch at the end of our kitchen, which I don't have the will to clean. It was the first time since my wedding that I actually doubted my marriage. I lay there looking at the white sky through the beautiful bank of windows at the back of our apartment (an apartment that we cannot afford since we don't have jobs or savings, let alone health insurance). *I have made a huge mistake*, I thought. *Mark is younger than I am, not ready for children, not ready to make money—what on God's green earth was I thinking by marrying him?*

But Mark *seems* older than me, doesn't he? I always think of my conversation with Basil (the one who really brought us together). "He seems older than me," I said. "Amy," Basil said with that decisive voice, "Mark seems older than everyone." Even your father said he was surprised to see that I had married an older man. And Mark himself says he was born to be middle-aged and tells me all the time that he despises the young. I love him; he does seem old. Anyway, it's not his fault that the University of Chicago doesn't have health insurance for grad students. I've never heard of such a thing.

Tonight I ran into a fiction writer at DePaul. He is about my age and is married (with two dogs and a two-year-old daughter). He invited us into his place, and looking around at his crazy life, I could suddenly see myself like that—dog barking, a baby, a desk in the corner that I was somehow still finding time to use.

We have to take it all in, Jess. We must have babies. Well, some day. We can't be so afraid of our futures and our livelihoods that we guard our time and resources so carefully. I think all of this is on my mind because of my job search (and of course the search for health insurance). I so much want to have a more steady life.

I pray that tomorrow I will pray and not fall behind again in our letters.

—Amy

March 2, 2005

Dear Amy,

I've fallen into the pit of despair. You said last night on the phone that we should stop trying to plan and just live our lives. Can I ever hope to achieve that? Days like this, I can't imagine becoming pregnant, having to be responsible for a child's happiness. I'm being horrible to Dave, filling with resentment at the sight of his back turned to me as he sits at the computer typing, typing, typing, calling out lines of prose for my approval as I lie on the sofa watching the entire *Brideshead Revisited* miniseries on DVD. I keep reminding myself of how wonderful it will be when he succeeds and I have time to work on my life, my work, my baby. Me, me, me, me. The little whisper inside alternates "It will never happen" and "You are hateful and heartless."

We are in the grips of another snowstorm, the kind where everything's flying horizontal and you just have to walk with your eyes closed and hope you get where you need to go. I can take only so much more winter.

When will light return?

There should be news for Dave this week from the Department of Theology at Notre Dame. Hopefully we will have cause to celebrate this weekend.

—Jess

March 2, 2005

Dear Jess,

I've been reading all day, driven into contemplation by the snow, and I just came across a passage in St. Teresa's autobiography that startled me. She begins the story of her childhood by recounting the tale of running off with her brother to the country of the Moors in the hopes of being beheaded, and then later of attempting to build twin hermitages in a nearby orchard with piles of stones. But in the midst of these stories, she says that she and her brother became fascinated with the notion of eternity and "had a pleasure in repeating frequently" the phrase "para siempre, siempre, siempre," or "forever and ever and ever." When I read that line I was so taken aback, I had to put the book down. There is an event from my childhood that has taken on mythic significance in my mind and has at its heart that same little chant.

When I was seven years old, my family took a summer trip to Mexico. It wasn't a vacation—my father was there for work—but the university paid for all of us to stay at a beautiful hacienda just beyond the city. When I think of that trip, I can still hear the sounds of strikers marching in the streets, feel the desiccated body of a little turtle we somehow let escape and die, and see the look of pain on my sister's face when she got sick and the doctor probed her stomach. I think I remember these things and the trip in general so vividly because I was seven and beginning to emerge from the shelter of my own being.

Our room had a tiny, circular pool cloistered by a high stone wall. We could look up from the pool and see the hot sky, the towering tops of trees and their lower branches resting on the wall, and the blooming pink and yellow vines that crowded in with the branches and trailed down the inside of the wall. My sister and I would float naked in the pool and stare up at the quivering tips of the high trees. The only sign of a world beyond our little paradise was the faint roar of the strikers marching in the streets, and the occasional lizard flipping down off the vines into the water. We would fish the wriggling lizards out and toss them half-drowned back into the thicket.

One time my parents got in the pool with us, and we all started to tread water together, our arms entwined, forming us into a tight circle. I remember us all laughing and the look of our legs kicking under the choppy surface. Then my sister or I said we wanted this moment to never end, and someone called out, "We'll be together forever." And soon this was extended into a little chant. We circled and chanted, "Forever and ever." The words began to run together, "andeverandeverandever." I remember feeling such a fierce loyalty and pride in my family, and such a happy freedom in finding myself part of it and adored. Well, that's the way I would say it now, but back then it probably just felt like an intense desire for our little chant to be true, for the moment never to end.

In her autobiography, St. Teresa goes on to say that it was through "the constant uttering of these words," "para siempre, siempre, siempre," that she received "an abiding impression of the way of truth when [she] was yet a child." That is really what I have been trying to say about the nature of my belief; rather than stemming from a single, dramatic encounter or even from any conscious, rational process, I feel sure that it takes its root in those early impressions that persisted through time. For if I have any real faith now, it can be traced back to that abiding impression I had growing up of the eternal nature of love. Death isn't hard to believe in because it is tragic, but believing there is a final end does violence to my very experience of love. Love seems to insist upon eternity, to demand it. I've heard it said that we know Jesus died from historical accounts, and we know he rose if we've had an experience of the living Christ. I am never sure if I've had that experience, but I believe I've had real knowledge of eternal love, and so I believe in eternity and in a God who sustains it.

C. S. Lewis says in his autobiography that, "it is not settled happiness but momentary joy that glorifies the past." But for me it is different; it is precisely settled happiness that comes back to me as glory.

Love,

Amy

March 3, 2005

Dear Amy,

I feel sometimes that my letters to you are written in ecstatic fits. After I drop them down the mail chute, I literally have no idea what I've said. I have a feeling I'd be shocked by some of the things I've written.

I've been thinking about last Sunday's Gospel: The Samaritan woman at the well. I can't seem to get away from her. Last fall, my confessor in Pittsburgh reminded me of her just before my wedding. My penance was to imagine myself in her story: me at the well filling the jugs and encountering Christ, who knows every detail of my life before I tell him and forgives my every sin before I confess it. Priests are always telling me of women and their jars of water—is this some technique they learn in the seminary?

I remember this episode as one of the few moments in my life when I felt that, yes, I was actually praying—not just distractedly mumbling the Our Father or trying to flood God with some sort of extemporaneous monologue. In imagining this woman's encounter with God, I could also imagine how he might speak to me as a woman who needed forgiveness and what it might feel like to encounter a Christ who knows me before I speak. I even felt startled by hearing him call me, "Woman . . ."

Last night, as I was engaged in my nightly practice of drinking beer and staring angrily at Dave's back while he works on his book, I watched the daily reflection on EWTN. Again, the priest emphasized the woman at the well, John 4:5. But this time I heard something different. It wasn't so much about what Jesus said to her. It was what she did later—she ran into town to tell everyone what had happened. She still wasn't sure what she'd seen, so she asked everyone: "Could this possibly be the Christ?" She wasn't sad or horrified that Jesus had known all her sins. (When we face the truth of ourselves with Christ at our sides, the priest said, we should not despair.) She was thrilled at the possibility that the Messiah was real and walking among them, and she wanted to talk about that possibility with everyone she met. "Many of the town came to believe in him because of the words of this woman," writes John.

God works even through imperfect witness. I thought of your conversion and how it seems to be affecting so many people in your life. I think it was good St. Teresa who said that we judge the efficacy of prayer by our actions, not by how it makes us feel.

Last year, the woman at the well was a story of forgiveness, a story about God knowing what I need before I ask. Now, the story begins when the woman leaves the well. That is the beauty of the Gospels, the liturgy, the sacraments, and so much else I find in the church. The story is never over. It unfolds and deepens in time.

Love,

Jess

March 3, 2005

Dear Jess,

Where did the idea come from that only edifying, pretty statements are enlightening? Your letters, filled with doubt, humor, darkness, fatigue, and moments of joy, show me God so much more clearly than any bit of cheerful spiritual wisdom ever could. They seem like prayers. I remember hearing about a group of Trappist monks who collectively decided to omit the curses from the psalms—all those passages in which the psalmist rails against God and the world. But without these occasional rants, how inhuman they would seem!

I loved your eucharistic adoration letter. As I read, a little chant to the tune of Monty Python's Spam song kept running through my head: "bread, bread, bread, bread" (pause) "bread, bread, bread, bread." Scott has a sketch of Jesus above his desk, an image of Jesus with his head thrown back, laughing. There must be such a thing as holy laughter, for it is staring not just at holy bread that is absurd but also so much of life. Maybe before sitting in contemplation of the Host, a period of hilarity should be required. Everyone should stand in the vestibule of the church and crack jokes until their stomachs ache from laughing.

I knew this woman once, a silver-haired hippie, who played guitar and percussion in a world-music band. She had a great sense of humor and a perverse imagination. At one of her gigs, a man showed her around the venue, a church, and said, pointing to the soaring pipes, "This is the largest organ in the United States." She had to crack "large organ" jokes for an hour before she could trust herself not to crack one on stage. But later when she heard the organ solo, I imagine the beauty struck her even more than it did the others—so much joy already even before the music began. Wasn't it Teresa of Ávila who said, "Deliver us from sullen saints?"

Imagining the laughter of God might help with my ongoing problem with prayer. When I was on my walk with Samwise (I interrupted my letter to answer his vehement waggings), an analogy occurred to me. I mentioned recently how I have come to love Mark's bald head. I used to stare at it, trying to will the hair to grow back. I would think, *How did I end up with a bald man?* (It's disgustingly vain isn't it? It horrifies me to write it here.) But lately, over the past months, growingly and consistently I have begun to love his head. Now I can't bear the thought of him being any other way. His bald head is absolutely beautiful to me. How could I have ever loved men with hair?

Hmmm . . . how was I going to hook this up to prayer? Maybe I was thinking of how things come to pass, how real change takes place. Maybe like in marriage, commitment comes first, then real love, and then transfiguration. First you stare at the Host. You stare, stare, stare (bread, bread, bread). And then at some point you begin to love it.

My ongoing struggle with prayer is primarily why I love St. Teresa. She had such a terrible time with prayer. "I was more anxious for the hour of prayer to be over than I was to remain there," she said. "I don't know what heavy penance I would not have gladly undertaken, rather than practice prayer." I understand that. I should rather clean the house, do laundry, write, even, than pray. "This intellect is so wild," she wrote, "that it doesn't seem to be anything else than a frantic madman no one can tie down." Isn't she wonderful?

Other reasons for choosing her as my patron saint: she suffered from chronic pain much of her life, and now she is the patroness of headaches (since I've had my own struggles with chronic pain, it might be nice to have her on my side). When she was a teenager, she cared mostly about boys and clothes, and later, in a rather corrupt convent, she got more involved in flattery, vanity, and gossip than in spiritual guidance. She believed in the transformative power of love rather than punishment. And finally, she made snide remarks all the time: "There is a time for partridge and a time for penance," she said when someone apprehended her gnawing on a roasted fowl. Or when she arrived at a convent in the middle of the night in pouring rain, and the archbishop ordered her to leave, she responded, "And the weather so delightful, too."

If she could find the love of God and the way to prayer, beyond all her vanity, and still have it in her to crack a joke, maybe she will be able to lead me to God, beyond my vanity, beyond my wild, stubborn thoughts, and help me dissolve my doubts in laughter.

With devotion,
Amy

P.S. This letter is long to make up for a missed day. In case you don't accept this offering as sufficient, also included is a stick of gum and the little pamphlet on the rosary I told you about.

March 4, 2005

Dear Amy,
I'm late with my letter today because I have an unholy hangover. Dave and I went to the Oaken Bucket last night and drank several pitchers of Bud Light while we listened to our friend Cara's man problems. I woke up in the middle of the night, half drunk and sweating and panicking, and Dave was so wonderful and comforting, as he always, always is. I was overwhelmed by feelings of love and admiration for him and ashamed of how distant and bitter I've been. I had to bring him to catch the shuttle to O'Hare at 5:30 a.m., and I could hardly bear to let him out of my sight. He is now in Philadelphia.

It's still terribly cold today, with twelve inches of snow on the ground. But the days are getting longer, and now, at 5:30 p.m., the sun is outside my window, and it seems miraculous. I'm just sitting here, staring, in the fog of my hangover. I don't think I have ever anticipated Easter and spring the way I do now.

My love for Dave has flared so intensely that I almost cannot bear it. If I love Dave this much, could I love a child more? And if I did, how could I bear it? I don't know how to love someone so much without worry, fear, and doubt.

Maybe it's another symptom of unbelief. There's a scene that's always haunted me in *The Daisy Chain* by Charlotte Mary Yonge. It's one of the Victorian domestic novels I love. When the eldest daughter tells her mother that she loves her more than anything in the world, the mother lovingly corrects her; she should not love any human more than God. A human love can only disappoint, while God's love is perfect and eternal.

When I first read it, I found this exchange completely horrifying. But I'm beginning to see the wisdom in it, even the comfort.

The great trauma of my life was placing my own mother at the center of my universe—even though I sensed the danger of that cosmic order even as a child. I've been scrambling since she died to reconstruct myself around some other human love. It will be too much for any child of mine to bear, won't it? And I'm so terrified of leaving a child alone in this world. *The Daisy Chain* says that the only cure for this is to love God first, and to trust him completely.

—Jess

March 4, 2005

Dear Jess,

Early this morning, Mark woke up from a dream. "I was in the elevator," he said, "and I knew that I was going to die. It was swaying off its course, and it was clear that it had detached from one of the cables. I looked around at the others, and we all knew we were going to die. I then tried to be philosophic. *We all have to die*, I told myself, *and I am prepared*. But then I realized I was thinking of God, and I knew I hadn't really been prepared, for I hadn't known that I would necessarily think about God at that moment."

"So what happened? Did you die?" I asked him later at breakfast.

"No. The elevator landed like a plane, just swooped in gently to the ground. And I knew that it was a dream, not real, and that it was just a vision of death, not death itself."

I'm worried that all my talk of death is rubbing off on Mark. He once joked to a friend, "Amy considers all time wasted that isn't spent meditating on her death." But Mark of all people should understand, which brings me to the second story. He once posted this on the blog he keeps with his friends:

> Somewhat incidentally, I would like to officially register a promise to leave any lecture, drop any book, or end any conversation which involves the idea that "it's not the destination of a trip that matters, but the journey" or that it is more important to be a "seeker" than a "believer."

So Mark may not call it death, but he does appreciate the value of a destination.

We were talking about his post this afternoon while listening to Gillian Welch's *Soul Journey*. Whenever I listen to that album, the line about driving around with the ragtop down always makes me think of us on our summer trip, the image split between Thelma and Louise and the way of the pilgrim. Well today, a verse in one of the later songs caught my attention. Singing about her parents who have already died, she imagines how lonely it would be if she couldn't meet them on high. I love this image of heaven (another working heaven), so simply imagined as a meeting place and the end of loneliness.

But then she goes on to ask what her life, her path, will have been worth if she fails to reach eternity. It's so striking to me that Gillian doesn't fall into the cliché that it's all about the journey, but instead explicitly reverses it. She says, what will the purpose of my life have been if I don't find eternity? if I can't meet my parents again?

I couldn't agree more with this song. If God isn't there, then what was the point? If we are all simply going to die and that's it (and all this love and beauty and suffering are just tricks of biology), then spare me.

Speaking of destinations, I hope you will call soon to say that Dave got into the theology program.

Love,
Amy

March 7, 2005

Dear Amy,

I'm not sure how to begin. On the way home from O'Hare, Dave and I got lost, missed the toll-road exit, and drove two hours out of our way into Michigan. The airline had lost his bag, and we worried it had been stolen with his favorite jeans and my favorite shirt. We were happy to see each other, but the tension was still there. As we drove, lost, I knew that at any moment I could start a fight. Erupt.

When we finally got home, it was after ten, and I went straight to the kitchen for a bowl of cereal, and he went straight to his computer. I called to him in the office, asking if he wanted some, or would he rather I made him a fried-egg sandwich, and I was prattling on endlessly and not even noticing that he wasn't answering, then suddenly noticing and becoming irritated. I walked around the corner with my bowl and spoon in hand and he turned to look at me. "I didn't get in," he said.

And I knew immediately what he meant, but wanted not to know. So I said, "What? Where?" "I didn't get in," he said again, and his expression was so heartbreakingly blank, his eyes bloodshot but not tear filled. We stared at each other in silence for a moment, in disbelief. "I got a form letter. It went to my junk mail by mistake," he said. I kept waiting for him to smile and show the gap between his teeth, hoping he was making a bad joke. I could feel the cereal stuck in my throat, the bowl still in hand. I wanted to scream, or bomb something, or cry. But Dave didn't cry. He just looked, I don't know, deflated. I was so angry that I almost couldn't comfort him, filled with disgust and hatred and regret, and I wanted to curse Notre Dame. But instead, I just hugged him, and we went to bed, and he slept with his head on my chest.

I did not go to work today. I called in with the stomach flu, although I know my boss knew I was lying. (Soon Dave and I will both be unemployed.) But I could not bring myself to go. I wanted to scream with rage, burn down the house. "What are we going to do?" I asked Dave. "Keep looking," he said. And Dave, good old Jimmy Stewart, was up at 8 a.m. and off to a job interview. How does he do it?

I stayed in bed, chanting "Lord Have Mercy" over and over in my head, as we did at St. Gregory's yesterday, and the sun shone weakly through my eastern window.

I want to flee! I have the old familiar impulse to pack it in and run. But where? It's no use. I'll get up tomorrow and go to work. I'll write thank-you letters for the vice president of development. I'll pretend to still feel a bit queasy. That will not be hard.

—Jess

March 7, 2005 (later)

Dear Amy,

Dave is downstairs looking for jobs online. He has decided that this is a sign. He will simply look for a teaching job, tirelessly, until he finds one. It's wrenching my guts to see him so hopeful. And yet there it is, tugging at my sleeve too, irritating in its persistence.

Sometimes I want the luxury of giving up, of unbelief. How can one be a Christian and remain properly depressed? There is always the threat of resurrection.

—Jess

March 8, 2005

Dear Jess,

Oh, wail, wail, wail. Can I just keep writing that and still call this a letter? I think if my letter could talk, it would only wail. But if it could sing . . . (cue handbells) . . . it would sing the Lenten, "Lord have mercy. Christ have mercy. Lord have mercy."

My throat is so sore, I can barely swallow, and today I went through six hours of interviews. The head of the institute turned out to be this fierce little woman who sat in her office in front of an entire gallery of awards and told me how she was single-handedly trying to bring peace to the Middle East. She was a tyrant. At the end of the day, I met with her assistant, who instead of interviewing me, told me a long story about his recent online ordination. He wants to be a minister so that he can marry people in Klingon.

Help. I don't think even a tenure-track job is worth this.

Anyway, then in a daze I got on the wrong train and had to wait forever in the bitter cold for a northbound train. When Mark finally picked me up, I couldn't say a word and sobbed loudly the whole way home.

Is this part of Lent? The last scrutiny is supposed to teach us how to throw ourselves upon the mercy of God. I have been reading and rereading the passage from Ezekiel that is intended to prepare us for this scrutiny:

> The hand of the Lord was upon me, and carried me out in the spirit of the Lord, and set me down in the midst of the valley which was full of bones, and caused me to pass by them round about: and, behold, there were very many in the open valley; and, lo, they were very dry. And he said unto me, Son of man, can these bones live? And I answered, O Lord God, thou knowest.

My bones—or at least the bones of my throat—are dry. I feel so beaten down by my sore throat, by work, work, work (which feels like endless hustling instead of anything productive), and worry. But all of this reveals to me my absolute need for God, and for mercy. How essential it seems right now that God have a human face and a human form and knows our tribulations. So many people talk of "the universe" as the abstract, vague recipient of their prayers and the orchestrator of their fates. But how can the universe be benevolent or compassionate, especially as it expands darkly and emptily out to its own doom? Seems to me the universe is in need of a little mercy itself. Have you ever noticed the skull beneath the crucified Jesus' feet? The passage above from Ezekiel ends like this: "And there was a noise, and behold a shaking, and the bones came together, bone to his bone . . . and the breath came into them, and they lived, and stood up upon their feet, an exceeding great army."

Tomorrow I will buy St. Teresa's *Interior Castle* and will read it all week.

—Amy

March 8, 2005

Dear Amy,

Today I am more hopeful than ever. Where does it come from? Yesterday morning I could not drag myself from the bed, could not imagine having the strength to return to Grace Hall. But somehow today I feel that all will be well and that God's eye is on me, and on Dave.

I've been reading good St. Teresa. She spends the entire introduction of the *Interior Castle* whining about how she has nothing to say, and how her head hurts, and how she cannot understand why she must undertake this process. But she asks God to guide her, and she is given the vision of the interior castle, the soul within the body. It gives me hope when she says that she will say many superfluous and foolish things in order to say something that's right. Maybe I, too, will manage in these letters to hit upon some accidental truth.

She says in the chapter on the fourth dwelling place that "the important thing is not to think much but to love much; and do that which best stirs you to love." I have been thinking of this advice in the context of the revelation that I must learn to love God above all else, even my family; it's the only antidote to fear. I thought of the tenderness toward the Host I have felt during adoration. I still wonder if it's really supernaturally inspired or just a trick of the light, but maybe it's not so important to settle that matter. If a practice helps us imagine ourselves in divine love, then maybe it's still a benefit to the soul.

You wrote that love must come first, then transfiguration. I thought immediately of the scene in *The Lord of the Rings* when Merry tells Pippin, "It is best to love first what you are fitted to love; you must start somewhere and have some roots." Maybe that sentiment is at the root of popular piety, all these processions and prayers and feast days. Divine love is unfathomable, but the faithful have developed so many ways of imagining it. And then there is that image of divine care that begins for us in the crib, with our parents. That is where our conception of God really takes root. Maybe I've had it all wrong, and it's not that I have to love God more than my family but simply come to see that my love of my family—past, present, and future—is a sign of the even greater love of God, which governs all.

Merry goes on: "The soil of the Shire is deep. Still there are some things that are deeper and higher, and not a gaffer could tend his garden in peace without them, whether he knows about them or not."

Well, since Tolkien hasn't been canonized, I think St. Teresa is a fine patroness, and I wish I could have her too. When I was confirmed at age sixteen, I wanted to choose Agnes, my old favorite from childhood, but my sponsor and godmother told me I should choose my mother's name, and I felt guilty for not thinking of it first.

—Jess

March 9, 2005

Dear Jess,

My sore throat is finally healed, and with it I feel a sudden strength. It seems Lent has finally begun to turn for me. I can't believe it is already March, the month this year of Easter.

Right before I went to the doctor last Wednesday afternoon, Mark and I went into the University of Chicago bookstore, beautifully called the Seminary Bookstore. I found *Interior Castle* there and began reading it as I waited for the CAT scan (they wanted to see if an abscess was about to explode in my throat). At first it seems so lovely, Sister Teresa, our friend Teresa (as you like to call her), leading us gently, reassuring us. "Yes, dear daughter," she seems to be saying, "you are vile and wretched, but at least you have made it into the castle and all the saints and Jesus are praying for your safe passage." I felt that following her would be so easy, especially now that she herself is among those saints.

But then at some point, and I can't remember the word or phrase that stopped me, an old uncomfortable feeling came over me, and I felt compelled to take down the book *The Fire Within* by Father Dubay on the mansions of St. Teresa and the writings of St. John of the Cross. The book is a call to laypeople, but the call is radical and complete; I could never bring myself to read much of it. You must simplify your life and become pure. I took this same book with me to a retreat with the Passionists (see, I have been carrying Sister Teresa around for awhile) and managed to open the book only long enough to lay a golden leaf from their walled garden in its pages. It's still there now, looking pressed and ancient, reminding me of that weekend and the nuns who are still circling the garden path.

Well, I opened the dreaded book and turned immediately, like I sometimes do to the terrifying part of a horror novel, to the passage on purity. Over the next two days, I would read the book literally in little glimpses, terrified to see more than I could handle. I'd read a sentence and slam it shut, put it back on the shelf. And soon, out of some sort of morbid fascination, I would sneak back into the pantry and pick it up again from the shelf across from the ginger and oregano. I would stand there and crack the book open just enough to be able to read the words, and I would hunt for a disturbing passage.

"I hate that book," I announced to Mark at lunch. I hated it because it seemed to be saying that we have to renounce everything good, that we have to shut our mouths and talk only about pious, bland things, and wear simple, bland clothes, and eat simple, bland food. We have to shrink our worlds down to those pure little boxes.

And yet, Christians are not alone in their demand for purity. All religions require purification as a prerequisite for reaching God or heaven or enlightenment. Buddhists call it *suddha*, a purification of the personality, a wiping away of the *kleshas* (anger, ignorance, and lust). Hindus refer to it as *sattva* (a state free of pollution). Muslims require *najasah*, or purity, and exemplify *najasah* with white dress. And almost all cultures have purification rituals: cleansings in living waters or *mikvahs*, in lavers or saunas, with ghee, rosewater, or milk. Almost all of these practices begin as physical cleansings to remove physical impurity, and then, as the religion develops, they become ways to achieve inner, or spiritual, purity. And it occurs to me that modern, Western countries have a new ethic of purity, the green movement, requiring various forms of dietary and lifestyle asceticism. We are starting to shun chemicals, additives, excesses, and waste in our foods and materials. We are searching for something simple, natural, real, and pure.

No matter what the case, purification has always seemed like something humans have sought intuitively. We must pass through some sort of fire or water or deprivation to get to the good life (or full or happy or true life) on the other side.

Love,

Amy

March 10, 2005

Dear Amy,

I love St. Teresa's fanaticism. I'm sure I would have chosen her as my patron if I'd known that story of her running away as a little girl to seek a martyr's death. That's the sort of thing that would have sparked my imagination as a child. I spent many long hours contemplating how I would make my mark.

I also had a lot of fears and compulsions that drove me regularly to prayer and invented religious practices. I loved St. Agnes, who was burned at the stake at thirteen. I had a book about her with graphic pictures, showing the burning and the blood. I loved that book. I wasn't horrified by it in the least. It filled me with longing to be a saint, to do something great and courageous not just in the eyes of the world but also in the eyes of God. I must have been in third grade—I remember well the position of the third-grade classroom, on the corner of the long, low-slung cell block of Our Lady of Lourdes, with lots of windows and a view of the graveled playground where I broke my arm the same year. One crisp morning, I wore a bright blue, zip-up polyester track jacket to school. I left it on all day, even after it warmed up and I began to sweat. I did it just to see if I could stand to be uncomfortable for that long. I didn't think it was enough to make me a saint, but I remember thinking of it as a test, and thinking that if I passed the test it would prove that I had the stamina for some greater test and that the whole project would somehow be pleasing to God. I made it through the whole day, but by the time I got home I had a fever. With great pride and satisfaction, I told my mom what I'd done. She, of course, thought it was ridiculous, weird, and annoying, since she now had a sick kid on her hands. I remember that she frequently shrugged at my religious fervor, not sure where it was coming from but hesitant to discourage it all the same.

I had my own formula for bedtime prayers, which I'd say when my mother left the room after tucking me in. I'd listen to the dishwasher swishing in the kitchen, the yellow light from the stove's hood illuminating my open doorway as I said an Our Father, a Hail Mary, and a Glory Be. I had my own coda that I always tacked on to the end: "Please, God, bless my mother and father and sister, and let them live long happy lives, and please let me sleep good tonight with no nightmares and no nausea or vomiting. And please don't let there be a nuclear war. Amen." That was it, to the letter. (If I forgot to say it, I'd wake up in a panic, feeling doomed to a night of nausea and vomiting and/or a mushroom cloud.) I reserved the rosary for times of serious trial, like a bout of the stomach flu. Once my sister got a terrible case of strep, and after my mother spent the night in her room comforting her and watching old movies on cable, which made me insanely jealous, I heard her explain to my father: "Jennifer just can't be alone when she's sick. Jessica's fine—she just grabs the rosary beads." I was still jealous, but I felt so proud of myself at that moment. I prized this image of myself as the strong, stoic child.

What a strange turn: when my mother got sick, they all got religion, and I turned away. But that's not really true. I never stopped believing. I remained private and proud, and I saw their turn to faith healings, Bible studies, and born-again revivals as desperate and embarrassing. Part of that was my age—at thirteen, everything embarrassed me. But I still believed in God, even that inscrutable God who wouldn't heal my mom. God—loving or indifferent—was eternal, and my mother wasn't. I sensed that from a very early age. That must be why I didn't call for her when I got sick but instead prayed.

Love,

Jess

March 10, 2005

Dear Jess,

Tonight I feel my spirit drooping. I didn't even bother to shower all day, and I just spent four hours in front of the television. Sometimes God seems so distant and the whole thing make-believe. I realized something last Wednesday night in the bright room with the whirring CAT scan doughnut around my head. During the past few weeks of sickness and job searching, I felt almost ecstatic, desperate for mercy, empty, and spent—and all of this gave me an odd pleasure, the sense of being strangely and maybe self-indulgently near God. But now, with the trials over and the mundane world returning, I think the real test will begin. The real trials must be in the long middays, the long stretches when nothing much happens.

Maybe the obvious trials—the presence of evil and the destruction of our careers and our husbands' careers and our own lives (OK, I am exaggerating)—have come to an end. Now maybe we will enter the trials of good fortune or the trials of the everyday. Which do you think is more severe, good fortune or the everyday? The former brings the risk of pride but the latter the risk of despair. How grim this all seems. Earlier tonight I wasn't in such a state.

I drove over to the Mustard Seed bookstore, a huge Catholic bookstore that is just blocks away from my old place in Rogers Park. I wanted to buy a better translation of *Interior Castle*. I also bought a little card with one of St. Teresa's prayers: "Let nothing disturb you; nothing frighten you. All things are passing. God never changes. Patience obtains all things. Nothing is wanting to him who possesses God. God alone suffices."

Hopefully later, after getting farther in her interior mansions, I will have more to say.

Love,
Amy

March 11, 2005

Dear Amy,

Thus begins the renunciation of my will. How's that for a grand resolution? St. Teresa wrote that "the whole aim of any person who is beginning prayer should be that he work and prepare himself with determination and every possible effort to bring his will into conformity with God's will."

Thy will be done. I've been stuck on this since the beginning of Lent. Reading St. T, I'm beginning to think it has been entirely appropriate. It may be the only prayer I need.

I'm now in the Lady Chapel of the basilica, sitting before the Eucharist. I wonder if this counts as adoration since I am not paying attention at all, but writing to you instead.

I realized yesterday that I felt the desire to be in the presence of the Eucharist. I'm afraid this means I'm completely insane. When I got to the chapel, the tabernacle was closed and the monstrance was not on display, and I was disappointed. I had the feeling of looking for someone, some *body*.

When I arrived today, someone was practicing on the pipe organ. Now it's quiet. The snow is falling outside, and I feel extremely happy and grateful. Where did this gratitude come from? Was it really only two weeks ago that I felt as if a black hole was sucking me into nonexistence? I can't help but think that what I went through after our Pittsburgh trip—that confrontation with evil—was to be expected according to St. T's vision for the pilgrim's progress. It was the old self-help cliché of facing your demons. I cringe to write it, but I cringe and soldier on, because God contains cliché—and legend, fable, fairy tale, and myth. I remember the Black Madonna hanging in the Snite Museum and know that God contains, and realizes, and perfects.

I'm sitting now before my favorite mural of Our Lady of Lourdes appearing to St. Bernadette in the grotto. Mary is bathed in the gentlest pale-yellow light. Lately, I've been so drawn to her. I find so much comfort in St. Teresa, too, in the way she calls her readers her sisters and daughters. I feel surrounded by a loving, feminine presence.

I've so yearned for a mentor all these years without my mother—I'm surprised I haven't been roped in by a cult leader yet. (Confession: I did call a telephone psychic when I was in college.) I've been searching for a spiritual director, but at least I have our letters to shine a bright light on my soul.

—Jess

March 11, 2005

Dear Jess,

The monthly depression seems to be settling in, but finally, bored with this wallowing, I sat down to reread, for the third time, "The First Mansion." Like you, I have been shocked to discover how familiar a voice she has. I had expected an austere, distant teacher, speaking to women who, having forsaken the world and sex and belongings and physical freedom, would have very little in common with us. But their struggles seem like ours. Teresa has me from the get-go with this:

> Would it not be a sign of great ignorance, my daughters, if a person were asked who he was and could not say, and had no idea who his father or his mother was, or from what country he came? Though that is great stupidity, our own is incomprehensibly greater if we make no attempt to discover what we are, and only know that we are living in these bodies, and have a vague idea, because we have heard it, and because our faith tells us so, that we possess souls.

Isn't this one reason we write our letters, and why we want to write at all? To find out from what country we came and attempt to discover our souls? Sister Teresa writes like a memoirist, aware of the point she has reached and that she is looking back but conscious always of what she went through to get there.

And the journey she is describing is the journey through the mansions of the soul. After reading the first several chapters, I have determined that I am squarely in the first mansion. Here is the description she gives of a soul in the initial dwellings:

> These are very much absorbed in worldly affairs; but their desires are good; sometimes, though infrequently, they commend themselves to Our Lord; and they think about the state of their souls, though not very carefully. Full of a thousand preoccupations as they are, they pray only a few times per month, and as a rule they are thinking all the time of their preoccupations, for they are very much attached to them, and, where their treasure is there is their heart also.

Infrequent prayer (me), lack of spiritual wisdom (me), terrible distraction (me), and attachment to distraction (me)—a pretty good fit, wouldn't you say?

Then following this description, she gives a wonderful catalog of the interior questions that plague beginners: "Are people looking at me or not? If I take a certain path shall I come to any harm? Dare I begin such and such a task? Is it pride that is impelling me to do so?" These questions seem precisely the mechanism of distraction: the endless doubt and stalling and mulling over of one's self-identified problems and hang-ups.

But the most beautiful idea in this first section is her notion that our souls are mansions and that we can progress through the rooms by means of prayer and meditation in search of God. And the God we seek not only is beyond us but actually dwells within, abiding in the innermost chamber of our souls. This alters the purpose of self-knowledge. What we truly seek within ourselves is not merely understanding but union.

And through this whole section she keeps referring to "the vipers that bite at our heels"—our blindness, our stupidity—and so urges us to pray: "Repair yourself to God and all his saints." I love that word, *repair*. Used in this way, it means to go, as to a place, and even more, to go frequently, literally to return again and again. But of course, one also hears the more traditional meaning: to restore, to mend, to renew.

When I come to the close of every letter, I am always filled with apology for the possible dullness of my letter and with gratitude for our friendship, and I begin to understand the old-fashioned formalities, those long openings and closings, full of apology, flattery, and goodwill. So, in the spirit of bygone manners: May our letters, even the dull, the crazy, the dashed-off ones, continue to repair us to one another and to God.

Love,

Amy

March 12, 2005

Dear Amy,

Today while procrastinating at work, I was reading the Gospel of John, and I got stuck on the verse "For God so loved the world . . ." This may be all I have in common with God, but I do so love this world—and I don't just mean my family or the majesty of creation, but the Boston song that's on the radio as I write this. It's startling to contemplate, really: God doesn't just love us; he loves the world we love, the world we know.

Maybe that is why an overemphasis on purity seems so out of order. My dad, for example, is always closing his eyes to the world and looking toward eternity. Not too long ago, we were driving in my car, the radio tuned to the classic rock station. For a moment he forgot himself and sang along, probably shared some obscure fact he remembered about someone in the band. But a moment later he was quiet, and I turned to find him with his eyes closed, murmuring softly to himself, "Jesus . . . Jesus . . . Jesus . . ." I don't know his soul or what really brings him joy and anguish—maybe the song called up some sad memory of my mom, or some past shame—but the sight broke my heart. It seemed that he was needlessly robbing himself of a perfectly innocent pleasure that even God wouldn't deny him.

I loved the poem you sent about God coming with a little joke. Reading it, I immediately imagined Mr. Sam. You met him at my wedding, where he read the second reading, Paul's letter to the Corinthians, with such gravitas. But I always remember him sitting at the head of his great oak table in his bathrobe, telling jokes and drinking condensed milk straight from the can, or ceremoniously dumping a bottle of Ancient Age into the Christmas punch before their annual party, or trying to turn the world around on Christmas morning so we could do it all again.

When I was little, Mr. Sam was the mayor of Slidell, and he had an authority that seemed Godlike to me. He was also a formidable physical presence; the bathrobe he favored was literally splitting at the seams. And that voice—if I rode my bike into the street, he had only to bellow my name from his doorway and I would steer safely back onto the sidewalk. He had a roaring laugh that ended in wheezing and tears, and he laughed a lot. But he was just as prone to melancholy tears. He wept openly over my mother's death when none of us could—sometimes with such regularity and force that we were uncomfortable. In fact, I often hung back at a safe distance, fearing his intensity, but I loved him all the same, loved his ways, which seemed particularly Catholic. He'd been preparing to enter the priesthood when he met his wife, who was preparing to become a nun. Their home always felt like a chapel, filled with things I'd seen only in church—bookshelves lined with leather-bound Sacramentaries and missals with brightly colored satin ribbons, a nativity carved from smooth, blond wood bathed in a soft spotlight in their bay window, even a miter (adorned with a crawfish instead of a cross) he'd wear on Christmas morning.

I'm not sure how all of this is related—my dad turning his back on life's pleasures, Ford's God and his little joke, and Mr. Sam laughing and wheezing at his dining room table—except that I think there is something simultaneously divine and humble in the reveling Christian. There is affirmation that we should love the world—the world God loves—but recognition that the pleasures we find here sometimes wound and, at best, never truly satisfy.

I've been thinking about our summer pilgrimage to Louisiana, and how taking you there will be like taking you to my mother. My sister and I always say her soul is there, although I guess we'd better hope it's in heaven.

I've done absolutely nothing today until writing this letter and reading. I can't wait to talk to you about the sixth dwelling place of the interior castle. It's a barn burner.

With love,
Jess

March 12, 2005

Dear Jess,

I worry sometimes that being Catholic will be a phase. I worry because there seem to be so many things that I am perpetually committing myself to: exercise plans, making the bed as soon as I wake up, grocery shopping on Sundays, writing at a certain time each day, staying on a weekly budget, and on and on. Not only do I hate the thought of putting faith on that list, because it would seem so cheap and common, but the list is really a list of failures, and I am terrified of having faith turn into a temporary project.

Part of the problem is the difficulty of acquiring any new habit. I have spent a lot of my life shying away from habit as if having habits would limit my freedom. But my mind and will can't take it. I can't order up enough desire or preference to have a clear notion of what would be best accomplished or most satisfying in every moment of every day. But worse than this, I tend to defer all decisions, stay outside all set paths, keep my options perpetually open, preferring to remain the critic rather than risk being a naive participant. If I went on this way, I fear I would defer the only life I have.

I just finished reading Coetzee's *Elizabeth Costello*, which touches on exactly this problem. The climax of the book is a sort of judgment scene. Elizabeth Costello finds herself, inexplicably, in a small Italian town, which seems to be something out of a Kafka story; "Kafkaesque," she says to describe the place, and she wonders if her purgatory has been designed perfectly to gall her, filled with literary clichés. Even the panel of judges who try her seems to be a literary parody of judges. But in the midst of this slightly surreal and seemingly trumped-up place, something real takes place. She is asked simply to write down what she believes. She refuses on principle, saying again and again, in a series of revised statements, that she is a writer and it is not her business to believe, that she must remain blank so that she can be "a secretary of the invisible."

After failing the first interrogation, she is brought up before a "special case" panel, to hear her plea for exemption from the statement-of-belief requirement. She makes a last-ditch effort to win the judges' favor by saying it is unfair for them to pin her down in this way, for there is no fixed person Elizabeth Costello. The second trial ends with this exchange:

> "You ask if I have changed my plea. But who am I, who is this I, this you? We change from day to day, and we also stay the same. No *I*, no *you* is more fundamental than any other . . ."
>
> Her interrogator waves impatiently. "I am not asking to see your passport . . . The question I ask is: you, by whom I mean this person before our eyes, this person petitioning for passage, this person here and nowhere else—do you speak for yourself?"
>
> "Yes. No, emphatically no. Yes and no. Both." Her judge glances left and right at his colleagues. Is she imagining it, or does the flicker of a smile pass among them, and a whispered word? What is the word? *Confused*?
>
> He turns back to her: "Thank you. That is all. You will hear from us in due course."

"That is all?"

"That is all for today."

"I am not confused."

"Yes, you are not confused. But, who is it who is not confused?"

They cannot contain themselves, her panel of judges, her board. First they titter like children, then abandon all dignity and howl with laughter.

At the end of the chapter, losing hope of ever making it through the gate (which presumably is *her* gate, *her* passage into eternity), she goes to the gatekeeper and starts to beg for an answer. "Do you see many people like me, people in my situation?" She speaks urgently, starting to panic. She begs him to tell her. Finally, the man behind the desk has had enough, and he "lays down his pen, folds his hands, regards her levelly. 'All the time,' he says, 'We see people like you all the time.'"

I hope I haven't bored you with this long summary. Costello is the quintessential critic, the one who remains perpetually outside it all. When called upon to speak for herself, she couldn't identify any belief as her own. But I fear acquiring belief is like acquiring any habit. That is why I worry. I don't have a good track record with habit.

A few things comfort me. By converting, I am joining a body of believers. When we say the creed we say, "*We* believe." The church is a community of doubters struggling to believe, relying on one another to make it real. And also, I will now be going through the motions of belief every week, "dipping, touching, singing," as you wrote, so hopefully, eventually, those motions will be ones I can call my own.

Love,

Amy

March 16, 2005

Dear Amy,

In an eternal meeting regarding the reconfiguration of our offices in Grace Hall. Having an out-of-body experience. Is this my life?

I feel desperate to prepare for Holy Week, but I have looming deadlines, and Dave needs me, and I must face the fact that I'm not a nun but a wife and a working girl. Maybe St. T *is* a bit much for me. You are right; the real challenge is not to love and desire God when I'm prostrate in the dust but when I'm in an excruciatingly dull meeting on the tenth floor of Grace Hall, or when I'm eating dinner in a chain restaurant with my mother-in-law, or paying a $300 gas bill, or peeling Dave's wet towel off the guest-room carpet. Is there a room in the castle that is so mundane? Or is this the very dryness St. T spoke of? Is this, in fact, precisely what she meant?

I'm embarrassed by how much I yearn for spiritual drama. It seems I won't be satisfied until I see a glowing vision of Our Lady of Guadalupe in my bathtub.

Dave finally snapped at me last night. "Why does everything have to be about God?" he asked. And I answered, "Don't ask me! It just is." He said that he wants to get something because he deserves it, not because God made someone give it to him. And I didn't know what to say, because I know that's not how providence works. But what else are we suggesting when we make prayer requests? Dave says he prays only for strength, and I suppose that is like saying, "Thy will be done." I thought about it for a moment and said, "You're absolutely right. We should work on conforming ourselves to God's will instead." It's something I've written in our letters, but I've never said it out loud. Dave looked at me like I was deranged. Oh dear.

Love,

Jess

March 16, 2005

Dear Jess,

My students are taking their final exams, so I am standing here at this broken-down podium watching them in various states of stress. So many of them are fruitlessly punching away at their calculators, as if trying to dial up an answer from some sort of technological oracle. A pager just buzzed. My best student clicked it off. I wonder if it was something important and now she will be fretting over it for the rest of class. And Linda is four months pregnant. I wonder if she is sick or tired. I know she left her house this morning at 6:30. Others are intent, serious, their faces blank. I wonder if any of them is feeling like I did during that test in college when the numbers blurred and then disappeared into the white page and I could think of nothing but my shaking hands.

Earlier today I took Samwise for a walk. The afternoon was dipping down. No more sun, everything colder, the afternoon shadows gone. We walked along, and the doubts began creeping in. Now that Easter is getting close, my doubts are intensifying. Maybe God really isn't there and the prescriptions of the church are just good psychology. Coming into communion with a body of people is just what makes us happy, not what is actually true.

This is the problem of faith, isn't it? The worry that it is just wishful thinking, a chasing after wind, and that the wind is a mere rushing of air from regions of high pressure to regions of low. And I seem to recall that there was a cold wind blowing up as Sam and I walked our three-block route.

In my prior model of conversion, doubt signaled a failed or incomplete act, like a fallen cake, as if something went awry in the conversion process and the whole thing had to be attempted again, done over. So, of course, doubt to me has always seemed like a serious threat to faith. I am now trying to see doubt as part of faith. "Religious faith *begins* with the discovery that there is no evidence," wrote Wendell Berry. "There is no argument or trail of evidence or course of experimentation that can connect unbelief and belief." But then why decide one way or the other? Why not just be agnostic? When I come to this point, I always think of Pascal. "Yes; but you must wager," he said. "It is not optional. You are embarked. Which will you choose?"

I walked behind Samwise through the darkening streets and watched him happily sniff and pee and trot along. I am definitely embarked. I guess if I really came to the conclusion that I shouldn't convert, that I am making a mistake, then I would turn back, but the truth is, I no longer believe in doubt. I often expect hurdles to be crossed, barriers to be felled, progress to be made. I expect to get from point A to point B and not have to look back. But that is not the way of the believer. The believer goes over the same ground again and again, the same cycle of the hours, the same cycle of the liturgical year, the same doubts, the same sins, the same reminders. And I am not trying to go against Mark's distaste for journey worship; I am just saying that in order to reach the destination the believer walks not in a line but in a circle.

I can't believe Easter is almost here—I hope I am ready. It seems like yesterday that I dropped my first letter to you down the box at Farragut and Ravenswood.

—Amy

March 17, 2005

Dear Amy,

St. Patrick's Day. On the north quad, Flogging Molly lyrics blasted from a dorm-room window, about sin going on the same "again and again." At Mass, the statue of St. Patrick was in front of the altar, surrounded by flowers. All the priests and old men were in their green sweaters and plaid pants. Outside, the noon bells rang, and the students shouted obscenities and "Erin go Bragh!" across the quad while the old ladies covered their ears.

I sat on a bench and read your letter. I wish I could conjure that soothing, mothering presence I felt a few days ago. I felt it like a shawl on my shoulders. But today it's gone, and I feel light and cold. In fact, right now I feel so light I might float away, like a helium balloon. I've got my stare on.

I'm trying to conform myself to God's will, but what does God want? He's only getting harder to figure out. It makes sense, though, that it would get harder as we go, because we develop a desire to see God's hand at work. We look for God everywhere, and we get confused.

This morning as I put on my makeup, I saw my profile in the three-way mirror and, for a second, saw my mother's face. I stared at myself for a good long while. How odd. I saw her in me and looked at my own reflection with longing. I think so much about her, and yet I worry that I'm forgetting her, that my memory of her is slipping away, coming now only in flashes.

When I was twelve, the year before Mom got sick, she and I made a Lenten promise together to go to Mass every day until Easter Sunday. I don't remember her going to church any other time besides Christmas and Easter, not even holy days. But I remember those Lenten Masses. We would walk from our house to Our Lady of

Lourdes on Berkeley Street, and the sky would be pink with sunset, the weather already warm in Louisiana. I remember feeling that this was something only she and I shared, apart from my sister, my father, my ever-present grandmother. My sister was sixteen and at the height of her teen snottiness, and my mother was finally turning to me, and I felt adult, walking with her and talking about our days.

I'm sure this is one reason I have loved our letters so much, because they are restoring this memory for me, that feeling of being one of two women talking, sharing something that is ours alone. In our own way, we too are walking together toward the church.

I'm sorry Lent is coming to an end. What will happen to our letters? To our hermitage of two?

With love,

Jess

The letter, written in absorbed silence, is an
act of faith.
—Vivian Gornick

Easter 2005

I began Lent by announcing my lack of desire for God, but now I think it wasn't that I didn't desire God, but that I failed to see that what I was desiring was in fact God. I failed to imagine St. Teresa's incarnate God who dwells in the innermost chamber of our souls, who permeates our loves and losses.

—Amy, March 21

• • • • • • •

I intended this week to be a week of constant prayer and fasting and contemplation of the mysteries at hand. Instead I've been eating pizza and chocolate and smoking forbidden cigarettes and getting my hair cut, of all things (God forbid I participate in the most important moment of your spiritual life with grown-out layers), and now here it is, the eve of the Triduum, and I'm feeling too bloated and privileged and blind to be of any use to you.

—Jess, March 23

March 18, 2005

Dear Jess,

I just returned home from first confession, and I feel like yelling from the rooftops. We need a word like *wail* but for the joyful times. *Yay* is too childish, and *hallelujah* a bit too liturgical or revivalist. How about *hooray?* Hooray! Why does confession make you feel so joyful?

I think I have always desired confession. When I was a little, I used to beg my mother to sit by my bedside and listen while I recounted my wrongdoings of the day. But often, too embarrassed to tell her outright, I would ask her to guess. She would patiently make inquiries while I would coach her: "No, no, worse than that," I would say. And when I was even younger, I would spend that same bedtime hour listing the many sins of my doll, Phyllis (named for Phyllis Diller), and discussing the possible penances I might suggest to reform her stubborn ways. I don't know where that desire came from; my parents weren't particularly punitive or accusatory. It seems in retrospect that I had a more basic, original need. These are silly examples, I know, but the need I had for this nightly ritual was real. And in many ways I still relate to it—that yearning at the end of the day to make things right.

We talked recently in my catechism class about confession. It is called the sacrament of confession. In some real sense it is the church's mechanism of ongoing conversion, of turning one's heart continually back to or toward God. I imagine the heart like some giant gear that we are slowly, imperceptibly turning. Prayer, confession, almsgiving, and service are our turning tools, our wrenches. But what exactly are we turning toward? Confession is also called the sacrament of reconciliation. When we confess, we are being reconciled to ourselves ("in our inmost being, where we regain our innermost truth" it says in the *Catechism*) and to creation and to God. So as we slowly turn our hearts to God, we slowly come into communion with ourselves and with one another.

When you are a child and you first recognize your own will turning away from your family, you feel a terrible loneliness. I remember sneaking out of my room in the early morning, the grass wet and the sun just hemming the horizon. I would climb into the top of our weeping cherry and sit up there in the forked branches just to feel the thrill of my own solitude. And yet I would also feel lonely and wish someone knew where I was. Now, looking back, I am sure someone did know. I am sure someone was peering out the back window to make certain I was there and was safe but also being careful to honor my little experiment in freedom. When I had my mother sit by my bedside to hear, or guess, my confession, it was this that I wanted. I wanted her to find me out, to see me as I really was (even when I was away), and to bring me back.

When I came outside from the parish center onto Paulina Street, the sun was bright and warm. I walked home keenly aware of the world around me and myself in the world, and even the shadows my arms made swinging over the sidewalk seemed to make the pavement a necessary part of my joy.

Love,
Amy

March 20, 2005
Palm Sunday

Dear Amy,
We spent Palm Sunday in Pittsburgh, where Dave was running auditions for the Pennsylvania Governor's School for the Arts. It was so

reassuring to see him there working, happy. I think he wanted me to see it.

I was so worried that our grad-school friends had dismissed us as religious fanatics, but Kathy asked me to meet her on the steps of St. Paul's in Oakland for Mass. She was on the verge of tears throughout. Meanwhile, I was cold as a box of rocks, noticing all the lame things that distract me during Mass—the rambling, nonsensical homilies (this one was something to do with no-money-down real estate scams and Christ being a fool; I didn't follow), the terrible choices of hymns, the careening cantors. I was so worried she would not enjoy it. I even felt self-conscious about how much we mention Christ in the Mass. We talk of him so little in conversation, fastidiously avoiding that potentially offensive, scandalous name: Jesus. I actually thought to myself, *She'll be turned off if she thinks this is what we're all about.*

What a faithless twit I am.

When we read the Passion and Christ asked the sleepy apostles, "Could you not keep watch one hour?" I looked at Kathy, and her eyes were full of tears and pain.

I picked up Dave on the corner of Ninth Street and merged onto 279-N toward Ohio. For the first time, I forgot to look back for one last glimpse of bridges and rivers and houses stuck on hillsides. I think that is a good sign.

Love,

Jess

March 21, 2005

Dear Jess,

I'm starting to panic—Easter is only five days away! I feel the need to get my reasons down in writing, so that if my knees buckle at the door of the church, you can whip this letter out and wave it under my nose like smelling salts.

I want to think more about that connection between conversion and communion (or reconciliation, which is just the return to communion). It was a revelation to me that confession carries both names, the sacrament of conversion and of reconciliation. This discovery gives me a way of making sense of what I will really be doing in a few days.

I began Lent by announcing my lack of desire for God, but now I think it wasn't that I didn't desire God, but that I failed to see that what I *was* desiring was in fact God. I failed to imagine St. Teresa's incarnate God who dwells in the innermost chamber of our souls, who permeates our loves and losses. I have always thought that my strongest motivation for seeking God has been, as Tolkien writes, that "oldest and deepest desire, The Great Escape: The Escape from Death." And not just my death, but the death of those I love. And even if I never had to endure a literal loss, still there would be unrest. Still there would be that insufficiency, that longing that persists even through good times.

So now when I think of God, I think of what works against loss; I think of communion. Tolkien calls "the desire of men to hold communion with other living things" one of the basic "primordial desires." And this makes me think of those beautiful lines of Isak Dinesen. "Will the air over the plain quiver with a color that I have had on," she wonders. "Or the children invent a game in which my name is, or the full moon throw a shadow over the gravel of the drive that was like me, or will the eagles of the Ngong Hills look out for me?" We are cut off from the world, one another, and ourselves. We long for reconciliation. And so this is what I desire: to come into communion, to be reconciled with the world, my loved ones, and myself, and so with God.

Conversion literally means turning around. But if I do finally manage to turn around, what am I hoping to see? "When the turn comes, it can give to child or man that hears it," writes Tolkien, "a catch of the breath, a beat and lifting of the heart." He goes on writing about fairy stories in general, but the Christian story in particular: "In such stories when the sudden turn comes we get a piercing glimpse of joy, and heart's desire, that for a moment passes outside the frame, rends indeed the very web of story, and lets a gleam come through." We turn and see that our deepest desire is answered, that we are not alone on the high road, that we were never alone.

Converting now is just the beginning of this turn. It is a declaration of hope, a hope in what I have glimpsed in the communion of my family, my marriage, my own heart. It is a declaration of hope that these partial unions are signs of what is to come, and, for that matter, what really *is*, period—not just tricks of biology, congregations of matter, but real, eternal things that we don't have to ever fully lose. And where does one find hope but in God? In the one who says *I am* and sustains all things in love.

So by converting I am answering the desire I first experienced when perched at the top of that weeping cherry—the desire to look back and see my mother standing at the window.

And now I must end with the same bit of poetry with which Tolkien closes his essay on fairy stories, for it is perfect. From "The Black Bull of Norroway":

Seven long years I served for thee,
The glassy hill I clamb for thee,
Thy bluidy clothes I wrang for thee;
And wilt thou not wauken and turn to me.
He heard and turned to her.

Pray for me.

Love,

Amy

March 23, 2005
Wednesday of Holy Week

Dear Amy,

I intended this week to be a week of constant prayer and fasting and contemplation of the mysteries at hand. Instead I've been eating pizza and chocolate and smoking forbidden cigarettes and getting my hair cut, of all things (God forbid I participate in the most important moment of your spiritual life with grown-out layers), and now here it is, the eve of the Triduum, and I'm feeling too bloated and privileged and blind to be of any use to you.

What a gift I have received from you this Lent, to come home from work every day and find your letters waiting for me, to run my finger underneath the flap of the envelope and unfold the papers. Each time I read one, I feel that God must exist; how could we both be so similarly deranged?

I don't know why I feel that this will be my last letter. I know I'll continue to write even now that Lent is over.

I will see you tomorrow, Holy Thursday.

With love,

Jess

March 29, 2005

Dear Amy,

It's Easter, and you're a Catholic, and I'm back in South Bend trying to return to life as usual. This is the first letter I will attempt to write. Where should I begin?

I think I'll start with Holy Thursday. I fasted, unintentionally. Why is it so hard for me to skip even one meal? I have managed today, only because I had an extra-large latte from Starbucks. Not exactly monastic. Anyway. I was sick with hunger and distracted by my terrible vantage point, behind the altar in a folding chair. After all my introspection, this was where I must begin the Triduum—behind the altar, with no view of the ritual taking place there at all? I flailed helplessly, trying to see beyond the throng, all these people, crowding holiness, wanting a piece, or more charitably, wanting to be a part of it, within it. I couldn't help but think of *Life of Brian*—"blessed are the cheesemakers? The Greeks? Oh, the meek!! . . . Oh well they have had a bad lot of it, haven't they"?—and also the Sermon on the Mount, scenes from *The Gospel According to St. Matthew* and *Jesus of Nazareth,* the faithful and the merely curious coming in droves, perched on the hillsides, on the rooftops, to catch a glimpse. I should have felt inspired but instead felt disgusted, wanting to shout, "Where were all of you during these six weeks of Lent while I was beating my breast and crying in the pews?"

After Mass I went home to the precious clothes and food that had been on my mind all night. A suitcase and a frozen dinner! Six weeks of preparation and this is what distracts me!

All Friday and Saturday my heart pounded away in anticipation. Again, I could not fast. At Reza's we feasted on grilled shrimp in lemon and oil, eggplant pureed with tahini. "At least it is the food of Jesus," you said.

That night, we knelt before an empty tabernacle. Doors open, revealing nothing. The horror! I felt the absence so keenly. When we stood from our kneelers, filing out in a line to venerate the crucifix, Kathy looked at me in a panic. "What do I do?" she asked. "Just touch your lips to the feet," I said. And immediately I thought, *How ridiculous! Kissing the feet of this little wooden figure. She'll never do it.* I waited my turn and watched. Some leaned forward with their hands folded behind their backs, barely grazing their lips to the feet. Some skipped the feet all together and went for the bottom of the cross—more sanitary? Others knelt or genuflected. I imagined grabbing the thing with both hands and kissing it with a loud smack. *Kathy will think we're crazy,* I thought. *She'll never do it.* As I approached, I wondered if she was watching me from back in the pew. And when it was finally there before me, in the priest's arms, I reached for it with both hands and brought the crucifix to my lips, and bowing gently, pressed my mouth tenderly to the little wooden feet. The series of motions felt surprisingly natural. When I returned to the pew, Kathy wasn't there after all. She was game and as eager as she has been in all other things. I watched as so many people knelt, or bowed, or genuflected, and kissed the feet. An elderly mother and her retarded son. She whispered in his ear, and he obediently followed her, bending and kissing. Another woman didn't kiss at all but pressed the palm of her hand full against Christ's chest. I remembered Nancy Reagan extending her hand to pat her late husband's coffin, gently, gently. The blind woman from the choir, approaching with her dog, following the lead of another red-robed friend, bending and kissing. All of us, bending and kissing.

It felt like a funeral, and I didn't know how we would recover from this experience. How would we socialize? Drink? Laugh? But we did. I imagine us throwing open the doors, emerging in a cloud of incense to breathe in the cold night air. The husbands walked ahead of us in charity. I see them under the street lamp, with hands in pockets under their blazers, walking in their steady, constant way.

Saturday felt like the day of the feast, with the same feelings we had on our wedding days, this intense need to concentrate, to fill the moments with meaning, to commit them to our memories, since we know they will pass so quickly in experience. Sometimes I look forward to things being past, so I can assign the meaning to them that comes only through contemplation. Looking back on it now, my wedding Mass seems beautiful, heady with incense and the rosy light of the church. But then, on the altar, I was just trying not to throw up.

I have a picture of you from that day, standing on the steps before the open doors of the church. You were opening the heavy door, and the photographer was standing just inside, and he snapped it just as you were pulling it back, chest expanded with breath, face lit with anticipation. I am standing in the blurry background, calling over my shoulder to you to hurry up. I have looked often at this picture, which is tacked to a board over my desk, while writing these Lenten letters. It has seemed like the perfect illustration of your conversion.

We arrived early for the Easter Vigil, and Sister Barbara gave us pink corsages, already wilting. Brian lit the bonfire on the street, and the wind blew, big Chicago gusts rustling our skirts, blowing the flame around so that he couldn't light the Easter candle, raising the prickly stubble on my bare legs. I stood closer to warm them, imagined a spark in my hair igniting me like a Roman candle.

We led the procession into the darkened church, Father Bart pausing here, there, to tip the Easter candle to the candles of the congregation, until the flame spread out to the corners of the church and the room became visible. I felt so proud to be there with you, so proud of this procession's ancient beauty. (It felt only vaguely like that scene in *Peggy Sue Got Married* when Grandpa takes Peggy to some weird Masonic ritual and they try to span time.)

We sat in the first pew and listened to the Old Testament readings, candles burning in hand. And suddenly I became dizzy. Hearing those readings, I got scared. I choked on their ancient dust. The candle in my hand seemed to flame hotter, and I couldn't escape the heat, no matter where I held that tiny flame. I tried to breathe deeply, to slow my heart. What if I had to run? What if I ruined this moment forever? What if your memory of the most important moment in your spiritual life was me running madly for the door—a hyperventilating, screaming streak of black and yellow, smelling faintly of Coco Chanel?

When the readings were finished, it was easier. The house lights came up and we extinguished our candles. I filled my lungs with cooler air. My heart slowed to normal.

Standing behind you at the baptismal font, I waited too long to deliver my big line. Someone whispered from stage right: "Say her name!" Father Bart smiled at me expectantly. I placed my left hand on your right shoulder, squeezed, and said, "She takes the name Teresa." He moved his thumb across your forehead, leaving the sign of the cross in shiny chrism.

Afterward, we walked to the Hopleaf, where we ate mussels soaked in ale and French fries with aioli and drank the most delicious cold beers. It was a wedding feast, and my feeling was indeed that our families had been joined, our bond now stronger than friendship.

It was so hard to leave on Sunday night. All day, my Easter joy was leaking out like a deflating balloon. Our families were resentful that we hadn't spent the holiday at home. Dave's mom called with her voice full of accusations. My dad was silent.

"Don't hold on to me," Jesus told the apostles when he rose again.

"Don't be afraid," the risen Jesus told the apostles, who loved him so deeply, zealously, clumsily, like a litter of puppies. And then, to Mary Magdalene: "Woman, why do you weep?"

At Mass today, the priest said that the paschal mystery is so unbelievable, so amazing, so overwhelming that the church does not expect us to fathom it. This week's readings are all stories about how the apostles didn't understand the Resurrection, at least not right away. They couldn't fathom it, either. Today's Gospel was from John—the one about Mary Magdalene and the empty tomb, about how Mary Magdalene doesn't recognize the risen Jesus.

I thought of Father Brian's Easter Sunday homily. The empty tomb. What did Mary see? Nothing. She saw nothing.

Remember the tomb.

Remember nothing.

We are now in the fifty days of Easter and facing the challenge of living with the Resurrection. I think it was easier for me to live with the Passion—Christ made real for me by pain, sacrifice, human flesh, blood, and bone.

I'm sorry; this letter was supposed to be entirely happy!

With much love and joy,

Jess

II

New Life

And none will hear the postman's knock
Without a quickening of the heart.
For who can bear to feel himself forgotten?

—W. H. Auden

Ordinary Time 2005

It seems like the world has been overturned since I wrote to you last. I am now Catholic and you are pregnant, and both of these events have changed everything forever. I want to remember everything as it was three weeks ago, but I know that already some things have slipped away and have been replaced by the life that keeps rising up around us and carrying us forward.

—Amy, April 15

• • • • • • •

I am acutely aware of being alone in here with this baby, this growing fetus that already has a heartbeat and little buds becoming arms and legs. . . . It's having to be with this constantly, even when you sleep. Even when you shower. Even when you most desperately want to be alone again, reading St. Teresa and scribbling notes in the margins. You've got to be here, doing it. You and your body, working, working, working to create this person, this baby, who already has a soul, although maybe that's just a bud, too. Or is that why the presence is so strong? Does the soul grow like an arm or a leg, or does it exist always in the same state? Is there another soul inside of me?

—Jess, April 25

April 12, 2005

Dear Amy,

Dare I hope that it's true? That it wasn't a fluke? That the crossbar was there after all, not just a figment of my imagination?

I sat on the toilet and stared at the stick for a full three minutes. Then I turned on the light and looked some more, so hard that my eyes hurt. The vertical line was undeniable. Definitely *not* negative. But where was the crossbar?

I'm afraid to hope that I am and afraid to find out that I'm not.

This is way ahead of schedule.

Every possible symptom could have some other cause. The spicy Thai food I ate last night. The period that could arrive at any moment. Would I be happy?

I can't bear to think of either outcome.

I can't bear to think.

More soon.

Jess

April 15, 2005

Dear Jess,

It seems like the world has been overturned since I wrote to you last. I am now Catholic and you are pregnant, and both of these events have changed everything forever. I want to remember everything as it was three weeks ago, but I know that already some things have slipped away and have been replaced by the life that keeps rising up around us and carrying us forward. Oh, Jess, it is so beautiful to think of your child (your child!) growing in there, and I think I understand what you said last night about death. Conception is the beginning, and every beginning starts time running toward an end: all stories and lives play out, and to be no longer the one conceived, but the one conceiving makes this all the more clear.

Today and maybe for the past three days, I have been having a small crisis of faith, wondering what comes now. The past three days—with your announcement, Dave's book deal, my out-of-the-blue job offer—have hardly been quiet. So maybe it is just today, in the wake of so many changes, with the house so still, that I have been feeling this way.

I want to tell you how it was for me at the Easter Vigil, but I keep thinking of my first, almost-inadvertent conversion. Back then I was feverishly working through arguments for the existence of God, historical evidence to "prove" the Resurrection, and endless apologetics. I was desperately trying to skirt the need for faith. In a last-ditch effort to make God undeniable, I decided I must have an encounter, but where was this ethereal God: In my mind? My heart? One morning, I sat beside Dru, the leader of the campus fellowship, in the vacant college chapel and begged God to appear. "Please, please, please," I managed to pray out loud. "I want to be done with doubts." I waited to feel something, some small thing—a shiver down the spine, a whisper—to see a glint in a dark corner of the ceiling. But there was nothing, just the hot air, the uncomfortable feel of Dru's damp arm too close to mine. God was indistinguishable from the rattle in my head of my own thoughts. And then suddenly Dru was hugging me. "Every angel in heaven is rejoicing," he said, practically in tears. Looking up, I realized he had taken that moment as *the* moment of my conversion. Was it? He was leading me outside, across the brittle summer grass and empty campus, a ghost town in July.

I tried to make the whole thing rest on me, my rational capacity and historical insight, or just my ability to gin God up. But Lent was so different. Instead of me rushing toward some conclusion and trying to force it to materialize out of thin air, I had the sense of something coming for *me*. Easter drew closer day by day, and the conclusion was already known in advance. The first time felt like an intensified version of waiting for the phone to ring. When would it happen? Now? Ever? When I walked up the steps of St. Gregory's for the Vigil, my stomach was churning, but not because I was wondering if God would show up, if it would all really happen. Instead, it was like the nervous anticipation of my wedding. The decision was already made; this was just the moment that would make it real and release me into the rest of my life.

And yet today in my quiet house, something of the old rattle is returning. The holy feast grows dimmer by the day. And like that morning in the airy silence of the college chapel, I feel alone and God distant. Last month I felt time moving with such purpose toward Easter, each day a little closer, a little weightier. And now your days are suddenly moving toward another great moment. You'll be operating on a new calendar, marking time by weeks and the growing weight in your belly. But for me, where is time headed?

Love,
Amy

April 16, 2005

Dear Amy,
I'm thirty-four thousand feet above St. Louis, Missouri, headed to Dallas, then to Baton Rouge.

I haven't slept in days, or at least not a satisfying sleep. It seems I've just lain in bed, staring into the darkness, pressing my fingers into my belly, my breasts, feeling for changes, some new softness or knot. I want to know so badly if it's true. I feel it is, but is that only my imagination? And what if it is not such good news but something bad: cysts, cancer? But I keep returning in my mind to the moment I peed on the second stick, holding my cell phone in the crook of my neck, placing the test on the bathroom counter and pausing just a moment before the display read "pregnant." So it must be true. You were there, on the phone, my witness.

All I have thought of is how my body is not really mine anymore—not mine to fill with beer and coffee and nicotine. Not mine to obsess over my expanding waistline, darkening nipples, and varicose veins. In some ways this is where the fear comes from, this loss of control. But maybe it's also a blessing. I belong to this child growing in me. I am no longer alone. Maybe this is how it feels to know that I belong to God, that I am no longer isolated and cut off from the living as I walk in my little death chamber. There's new life in me, with a heartbeat.

And yet I'm so aware of death! It's no longer a mere possibility but a real thing taking root in my uterus, a being that will live and die. I remember a painting of the Annunciation I saw in the Carnegie Museum in Pittsburgh, the angels coming to Mary with the news. They also carry the implements of Christ's death: the crown of thorns, a nail. Mary tries to shield her eyes, her body. How did she manage to rejoice, to say yes?

Now, I'm on my way home, where I'll be nearer the memory of my own mother. How like her I feel at this moment, in my big sunglasses, popping my gum, right leg crossed over my left, gently bouncing as if of its own will. Still I feel so unprepared to be a mother, so mystified by life and how quickly it is taking and then changing shape.

With love,
Jess

April 17, 2005

Dear Jess,

I am struggling to go joyfully forward. You are now in Louisiana, and your physical absence seems to underscore the odd sense of separation I have felt since we found out you are pregnant. Before, I think I drew too much sustenance from the joint nature of our spiritual journey. "Whither thou goest," we said to each other as a way of walking together toward God. But it seems that wasn't quite right, or wasn't the whole story. Really it's "whither *Thou* goest"—the way of the cross, not a road of our own making. Yet it unsettles me that suddenly you have jumped ahead, and I am still back here, pre-parenthood, pre-family, pre . . . I am still seemingly free to make plans as I see fit.

I felt this same way right after my sister's wedding. She had a tiny ceremony in a country chapel just a few miles from our childhood home. The whole group managed to crowd around one table in the only nice local restaurant. We laughed and made merry, and then my sister and her new husband drove off, headed ultimately for England, where they would live for the next six years. Just like that, everything had changed. My sister was no longer mine but his. It was his life and their life together she would have to honor above all other claims.

Back in my parents' house, we all spent the rest of the day milling about, mostly silent. Remembering it now, it seems to me that we left all the lamps off. The white, diffuse light that comes through windows on a cloudy day filled the rooms. I remember sitting at the kitchen table alone. Everything around me seemed to have dwindled down into ordinary shapes and placement. The square salt shaker over there, the few crumbs scattered from a rushed breakfast. I tried to pin down what was wrong, but my thoughts were vague, floating, as if I'd been cut loose. I felt an occasional tight sting at the back of my eyes.

I know this must sound so melodramatic; I am really not trying to be. Of course, I know I have my own claims. I am married, I have committed myself to a spiritual path, but the question of having children, made suddenly so stark with your pregnancy, gives me that old feeling of standing on the brink, undecided. A boyfriend once told me that I was all potential, nothing decided (I almost punched him). I yearn for a life that is anchored by commitment.

Please don't take any of this the wrong way. We've both been considering starting families; this has always been in the cards. It's only fear of the unknown (or maybe just fear of the everyday, without any obvious adventure) I'm balking at. Forgive me.

Love,
Amy

April 25, 2005

Dear Amy,

Since I got back from my trip, I've been so tired and lazy that I've been going to bed every night at 6:30 pm and then lying here sleepless, stomach churning, muscles aching, reading absentmindedly through the stack of books on Dave's nightstand. Tonight it's

John Cheever's journals. Though bleak, somehow they comfort me. Maybe because the moments of real joy are in the descriptions of his children: watching his son, barefoot and in chinos, lighting a Roman candle on the dock on the Fourth of July. Playing hockey with him in the winter.

I must have faith that one day I'll feel it too—that admiration for my child. Right now it's all fear and dread and worry, each thought more selfish than the last. How will I write if I'm always sick, or sleeping, or doing laundry, or nursing? How will I work and write and raise a baby? Apparently, all these thoughts are supposed to magically disappear when I hear the baby's heartbeat, at least according to *What to Expect When You're Expecting*. But it's four more weeks until my first appointment with the OB.

I'm still trying to make sense of my trip to Louisiana, to get to work on my story, but I feel oddly disconnected from reality at the moment. This pregnancy has webbed around me so that everything else and everyone else seems far away. I am acutely aware of being alone in here with this baby, this growing fetus that already has a heartbeat and little buds becoming arms and legs but isn't quite looking human yet. That's really the feeling—alone with it. No one and nothing can help, or ease the anxiety or the side effects. It's having to be with this constantly, even when you sleep. Even when you shower. Even when you most desperately want to be alone again, reading St. Teresa and scribbling notes in the margins. You've got to be here, doing it. You and your body, working, working, working to create this person, this baby, who already has a soul, although maybe it's just a bud, too. Or is that why the presence is so strong? Does the soul grow like an arm or a leg, or does it exist always in the same state? Is there another soul inside of me?

On the way to Baton Rouge from my dad's house in Slidell, I stopped at the cemetery to sit pregnant before my mom's grave. It just seemed like something I should do; I'm not sure if I manufactured it for drama or if the impulse was genuine. The flowers I'd put there on my last visit were gone, and I didn't have the time to replace them, so the urn stayed empty except for the white bow I'd tied around it. That was still there. Cobwebs had formed over her name (don't they clean these things, or is that my job, too?). Suddenly a bright streak of green raced across the granite: a gecko. I haven't seen one in ages. Bright grass-green, with that red balloon under his jaw. He just sat there, panting, staring at me, looking new and strong, lean, muscular, indestructible. I hate geckos.

I said a Hail Mary. Never before had the cemetery felt so pointless, so dead. I used to feel something when I went. This time I felt nothing but absence, dust, void. And new life running it over. A bright green streak across my mother's grave.

So this is the way it works, I guess. Life marching relentlessly, burning through families and seasons and years, creating, dying, creating again. Now, something growing inside me that I can't stop.

No wonder women want the right to choose. I've never understood it so plainly. Your body is no longer your own. And it's scary. If the baby were gone, would I feel in control again? Can you ever go back once you've felt it?

Then there were the caterpillars. Did I tell you about the plague of caterpillars? They were falling from the trees. They were in my hair, stuck to my clothes. One crawled out of my sleeve as I was driving home.

Everywhere I turned, life was going forward, life literally raining down. But my mother's grave was hopelessly dead and pointless. Maybe it's better to be scattered to the wind than to erect such a pathetic monument that will become a playground for a gecko. Damn that gecko.

And then I saw my old boyfriend, the last man I was with before Dave. He walked right by me in the airport, messenger bag slung across his shoulders like a proper hipster, but his hair was short—clean-shaven, grown-up. I was mid-sip on a forbidden Coke, sitting there pregnant with my Yankee husband's baby, just inches away from what might have been so different. How quickly it all rushed back! The solid feeling of his body, the fiercely bitten fingernails, the click of a Zippo lighter, the indecipherable French accent of our housemate, the two-step at the newspaper Christmas party—all scenes from some other lifetime. He just kept walking, and I kept staring, invisible, like George Bailey. He didn't see a thing.

Love,

Jess

April 30, 2005

Dearest Jess,

I am thinking of you right now and wondering if your aching toes are any better. I read about fifth disease online. The statistics don't sound nearly as bad as you thought. But I am glad you are seeing the doctor on Wednesday morning. Even as I write this letter about things that have nothing to do with your plight, know that I am thinking of you and praying that you are well.

I want to write to you about the horror of the everyday. How's that for a cheerful beginning? I'll warn you from the start—I'm not in the best of spirits, but hopefully I will write myself out of the little hole I seem to be in. My mood began about an hour ago. I returned home from work feeling springy, sunny. Birds chirping outside. A four-day weekend in front of me. Then I checked my e-mail, and there was a message from a fellow in the St. Gregory's book group. Last night while we were discussing Chesterton's chapter on suicide versus the martyr, he told two stories: one about his own near attempt at taking his life; the other, about his sister-in-law, Jin, who almost, through the help of a Dr. Kevorkian type, committed suicide. Jin is still alive but is truly dying this time from cancer. His e-mail contained a link to her web page, part of a hosting site that sponsors live journals for the terminally ill. I read her most recent post. She has decided to discontinue radiation and chemo so that in her last months she will be healthy enough to enjoy her two little girls. She is making a box of letters and journals for both of her children and her husband. When a mother goes away, Jin writes, she leaves dinner in the fridge. She is trying to extend the same gesture through time with the boxes. I couldn't help thinking of your mother as I read, how she must have felt as she prepared to leave you and Jennifer. Jin went on, writing rather cheerfully about death, mentioning karma and spirit and suffering, but ultimately pinning her hope on the belief that her family would be reunited in the spirit world.

I stepped away from the computer and found myself in the everyday world. The common floor beneath my feet. The common sun on the porch railings. A common, everyday dog barking in a nearby yard. And it is not the commonness, really, that bothered me, but the overwhelming feeling that this is it. Maybe that is something like what you felt watching that wretched gecko. The world, in all its stark familiarity, seemed to be saying, "Here it all is, all of it—don't look for anything more." The idea of Christ and his suffering and death, the need for sacrifice and resurrection, suddenly seemed impossible. How could such a grand, terrible, awesome thing be demanded or even desired in this everyday world?

I hope I am making sense. It is so hard to get across the horror I feel when I lift my head from a book or from writing and find a world grown loudly dull. And it's not that there is not beauty or love to be found, but that mystery has somehow been banished; the sun has stamped out the unseen.

How does this relate to Jin? Well, although quite different from my beliefs, Jin's faith seems to rest on a supernatural belief—a faith in the eternity of the soul and the possibility of reunion beyond death. But it is so hard to sustain this belief through the course of a day. And I guess I should say a typical day, one not threatening to be your last. We live in a world that worships nature; we look to nature to see how things are supposed to be. We suspect that we humans have messed it all up and must return to the natural way of things. And yet when it comes to death, where does this faith in "the natural" leave Jin, or your mother, or all of us who are ultimately dying?

This problem of the everyday is related, I feel sure, to an experience I had repeatedly as a child. I would wake up and see the sun shining on the edge of the curtain above my head, a bit of blue sky gleaming at the top of the window, and invariably the sound of an airplane overhead. I would lie there and feel sickened by the day, that same sense of the commonness of things. The best literary description I have ever found is in *Hopscotch* by Julio Cortázar (this passage is actually the sole reason I haven't yet burned the book):

> I woke up and I saw the light of dawn through the cracks in the Venetian blinds. It came from so deep in the night that I had a feeling like that of vomiting up myself, the terror of coming into a new day with its same presentation, its mechanical indifference of everytime: consciousness, a sensation of light, opening my eyes, blinds, dawn.

> In that second, with the omniscience of half-sleep, I measured the
> horror of what astounds and enchants religions so much: the eternal
> perfection of the cosmos, the unending rotation of the globe on its
> axis. Nausea, the unbearable feeling of coaction. I am obliged to bear
> the daily rising of the sun. It's monstrous. It's inhuman.

Everything rings familiar except his suggestion that it is the perfection of the cosmos that appalls. What horrifies me is the cosmos
stripped of mystery, bare-boned and normal. Maybe it is the plane
overhead—a sign that we have even understood the heavens enough
to pierce them, to fly through them on the way from here to
there—that really gets me.

It is in this mood I often find Chesterton marvelous. Here is
a passage that could be read as a direct answer to the grim
vision above:

> The sun rises every morning. I do not rise every morning; but the
> variation is due not to my activity, but to my inaction. Now, to put
> the matter in a popular phrase, it might be true that the sun rises
> regularly because he never gets tired of rising. His routine might be
> due, not to a lifelessness, but to a rush of life. The thing I mean
> can be seen, for instance, in children, when they find some game
> or joke that they specially enjoy. A child kicks his legs rhythmically
> through excess, not absence, of life. Because children have abound-
> ing vitality, because they are in spirit fierce and free, therefore they
> want things repeated and unchanged. They always say, "Do it again";
> and the grown-up person does it again until he is nearly dead. For
> grown-up people are not strong enough to exult in monotony. But
> God is strong enough to exult in monotony. It is possible that God
> says every morning, "Do it again" to the sun; and every evening, "Do
> it again" to the moon.

Chesterton is crying out against automatic necessity. "The repetition
in nature may not be mere recurrence; it may be a theatrical encore,"

he writes. "It may be that our little tragedy has touched the gods . . . and that at the end of every human drama we are called again and again before the curtain." If life is mere, just an animal fate, it could hardly even be called life. Life involves will, joy, contingency. And this is exactly, I think, what horrified me when I peered up through the window at the day. The possibility that it was a blind day, a dumb day—unaware and automatic—turning through someone dying, someone being born, turning without regard for life. And to see that sky and suspect for an instant that our lives, too, might be of the same type: mere, the result of molecules and genes and quantum mechanics, carbon chains, and electrical signals. But Chesterton rescues the sun. He imagines behind it a magician who delights in its course.

If all is natural, like many appear to believe, if life is natural, cancer is natural, and death is natural, then everything becomes common as an automatic sun, everything (for me at least) loses its life even before it dies. By positing something supernatural, beyond nature, suddenly nature itself changes. Some things seem right and good and glorious—the sun, for example. And others—cancer, death, separation—seem terrible. Nature is put in reference to something else.

It still bothers me and causes me to question my faith that some people seem to feel no need for this kind of supernatural belief. But then again, I do not know these "some people" individually. I don't know how each one comes (or doesn't come) to a point of peace. I don't know what beliefs guide them on the way. So to use what I imagine to be in all those hearts and minds as a stumbling block for my own faith would be the mistake I have made again and again. We are made privy only to one heart in our lives.

—Amy

May 24, 2005

Dear Amy,

Today was our first real doctor's appointment, and I was nervous. I shaved my legs and the stubborn hairs that keep sprouting on my abdomen. I tried to wear a dress, but they've all gotten so tight. I wore the black linen one, only half zipped, and a cardigan to cover the exposed skin.

They weighed me. I've only gained two pounds since my first visit, when I saw the nurse, four weeks ago. How could it be only two pounds?

Deep down I was still convinced that this would be the day I learned that I wasn't pregnant after all, that my expanding stomach was home to an engorged malignant tumor with teeth and hair. I wanted to save face and tell the doctor it was OK, I knew I probably wasn't pregnant after all. "It would be just like me to get psychosomatic morning sickness," I told him. He just shook his head and kept prodding my belly with his fingers, kneading me like a cat. Then he did a lightning-fast cervical exam and said, "Yep!" Then he didn't say anything. I kept waiting for him to confirm. He got out the Doppler and rested it on the table, squirted something cold on my belly and rolled the thing around, looking for a heartbeat. Nothing. Then a pounding. "That's your blood flowing to the placenta, feeding your baby," he said. "Sure it is," I wanted to say. The "baby." I hadn't seen any proof of this "baby" yet. And wouldn't it all be so ridiculous? This doctor carefully listening for nothing? He couldn't find it. He searched and searched for that feathery, rushing, swishing noise, which sounds a little like horses running, from what I've heard on the pregnancy websites. I downloaded an audio file a few weeks ago at Dave's parents' house. But there was nothing but my own loud, intrusive pounding, pounding away. "Give me five minutes," he said. "We'll do an ultrasound."

They brought me across the hall. I stripped down again and got on the table, feet in the stirrups. Dave sat in a chair next to me. They hit the lights, squirted more cold jelly, and before I could protest, they had the wand in me and there it was on the screen: my womb, misshapen and tilted the wrong way, and in it, a baby, with a giant baby head and discernable arms and legs. And it was *moving*.

My heart lurched. What was that feeling? It was not quite love or even happiness. It was something I've never felt before. I was suddenly crying and I didn't know why. The doctor smiled and pointed to the giant baby head and wiggling baby arm and said, "You're eleven weeks."

I could have looked at that screen all day. That giant alien head and that waving arm. "What did you feel?" I asked Dave after we left the office. I still wanted to name that emotion. Was it sadness? Gratitude? Wonder? "Relief," he said. And it seems right, or at least the closest I can get. I haven't screwed this up yet. It's alive in there, and waving.

—Jess

May 24, 2005

Dear Jess,

Now that you are pregnant, and I am actually living a particular faith, everything seems more real, or at least I think it *should* seem more real. But it is still so easy to slip into complacency and forget all about faith, to act as if life were still as undecided as it once was. I imagine, in some sense, this is true for you, too. You are in this strange middle period, not exactly *without* child but not living the life of a parent yet. You might go on for a time, tricking yourself into believing that nothing has changed.

I think my last letter, eons ago, was about death. (What a surprise.) I might as well pick up there. Last week during our book group, someone said that he is always trying to find a way to be happy about death. He figures the only way to be happy at the prospect of death is to love not only your neighbor as yourself but your unborn neighbor as well. If you love these potential humans, you will want to give them their turn, make way for them by vacating your spot. Maybe it is a way of projecting the communion of the saints into the future and letting all, in turn, have a go.

Of course, I immediately told him my thoughts on the matter—that death is not something anyone could ever be happy about (unless, I guess, it is the end of some sort of greater evil, like terrible pain). Death is always terrible. But Christianity gives us a way to have hope beyond death and a way to transform the actual act of death into life.

Mark was mostly silent during this exchange. Several others were absent. Scott piped up to agree with me, in his pastoral way, that, yes, death is always a terrible thing and is exactly that (nothing more) if our souls are not eternal. The oldest member of our group, Tom , just listened. After we'd gone on and on about death, he spoke up.

There was a man he had known when he was young, a youth leader and guide. He looked up to this man as a father figure. "He took us to Mass, guided us through first communion, coached us in all aspects of religion." Tom went on, describing how central this man had been in his religious upbringing. "He was my pillar," Tom said. But then, years later, maybe about ten years ago, the man became very ill. Weeks before his death, Tom went to visit him. At one point during their conversation, the man looked up at Tom and said, "Do you really think there is a heaven out there?" Tom stared back at him, incredulous. Here was his pillar, his guide, his rock, and even *he* didn't know? Had it all been a ruse—all that sturdy faith and direction? "I was devastated," Tom said. "I still think about it now." He was silent again, staring down at the book we had long ago given up trying to discuss.

The meeting soon broke up, and we all left. I walked in the night air back down Paulina Street with Mark and thought about Tom. This grave, elderly, dignified man—not unlike my father—yet still so anxious for faith, for someone to be older, wiser, surer than he is. My father often tells me that he feels as if he were still just some young upstart, a fledgling member of the math department. But then he looks around and notices that there is no one left who is older than he is. He is the one all the young guys are looking to. He is the thing they hope someday to be.

Who holds this faith for us? And will we someday be strong enough to hold it ourselves, bear it for the younger people who are looking to us?

We are so dependent on one another for faith. We hold faith communally, but there is no such thing as a faith held communally but by no one in particular. There is nothing that completely transcends the individual. It is true that this or that person may waiver from time to time. But at all times there must be someone holding it up. Jesus chose Peter for exactly this purpose. "You will be my rock," he said. And Peter had to bear faith, believe even when no one else could.

It's like that scene in *Superman*. Christopher Reeve is holding up Margot Kidder. "I've got you. Don't worry," he tells her.

"Great," she says, "but who's got you?"

We never know when we will be called upon to be that support, that pillar for another. And we will never know what our lack of faith has cost others. So, when the time comes, and I think it is coming soon—we saw the first glimpse of the life to come in those little hazy ultrasound images—will we hold up, Jess? Will we have enough faith to give it to another?

With love,
Amy

May 25, 2005

Dear Amy,

This afternoon I was feeling surprisingly well—it seems my morning sickness usually kicks in at about 3 p.m.—so I went to the basilica for Mass. When I entered the narthex, the sun was streaming through the stained glass in broad beams, illuminating the pews like spotlights. It was early, but many people were already there, kneeling and praying intently. I sat in the fourth pew and tried to clear my mind. But I noticed the priest heading in my direction and immediately panicked, thinking that he was coming to interrogate me about that story I wrote about the stations of the cross. Silly, I know. Instead, he leaned over the pew and whispered to me, "Would you lead a decade of the rosary?"

My stomach coiled into a hot, tight knot of irrational panic. I didn't even have a rosary. I considered sneaking out after he walked away, but then decided I didn't care. I realized that I wanted nothing more than to walk to that lectern and say, "Hail, Mary."

It turned out that the other four people he asked didn't have rosaries either (apparently I'm not the only Catholic who doesn't keep a rosary in her pocket—go figure), so we went into the Lady Chapel to find the rosaries kept in baskets there. And in case we panicked and forgot, the priest gave us each a slip of paper with our lines on it. So the five of us sat in chairs on the altar while the priest stood at the lectern to our left, alternately announcing the joyful mysteries and kneeling on the first step of the altar. I had the fourth mystery: the presentation in the temple. But of course I didn't hear a word of the mystery, because my hands were sweating and I was wringing my little slip of paper, waiting my turn to ascend the steps, imagining tripping, puking, something horrible.

And then suddenly it was my turn, and it was the strangest feeling, to be up there leading people in prayer. What do you do with your voice? I can't stand it when pious ninnies say the Hail Mary as if it were some happy jingle: "Pray for us sinners, now and at the hour of our death, amen." Why should we sound so happy? I think we should sound desperate. But how do you convey desperation from a lectern? I settled for mournful. But I worried the whole time that I sounded like a robot or like a child reciting her lines in the school play. I thought of Gabriel and Elizabeth saying these same words—"Hail, Mary, full of grace!" Angels and saints! My heart pounded and my stomach churned. Then I lost track of how many Hail Marys I'd said, so I said an extra for good measure before launching into the Glory Be. Sure that I'd screwed it all up, I returned to my chair, but I couldn't tamp down my ecstasy and feel dejected. Even though the prayers continued without me, tumbling out of mouths by second nature, what a feeling it was to call out, "Blessed art thou amongst women, and blessed is the fruit of thy womb, Jesus." And to hear the congregation call back, "Holy Mary, mother of God . . ."

When it was over, the priest thanked us and told us to keep the rosaries. I must have looked like I'd just gotten a gold star. What a ridiculous fool I am.

The Mass began shortly after. It was a memorial Mass, and it began with the choir chanting the "Funeral Ikos," which is one of the most beautiful meditations on life and death I've ever heard:

> Why these bitter words of dying, O brethren, which they utter as
>   they go hence?
> I am parted from my brethren. All my friends do I abandon, and
>   go hence.
> But whither I go, that understand I not, neither what shall become
>   of me yonder;
> Only God, who hath summoned me knoweth. But make
>   commemoration of me with the song: Alleluia

I thought of my child coming into and leaving this world, of our inevitable parting.

> Youth and beauty of the body fade at the hour of death, and the
>   tongue then burneth fiercely and the parched throat is
>   inflamed.
> The beauty of the eyes is quenched then, the comeliness of the face
>   all altered, the shapeliness of the neck destroyed:
> And the other parts have become numb, nor often say: Alleluia.

I thought of my mother, her frail body, her shorn gray hair, her weakened voice.

> With ecstasy are we inflamed if we but hear that there is light
>   Eternal yonder;
> That there is paradise, wherein every soul of righteous ones
>   rejoiceth,
> Let us all also enter into Christ that all we may cry aloud thus
>   unto God:
> Alleluia!

But I don't want paradise. How could I love anything more than Dave or the baby growing in my womb? How could anything be more precious than the memory of the soft skin on my mother's forearms?

Oh, it's too much to bear. I don't want to imagine an afterlife without my earthly loves!

In flames,
Jess

June 19, 2005

Dear Jess,

It has been so wonderful to be home with my parents in Pennsylvania. Right now I am writing this letter in the hammock in the pine grove, listening to the breeze in the corn and the cows hollering in the distance. Sometimes I wonder how I manage to think at all with the clatter of the city all around.

Last night I did something I haven't done for years. I drove back to the house I lived in when I was little. Our old house is at the end of a road on a cul-de-sac next to a huge, open park, which is mostly green grass, spread out between two small playgrounds. When I was a child, the park almost felt like my backyard; you could tell where our place ended and the park began only by the pattern of mown grass. I didn't even have to cross a street to enter it.

I parked my car under the street lamp in the cul-de-sac and then made my way in the dark to the upper playground. All the equipment is new: a plastic version of the old, wooden fort; a safe, buttressed slide in place of the too-tall, too-steep metal ramp; a new set of swings dangling in the same places we to used sit. The only remaining piece, pinning the present assembly to the past, is an old stone tortoise. She stands there, feet planted in the bark chips, just as she did when I was small enough to crawl under her shell and chalk my name on her belly.

I threw my leg over her neck and pushed myself up onto her back. And then everything started to feel like a repetition of what always happens when I return. I run my fingers along the grooves on her shell. I sit there for a while and feel the night around me, the lights from the houses circling the park, the stars above, and then, pretty soon, I look back, across the cul-de-sac, to the windows of the ranch house at the edge of the grass. It is so easy to imagine that my young life still fills that house. I can almost make out the face of the girl I once was peering back at me through the window. I used to sit on my bed, face pressed into the screen, smelling its dust and weather, and imagine my future and what I would one day be.

And then, sitting on the tortoise, I realize that I am the woman she had already predicted. My arms stretch down a little longer, my eyes and nose and lips trace over hers, and she sits there straight-backed and slight inside of me. And around us both, I feel the skin of an old woman forming, lying wrinkled and loose over our hands and neck, our young bones caught within her tired ones. It is really for this moment that I always return to the park: to sit there with them, our bones within bones, our minds within minds.

As I write about this now, it seems so sad, and yet I go back again and again. There is nowhere else on the planet I can feel as connected to what I once was and what I will become. Sitting there in the park, I can feel that I haven't lost my younger self, that I won't lose who I am now, as if all my moments have come home to roost with me for a short while.

But later, like now, it does seem sad. I look back and see us being carried forward through time on the back of that tortoise. Now in my imagination it's Aesop's tortoise, feet lifting and stamping, keeping time, moving steadily toward the finish line, that future point at which all our forms will have been taken.

We are now in the fifth week of Ordinary Time, and I feel unmoored. I know this is part of the liturgical year. I've read that it is in this period we are supposed to experience "the mystery of Christ in all its aspects," so the narrative is no longer a clear story but broken up. We get fragments of important moments, but nothing obviously hangs together. It makes sense but seems too much like everyday life. During Lent I could really feel the perpetual cycle of the liturgical year. Even though it was my first Ash Wednesday and my first Palm Sunday, I experienced the weight of those days that seemed to be anchored by repetition to the "immeasurable eternity of the day of God." But come Pentecost, the last day of Easter, it seemed the tethers were somehow cut and the overlay of God's time lifted off, leaving me alone to count the days as I always have. I am back to feeling time as mere forward progression.

But speaking of time, it's getting late—the mosquitoes will be here soon. I hope you are feeling well and not too tired at work.

Love,
Amy

June 21, 2005

Dear Amy,

Today I had lunch in the dining hall with some colleagues. I ended up talking mostly to one woman, who is in her late sixties and has big blue eyes with sleepy lids and speaks in this comforting, velveteen Baton Rouge accent. I was trying to speed her along so I could participate in another conversation going on slightly to my right, but then I realized that she had something to say to me and that I should listen.

She told me about how when she was pregnant with her second child, her own mother died. "What a horrible experience," I said, and she said, "Yes, it was; it was the watershed experience of my life. I was thirty-five." Then she said, "You can't really know yet if your mother's death was your watershed—you're too young." And I almost corrected her and said, "Oh boy, do I ever know," but then I realized, she may be right. My head got full of the idea that something worse may happen to me yet. I got terribly sad. Suddenly everyone else seemed to go behind a glass, and I, on the other side, just listened to them talk and felt myself becoming more and more distant, until lunch was over, and we dumped our trays, and I walked out alone, back to my office.

How could it be that my mother's death was not the watershed moment of my life? I suppose I was already basically who I am: by turns shy and obnoxious, introverted and yet starved for attention. I suppose I was already obsessive-compulsive, superstitious, Catholic. I was all those things when she was still alive. What was it that her death accomplished in me? It must have had some tremendous effect, right? Why does this make me so sad? I guess because if I am essentially unchanged, then there was no reason for her to die. The world—even her daughter—went on, unnoticing.

It was not her death that made me so conscious of being alone in the world; I discovered that before, when I would lie in bed at night and try to imagine things that were impossible to imagine, like eternity. My heart would start to race, and the glass would go up between me and the physical world, and my stomach would turn, and I would sit up in bed and frantically call her name. And she would come into my room and sit on the edge of the bed, and she would scratch the inside of my forearm until the impossible thoughts went away.

It was my father, I guess, who had the real effect. And yet he is the one who remains curiously absent from all my tellings of the story. I never cry for him. Maybe because I'm too angry. But more often, I've felt that it's useless to hold him accountable, because he's just a man, and he couldn't deal with the loss of her anymore than I could. But how do you abandon your child? How do you turn your back on your youngest girl? And even more confusing, how do you love Jesus so much and despise your own child?

And that is the problem, there. So pathetic, I know. But I still have this feeling that he hated me. To me, back then, it was quite undeniable. He couldn't stand my presence after he married Angel. I was convinced that I disgusted him, and the only way I could cope was to revel in it. That was when I pierced my nose and began to do all the things that I felt a disgusting child would do. Why not? I'd show him what disgusting was.

But no, it happened even before he remarried, the night the world cracked open and I felt for real the pain that I had imagined when I had tried to fathom eternity, but this time there was nobody there to come in and make it disappear.

It was my sophomore year, early fall, the first cool snap, which, in Slidell, was a great and momentous occasion, a night when you would dig out your one sweater and go and lie in the driveway, listening to the rustle of leaves in the breeze. Except this day was terrible for whatever reason. Probably because my boyfriend had done something awful to me. Could this have been the day he passed me the note at my locker that said something like, *I never loved you . . .*?

I was in a state of complete despair, and I came home to a dark, empty house, my sister away at college, my dad at work. By the time he came home I was doubled over on the bathroom floor, clutching my stomach. I did this often in those days, suffering from some horrible psychosomatic manifestations of grief and anxiety. I would get stomachaches that felt like being flayed by a burning sword. And he came home, but only for a change of clothes before he headed out again. I don't remember much of what passed between us that night, but I do remember dropping my act, too tired to be sullen and angry and disgusting. I was exhausted and scared, and I wanted comfort. I remember I was earnest, and I begged him—"Please, don't go. I don't want to be alone." I was fifteen. But he was going. When this was clear, I became hysterical and chased him out of the house in tears, holding onto his sleeve, saying, "Please, please, don't go. I don't want to be by myself." And he was cold and didn't want to look at me, and he actually shook me off and got in the car, and the headlights receded down the driveway, and I collapsed there—I remember this part so vividly, the feeling of the cold concrete scraping my bare legs—and cried. I cried so loudly that Mr. Sam's wife came out of her house to see what was the matter. She didn't say a word. She picked me up and led me inside and directed me to the sofa, where I clutched my stomach in agony. And she went to the bathroom and got a rag and wet it, and sat on the sofa and brought it to my forehead and my throat. And I was so embarrassed, so mortified, I couldn't speak. She didn't either, and I was grateful for her silence.

Now that I've written it, I think this scene must've been what broke my heart, even more than my mother's death, because it made her death that much more tragic. It was the first time I realized I was truly alone and that even my own life had ended in a way. I had entered that terrible nightmare of eternity, that place that I couldn't imagine when both my parents were alive and in the other room as I tried to go to sleep. When my mom died, she took everything with her, including that reliable transaction—I call your name, and you come.

But that is enough for tonight. Indeed. It is way too much.

Love,
Jess

June 29, 2005

Dear Jess,
Today is one of those days when the sun seems callous.

I have been thinking of you as a child, lying in bed meditating on the idea of forever, and then that horrible image of you, crumpled on the cement, weeping, feeling cast into an eternity you never wished to enter. I was thinking about it when I went to Mass in Bellefonte, Pennsylvania, on Sunday. The church was packed, not a single empty seat, and my father and brother were beside me on the pew, looking terribly awkward as they went through the unfamiliar motions of Mass. Every time I see my parents, especially lately, they are older—my father nearly seventy—and with each passing year I become so much more desperate to keep them alive. The idea of either one of them dying seems like a cataclysm I couldn't bear. Yet I look around and see so many, including my dearest friend, bearing losses like this already.

It will happen, I thought, as I sat there in the crowded church. *No, it really will happen.* I looked up then and saw Jesus, at one of the stations of the cross, stumbling under the weight of the wood on his shoulders. And above this scene were the words "Come to me all you who labor and are heavy laden and I will give you rest." If it were just that statement, without the image of Christ in the dust, then it would make me as furious as the sun often does, as if God were trying to toss some indifferent sunshine on our misery.

No one close to me has ever died, but I have witnessed my parents lose their parents. I never knew my grandparents well, for they lived on the opposite coast in Oregon, and I probably only met them five or so times in my life. But I still remember that day, when the phone rang in our kitchen and my father picked it up and let out a silent gasp and caught himself on the counter. It was my grandmother on the phone. My grandfather had fallen down on the gravel path to the barn and had died before she could make it out to him. She had been watching from the window. Later, my father stood with my mother in the kitchen, right out in the open in the afternoon, his head in his hands, and cried. My sister and I were too scared to go to him, our steady father who never shed a tear in our presence, weeping.

"Come to me all you who labor and are heavy laden and I will give you rest."

It is hard to believe that there is peace or rest or joy there, buckled under the cross, yet that image is the only thing around that seems to tell the truth about life. The suffering at the heart of Christianity makes its promise of peace easier to believe.

Sometimes I try to imagine what somebody who had never heard of Christ or any other religion would make of the cross. I imagine a person who has lived a long life and had her share of hardship and loss being presented with different philosophies and religions. Image after beautiful image of glory or mystery or peace is presented until someone holds up a crucifix—a man nailed to a piece of wood, head bent against his chest. Even if she knew nothing of the story surrounding it, nothing of churches, wouldn't this image, a clear depiction of human suffering, stand out from the rest?

Oh, Jess, you've had to bear so much more than I have. I hope you are well tonight, and not too lonely with Dave away.

Love,
Amy

July 3, 2005

Dear Amy,

There was a package waiting for me on the doorstep today. My sister had sent me some things for the baby, some old pictures of us when we were kids, and some pictures of my mother. These were gift enough; I have so few pictures from those times, so few pictures of the two of us sharing the same space. But she also sent bags of letters my grandmother wrote to her own mother. I've been reading them all night, fitting them together to make sense of the story they tell.

She wrote pages and pages every day, sometimes two or three times a day. She took the pad and paper on the road from New Orleans to Houma, driving with my grandfather while he chased down people who'd defaulted on loans. She took them on a ferry over the Mississippi River. She took them on the Huey P. Long Bridge to the west bank of the river. She wrote of her morning sickness. She was very sick in the first trimester but never threw up, except for that morning she craved pancakes and a hot dog (a "winnie," as she called it). She fried them up together and loved every bite, then she threw up and passed out. She wrote on the toilet in her fourth month. Around Christmastime, she wrote about blood clots and spotting. She called her baby Petunia, and Carrie Mae, hoping always for a girl, and then quickly took it back, not wanting to jinx her chances.

The letters go on for ten years and then some. She includes newspaper clippings: the time she was in the paper for a screw-up at the DMV; the article about Father Tim leaving Our Lady of Lourdes. She wrote when they struggled to pay $40 in rent and when they opened the fourth location of my grandfather's business and when they bought their second home on Bayou Bonfouca. She wrote of my uncle, her older son, and his "spells," his sleeping until 1:30, his psychological decline.

As the years pass, the letters get shorter until they are just scribbled on note cards. I begin to recognize her voice. There's barely a trace of that girl missing her mama and little sister, that girl who was so homesick for Georgia. The time grows between postmarks, until I'm reading letters from a woman in her fifties, disappointed and ailing, jotting quick notes to her dying mother. That's where the letters stop. But I know how the story ends. Not well.

I came downstairs and found a letter from you on the steps and felt a surge of relief. I'm terribly lonely for my mother and grandmother and the way her house smelled like bacon frying in the cast-iron skillet and coffee percolating on the stove, and cigarettes—lots and lots of cigarettes, even when she was nine months pregnant with my mother, those goddamned cigarettes.

In a state of utter connectedness with the communion of saints, feeling oddly soothed and yet teetering somewhere near absolute despair,

—Jess

July 4, 2005

Dear Jess,

I've been thinking more seriously about getting pregnant, wandering around the children's section of bookstores, trying to get my imagination on board.

This morning I came across a book by Arnold Lobel that gave me a jolt of recognition, as if I were three years old again, lost in the world of Frog and Toad. So magically familiar, the illustrations seem almost like snapshots of my imaginative life as a child. I must have studied the details of those green and brown sketches, the little winding roads and oversized reeds, for hours.

There is one story about letters. A perpetually cheerful Frog pays a visit to Toad but finds Toad glum, sitting on his front porch.

"This is my sad time of day," says Toad, "when I wait for the mail to come."

"Why is that?" says Frog.

"No one has ever sent me a letter. My mailbox is always empty. That is why waiting for the mail is a sad time for me."

Then Frog and Toad sit "on the porch, feeling sad together."

Frog rescues the situation by running home, writing a letter to Toad, and sending it literally by snail mail. The little snail brings it four days later.

Even though Toad saw Frog every day, he longed for the strangeness, the otherness of a letter, for something to come from out there and address him, "Dear Toad." Is that the thrill I feel finding a letter from you in my box? The address of a friend is made into a physical fact and every letter an artifact of the otherwise invisible communion of friendship. That must have been part of the thrill you felt holding those letters your grandmother wrote.

This makes me think of another story about waiting for a letter. In the poem "A Sick Child" by Randall Jarrell, a little boy lies in bed and tries to imagine a letter he would most like to receive, but none of his ideas seem good enough, even imagining a letter from outer space, because no matter how far-fetched, every idea is of his own making. He finally hopes that somewhere out there, beyond outer space, beyond already imagined lands, there must be something unlike anything he has ever known or seen or even dreamed of before. And he calls out, almost like he is praying, "All that I've never thought of—think of me!"

In the end I wouldn't be surprised if that letter from Frog didn't completely satisfy Toad. Although I'm sure it helped ease his loneliness, I bet Toad still had a lingering desire for something to come that was different from everything.

When I came into the church last Easter, I think I was naively hoping to relieve myself of that old experience of sitting in the airy space of a room waiting for God to show up. Yet that experience has not gone away. Becoming Catholic has given me a place to wait, but has not erased the fundamental problem of solitude.

On the website for Gethsemani, next to an image of the plain stone walls of the monastery, is a couplet from Psalm 62:

Alone in God,
My soul waits, silent.

That is what intrigues me most about going there—to be surrounded by so many people who have devoted their lives to waiting for all they have never thought of to think of them.

When I am there, I will pray to have the tenacity of Toad.

Until the next letter,

Amy

July 5, 2005

Dear Amy,

Dave is home, and I'm basking in his love and attention like a lizard sunning herself on a warm rock. I really was languishing here without him. I can't bear the thought of him going away for another three weeks to teach the brilliant young writers. How do our cloistered sisters manage, with no one to look at them, to sleep with a hand on their stomachs, to prove they exist and are loved?

I just received your letter, in which you wrote of the Gospel according to Matthew: "Come to me, all you who are heavy laden. My yoke is easy, and my burden is light." I don't know that I've ever properly understood these Christian exhortations—are we supposed to take up our crosses or give our burdens to God? Which is it?

I guess grief is the cross I'm bearing and have borne for more than half my life now. I love the idea of bringing that burden to God. I really do. I want to pray. Every day I say, "I'll start . . . tomorrow." There's a quote from one of the desert fathers that goes something like, "Each day, I begin." I don't even get that far.

Don't I want God to take this burden? Don't I want to cast off this cross? Maybe I don't want to be relieved; maybe I cling to grief because it's all that remains of my mother. But this mourning has become so predictable that it sometimes seems more like tedium than suffering. How many times can I rehash the same memories, retell the same stories? Sometimes I think I have unearthed a new one, and then I look through my journals and notebooks and find it sitting there stupidly.

I've been reading *The Seven Storey Mountain*. Merton writes of being so tired and uninterested in the life he was leading, of its futility. And yet, "What was this curse that was on me, that I could not translate belief into action, and my knowledge of God into a concrete campaign for possessing Him, Whom I knew to be the only true good?"

Merton got to become a priest. I'm going to be a mother and a wife and a working girl. How do I possess God? What are my options for a concrete campaign?

I eagerly await our weekend of silence in the home of Merton himself. Maybe he'll haunt me.

Love,

Jess

July 10, 2005

Dear Jess,

I finally know what I have: acedia and vainglory. But mostly acedia. Acedia feels like giving up, like nothing is really worth the struggle, and the whole God thing suddenly seems absurd. The ordinary world and my ordinary self seem to be all I can hope for. I think I get a bout of acedia about once a day, and occasionally whole days are taken up by this glum, slothful mood.

When I was looking around in the Gethsemani library, I found a book titled *A Rumor of Angels*, by Peter Berger. He talks about the slow receding in modern times of the supernatural from our awareness. When mystery draws back, we are left with what he calls the *Lebenswelt,* or life world. It is the common world of our senses, "the arena of most of our projects in life, whose reality is strongest and thus the most 'natural' in our consciousness." When you are in a state of acedia, the *Lebenswelt* is all you've got. The world sings its being—"This is all there is. This is reality and nothing more"—and drowns out any rumor of angels.

Sister Funk (who you would think from her name would have a lot of experience in this area) says that the remedy for acedia is manual labor. So I tried it. I cleaned the house and even forwent the mop, getting down on my hands and knees to scrub. Then I went outside and started pulling weeds. After a couple of hours, I realized it was working. I was enjoying the sun on my face and the look of the black, damp earth my trowel upturned, and I noticed I was thinking of my mother.

My mother is a gardener. The thing that startles me about her gardening is that it is so radically private. She lives in the middle of fields tilled by heavy machinery; there is no sidewalk with passersby; there are seldom visitors. But over the years she has single-handedly converted acres of grass and weed into flower beds and hidden gardens. I walk around her place and feel overwhelmed, as I did at Gethsemane, by the combination of beauty and hiddenness. The seclusion makes it seem holy, set apart.

And this makes me think of Saint-Exupéry's *The Little Prince*. There is a scene in which the little prince comes across a lackadaisical fox. "My life is very monotonous," says the fox. "I hunt chickens; men hunt me. All chickens are just alike, and all men are just alike. And, in consequence, I am a little bored." The fox is in a state of acedia. But he also knows the cure for his state. "You must tame me," he says to the little prince. Taming is done by following rites, those actions that make "one day different from other days, one hour from other hours." The result of being tamed, says the fox, is that the sun will come to shine on his life, and he shall know the sound of a step that is different from all other steps. The world that had once felt filled with sameness will suddenly break apart into separate and cherishable pieces.

In the end, the fox says, it is the time you waste on something that makes it so important. So I don't think it is just manual labor that combats acedia, but labor done in secret, for what makes something seem like waste or loss, and thus important, is the hiddenness of it. "What is essential is invisible to the eye," says the fox.

I see my mother in her white hat and tattered oxford rolling out the wheelbarrow to bring a load of mulch to the beds, carrying out the rites of the everyday in an act of faith. I imagine her breathless as she steers the unsteady weight of the barrow, her face red from the effort and her legs and arms bracing. She shovels for hours and makes trip after trip for more mulch. Then she hauls the hose to the edge of the bed and the first water sputters out, and then begins to arc and spread from her hands, and to light up in the sun as bright and sheer as if a spirit were raising its silver wing over the chips of bark.

By wasting our time, our love, in secret, we participate in the resurrection of the everyday. I heard someone say once that we should not think of the risen Christ, as if it were a finished act, but of Christ rising, *Homo resurgens*. When we work in secret, we participate in this rising, in the great taming of the world as Christ ascends.

I wish I could take my mother to Gethsemani. She is too private for most churches. She is more like a monk than most people I know. I found a book of hers once, a collection of sermons by J. Wallace Hamilton, in which she had marked this line: "Life is what we are alive to." She has never needed the eyes of others on her to feel alive. I wish I could be more like her, to live more of my life in private—because vainglory, my other condition, is precisely the need to view myself through others' eyes. It seems the cure for both of my states is the same: to work in private and not wait for the world to tell me it is all worthwhile, to somehow become comfortable with the apparent waste of unacknowledged labor.

I hope we will someday be able to return to Gethsemani.

Love,
Amy

July 16, 2005

Dear Amy,

It's the middle of the night, and I can't sleep. Dave is back in Erie, and I stayed up late reading *The Power and the Glory*, by Graham Greene, which was a mistake because it's completely terrifying.

I slept briefly and had the most vivid dream of my childhood home in Slidell. There was a wedding going on in the yard next door, and I was in my mother's blue bathroom, putting on makeup, drying my hair, and frustrated at how long it was taking me to get ready. I couldn't find any dresses to fit over my pregnant belly. Through the bathroom window I could hear the music outside, the voices and laughter of all my childhood friends. I suddenly realized that I wasn't going to make it to the wedding, and I began to cry. I woke up in tears.

Why is it that I still dream of that house? Has it become a symbol of everything lost and yearned for? It is literally the house of my dreams, even when those dreams are not explicitly about the place or even my childhood. And I wake with the same longing and home-sickness I felt when I was fifteen.

On our last trip to Louisiana, my sister and I actually drove over and stole the house numbers off the bricks. It was dark except for the streetlight at the foot of our sloping driveway. It shone like a spotlight on the same empty patch of cracked concrete where I'd watched, from my bedroom window, the beloved neighbor boy turning 360s on his skateboard. The grass had grown tall, and some-one had chucked a large foam daiquiri cup into the weeds. The shutters had been removed from the windows and were stacked on the front porch, where we once stowed our bikes. Sheets hung from the windows inside.

I stood on the porch, struck by the smallness of the place. It was clear nobody was home and hadn't been in ages, so I tried the door but found it locked. I ran around to the side door—also locked. But the gate was open, and I could see the overgrown backyard, and our playhouse, where we'd tried to conjure spirits with our Ouija board, had collapsed. I climbed the rotting wooden steps of the deck and peered through the sliding glass door into the kitchen, saw the same appliances, the old faux-brick linoleum, the snack bar where we ate our morning Pop-Tarts.

It had been hard to imagine anybody else living there, but it was harder still to think that nobody cared for it anymore. It seemed that it might crumble before my eyes. I wanted something, some souvenir, a piece of the place—a brick, or a clump of earth.

That's when I thought of the house numbers, 261, faded and chipping next to my old bedroom window. I reached up and gripped the six around the edges and yanked it too hard; it came off easily, and I fell backward into the bushes. I tore the remaining numbers from the house, some long-dead creature's desiccated nest crumbling in my palm.

Satisfied, I ran for the minivan. My sister backed down the curving drive, navigating the curves instinctively, the way your muscles remember a dance. I felt victorious then. Now it strikes me as awfully melodramatic, but there you go. I'm glad I have them. They seem like relics, pieces of a once-living body. Just a look at them transports me to that old world, and my life from that time no longer seems like a dream.

It's nearly six now, and the darkness is fading, so I might sleep.

Love,

Jess

July 20, 2005

Dear Jess,

I got a beautiful letter from you today. The arrival of a letter is often the only sacramental thing in my day. I sit down quietly, by myself, for often I have saved it up for just the right moment, and then I lose myself in the world we have created between us—a world that includes our lives but cherishes them, and a world that includes God but makes him more explicit, which really means—I just looked it up—to unfold, smooth out, unroll him. We press God out in the pages of our letters, ironing and ironing, like two old-fashioned women. We mail him back and forth, and pile him up, like a basket of linen.

It seems that you and I have two friendships, which we keep loosely separate: that of our letters and that of our encounters. I wonder if we have instinctively made this division. We worry that we might miss our lives by obsessing over our souls (and over death), and so, in person, we rarely talk about God.

But forgetting about death, even in daily life, never really seems like a possibility for us. Lately, it has come to us in dreams, in the stories we hear of others, or up close: a pain stabbing my mother in the hip, a cancer slowly taking the mother of Mark's childhood friend, your mother's death never gone, the father of one of my coworkers suddenly collapsing in hysteria for no apparent reason. I know this line of thought is all too familiar to you, sickening really.

Maybe the best approach is to lose ourselves in work and hope. Too much staring death in the eye might bring death, like devils, too close for comfort.

Thomas Merton was like us in this respect. He felt death as an ever-present reality, not just the final end. It drove him into solitude, into contemplation. It drove him to write things like this:

> How tragic it is that they who have nothing to express are continually expressing themselves, like nervous gunners, firing burst after burst of ammunition into the dark, where there is no enemy. The reason for their talk is: death. Death is the enemy who seems to confront them at every moment in the deep darkness and silence of their own being. So they keep shouting at death . . . never discovering that their hearts are rooted in a silence that is not death but life. They chatter themselves to death, fearing life as if it were death.

But I guess it really wasn't death that drove him to this clear thought, but eternity—the reality, he said, that many mistake for death. That is what I long to find here and now: life, eternal life. You fear you might miss life by focusing on death, and I am sure you are right. But we also might miss life by living. If life, like Merton said, is there for the taking, for the hearing in silence, I want to take and hear it.

Our letters, I think, are not those nervous bursts into the dark. Our letters are excavations, slowly uncovering this life that must already be in our possessions, trying to make it explicit, to unfold it for our eyes to see.

Love,
Amy

July 27, 2005

Dear Amy,

It's Thursday night, and I'm lying in bed with my laptop. The house feels different somehow after Dave's mom's visit. She made it feel more like a home where a family lives. And she also drove me absolutely out of my mind.

Is there a feminine equivalent of the word *emasculated*? I felt utterly superfluous the entire time she was here. So yesterday, I left work a little early and drove out to the mall and spent nearly $400 on maternity clothes. I didn't really know why I was doing it at the time, except that my stomach seemed to have grown over the course of the workday, and so even my elastic-waist hippie skirts are pulling at the seams. But then I realized that it was merely an act of rebellion, spending money on myself this way. It felt like the only thing left for me to do; she'd sanded and painted the furniture, made the curtains, lined the drawers with shelf paper, washed and folded the clothes. So I went and did the only thing I know how to do: shop. Then I came home and sat across from Dave at the dinner table and cried. I'll be returning it all tomorrow.

I'm so grateful that you were here with me when I found out this baby is a girl. I can't begin to express how important that moment was for me—how each time I think of it my heart leaps in my chest. Seeing her face, naming her, it seemed I was meeting someone for the first time whom I had always known. I guess she *has* been with us for a while now. Doesn't Lent seem like years ago? Charlotte was with us in those later days of your conversion. She was with us that night as I put my hand on your shoulder and named you Teresa. But it's more than that. It's like her soul has been in my soul my whole life. And yet I also felt my life beginning in that ultrasound room, my real purpose broadcast on the grainy black-and-white monitor. How could it be possible to love so much, already?

I can't wait to hear Charlotte call you Nanan. I want to call you Nanan myself—it seems insufficient to call you "friend" or even "aunt." My sister calls her godmother Nanan, but I call mine Joan, so this is a Louisiana tradition that I missed. Still, it's important to me to connect her with where I come from. Otherwise I fear it will all be lost.

With love,

Jess

July 31, 2005

Dear Jess,

I am still reeling from that vision of Charlotte—already looking like you, with big eyes and long legs—turning and turning inside you. I thought that I had already imagined her fully, that I really believed that a baby was in there. And, of course, I did believe it. But then I saw her for real! How precious your body suddenly seemed, some sort of holy vessel. As we walked around for the next two hours, I felt her hidden presence with us: Charlotte's heart beating, her spine twisting in somersaults, her little mouth opening and closing.

Sometimes I go through this mental exercise: I try to stake out God, make God's length and breadth big enough in my mind. It doesn't help to picture the outer edge of the still-expanding universe, the millions of galaxies, all those oh-my-Lord-can-you-believe-how-big-creation-is number games. Instead, it helps to think of things that are living, working, breathing beyond my sight. Not anything will do. I have to pick my candidates carefully. But really, it is not a matter of picking; certain people or events make an impression and continue to exist in my mind long after they are physically before me.

For example, I think often of the Passionist nuns going about their day, climbing up the spiral stairs, coming into the chapel, counting off the beads of their rosaries again, and again, and again. I think of emperor penguins, marching like noble soldiers, across the Antarctic, dropping to their bellies now and then to row themselves along with their flippers. At what stage of life are their chicks? Are they still huddled on their fathers' talons, underneath their stomach rolls? Or waddling around and hurling themselves like puppies at other chicks? Or standing now at the edge of the sea waiting to take the first plunge? And now, Charlotte is part of this staking out of God.

What is common to all of these? Each is an instance of life beyond everyday experience, so each is, in a way, hidden. Each represents a certain stoic engagement with life and seems to be carried forward by faith alone, or by instinct, which might just be God-given, perfect faith. Each needs no gaze to make it tick. I think of the nuns kneeling, and then the penguins trucking over the ice, and Charlotte spinning and kicking, unseen in South Bend. It seems plausible that one of these things might happen in a godless universe, but not all three simultaneously. You can call the force that drives those penguins instinct if you like, but that is just a name (trying to trick us into thinking we understand) for something we don't understand at all. That force seems much more like faith to me. It is definitely not instinct that trains a life to the liturgical year, to that supernatural time that overlays our ordinary hours. And Charlotte, what keeps her growing?

How does this indicate God and not just mass delusion? Well, faith is certainly not something we cook up; the world is much too terrible for that. Faith has to be a gift. And so there it is, the long lines of penguins to the north, the nuns to the south, and Charlotte in between, all marching and counting and spinning on faith.

Adoringly,
Amy

August 4, 2005

Dear Amy,

I drove home from Chicago today feeling terrible: the cramp in my left side still there, the rain pouring, the traffic bumper-to-bumper on I-80. By the time I got home, I couldn't bear to stay at the office, so I made my excuses and came home to a can of soup and a long nap.

When I woke I reread your letter, in which you wondered about faith as a gift or a mass delusion. I've been reading a book of homilies by Father Matthew Kelty of Gethsemani, and your letter brought one passage in particular to mind:

> What proves the reality of faith as much as the power of its substitutes when true faith is lacking? People will believe almost anything. Once they have assented to some sort of supernatural dimension in their lives, they will get on with the business of living and do pretty well. The doing pretty well does not prove the verity of their beliefs—it proves that belief is natural and healthy.

I thought of how my dad, sister, and I all turned to different faiths after my mother's death. Our faith had been rooted in her; she was the center of our family's universe. What would fill that gap? We plugged it with parapsychology and the *Celestine Prophecy* (my sister), biblical fundamentalism and end-times theology (my dad), and me—what? Kelty goes on:

> We as Christians are a bold lot in attesting to what we believe, and as Catholics we are at the head of that lot in the extravagance of our claims. We make more demands on the depth of our faith than any who profess Christ.

Maybe I need an outrageous faith to fill the hole left by my mother's death. Sometimes I wonder if this is all I've done in choosing Catholicism—presented myself with some impossible challenge, some obscure mystery that I'll never unravel. Catholicism makes wild claims on the imagination and the intellect, and I seem to thrive more on that struggle to understand than on prayer or any sort of personal relationship with God. It is, for one thing, very time-consuming. It takes your eyes off the *Lebenswelt*.

But are we missing our lives by obsessing over our souls? Sometimes I have the same fear. Suddenly the fog will clear, and I'll see Dave sitting across from me or lying next to me in bed, breathing, fully present in all his flesh-and-blood mortality, and I regret that I've lost a second of time with him. If eternity is coming for us anyway, why shouldn't we love the world, and love it hard? Why should we spend our short time wondering about what is to be lost and the unknown to come?

Somehow, even after losing my great love, the world kept turning—sun rising, Passionist nuns climbing spiral stairs, penguins marching—and although it took some time, I found more and different love but just as strong: love of husband and child and true friendship. Somehow, the world, though terrible, did not turn ugly, even after my worst fear of mortality was confirmed. This is how I can still have faith that God is keeping this transient place good, and he wants us to enjoy it. Does that sound too simple?

When you said the other day that we can never look at the world from the point of eternity, you were right. So we simply have faith, and—despite all—love now.

—Jess

October 16, 2005

Dear Jess,

Joy, joy, joy, joy! I can't believe it. I haven't advanced one iota since we talked this afternoon—I am still in dumb shock. How odd to sit there and see the test overcoming the stick, uncovering one—no, two—stripes. I finally took a second test, sure the first was a fluke, but again there were two lines. It is not real at all. Nothing is real. I know that I will fall asleep tonight and it will go away, slip into the dark, back to some magic land where it came from. I will wake and realize it was all a crazy dream. Two thick pink lines of chalk on a block of cement from my childhood, drawn and redrawn in hopes of some far-off future, and then forgotten, hopscotched over on the way to the heaven square.

Last night at that infernal academic party, the famous professors were trying to mingle. One of the towering, silver-haired giants came over and looked down at a trio of us: me and Mark and one of Mark's old roommates. The giant was a classicist and supposedly the wisest, oldest man on the committee. To relieve what must have been our obvious discomfort, he told a story: "In one of the few successful teaching moments of my career," he said, "a student came to me in my office, full of consternation—dark circles under his eyes from a sleepless night of reading Plato. And he told me that he'd been thinking about it for hours and had come to the inescapable conclusion that there were no reasonable grounds for believing that the world exists. I looked at him and said, 'What else would it do?' 'Oh, of course,' the student said, and left my office."

I love that. What else would it do? The world with its single purpose: existence. I guess it is not too far-fetched to believe in what already is, but what about what is coming to be? How could something come from nothing?

Have you realized yet that our babies will be in the same grade?

Ecstatically yours,

Amy

October 25, 2005

Dear Amy,

Now that you're pregnant, I realize how much I've already forgotten. How sick did I feel, and when did it start? What foods made my stomach turn? What made me cry? When did I finally start to grow? How have I changed? Am I different, more than just physically? I'm afraid that pregnancy has become routine, and that I am not as vigilant as I was in the beginning.

Every day, I say, "Today I'll write a letter." And every day, I get home after 5, eat dinner, sit on the sofa, and stare into space. Or, I get an overwhelming urge to clean the kitchen floor. Or Dave asks me to read yet another draft of the book. This should be banned by the Geneva Convention: forcing your eight-months-pregnant wife to read drafts of your essays about torture every night.

So there: I'm writing. It feels pretty good. I think I'll start by contemplating my navel. I am thirty-three weeks pregnant, and my stomach has rounded into a nice, firm basketball, and my navel, once deep and cavernous, has puckered shut. I haven't found any stretch marks, but my skin is taut and oddly hairy. The linea nigra has extended so that now it is both above and below my belly button. I'm spilling out of my bra. Every day I check for colostrum, wondering if I'll be able to breast-feed.

My feet have swollen a half size, but my ankles have always been so weak and skinny that the extra fluid makes them look normal. I don't have that stuffed sausage look below the knees just yet. But there are still seven weeks to go.

The mornings are getting later. It's still dark at 6:30 a.m., and it's harder to get out of bed, so Dave hits snooze until 7:10, and then we turn on *The Today Show* to make fun of Katie Couric (whom we secretly love) and see the weather. Then I drag myself out of bed. Literally. I have to build momentum to get myself into an upright position. While I'm in the shower, Dave makes my waffles and brings them upstairs with my orange juice, so they are waiting for me.

In the shower, I massage my belly, back, and neck, all stiff and sore from the contorted positions I sleep in. I find that I wake now every two hours, either to pee or to flip or to get a drink of water (I'm so parched these days—water and ice have never tasted so good). Dr. Shah told me this is nature's way of preparing me to sleep less before the baby arrives and wants two-hour feedings. Another amazing thing that our bodies seem to know how to do without any instruction.

I tell Charlotte hello every morning, patting my belly in the shower. It is too big now for me to shave my legs or even wash my feet.

I want to remember every detail. It will all be over soon. Will I have made the proper memories or taken the right notes? I'm still amazed each day when I look in the mirror and see something that wasn't there before. Or when she moves in a new way or finds a new space to fill inside me. At night I lie in bed and use the monitor I bought to find my heartbeat, and then hers, and listen. I let Dave listen sometimes, and he smiles boyishly and pats my belly, but he never seems as deeply satisfied by it as I am. How could he be? It seems like he won't realize the gravity of what we've done until he sees her in this world. For now, it remains exquisitely private. So much my own.

You must write to me every day, with every new symptom and fear and craving.

—Jess

November 1, 2005

Dear Jess,

I'm worried about you. Are you still feeling breathless? Maybe you are there right now at the hospital waiting for the EKG. Anyway, I'm worried that you have been through an ordeal and won't be up for the drive. Please, please don't worry about it if you are too tired. I can come down there and bring the baby shower to you.

I feel so sure that Charlotte is going to be healthy and perfect. Remember the withered Jesus from your dream, lying next to you in a hospital bed. "Be at peace," he said. I wish he would come to me! I need to calm down.

What was I thinking, wishing to be sick? I'm so sick now. What's it going to be like when the hormones get even higher? I hear they don't peak until around the tenth week. I'm giving a quiz right now, and it is all I can do not to run from the room to the bathroom. I only brought one Blow Pop today, and of course that is already gone. They work so well—how did you know?

Love,

Amy

November 1, 2005

Dear Amy,

Yesterday was Halloween, and Dave and I sat on the front porch with our glowing pumpkins and passed out candy to the neighborhood kids. The ground was covered in orange, yellow, and red leaves that crunched under their feet, until the rain came. Growing up in Louisiana, I never saw such colors. The leaves, if they dropped at all, seemed to just blow off the trees overnight and lay in wet clumps of brown on the ground.

My dad sent me pictures of the damage from Katrina, and they included some shots of my old house. When I saw the first one, I felt as if I'd been punched—the image literally took my breath away, and I sat on the sofa and sobbed. I recognized it immediately, even though it's nothing but studs. The light was pouring into what used to be the kitchen, just the way I remember it, all golden and dreamy.

I haven't dreamed about my mother in a long time, but I have started, again, to wake up tracing my fingers up and down the inside of my arm, which I find extended straight up into the air. She's still here, still bringing comfort, even as I am forgetting her.

The void in me is aching. It isn't getting easier. It may hurt even more now, because I'm becoming a mother. I'm going gray. I'm getting varicose veins in my legs. My eyes are crinkling when I smile. I understand how she must have felt, knowing but not believing she would die. The heartache of leaving her girls in the world without her. What would I tell my own daughter? It will be the hardest thing, the worst thing that ever happens to her. It will define her. But if I love her as my mother loved me, she'll be OK, somehow. She'll have a lot to go on.

I wish I could remember her more, tell you more. I wish there was a conversation we'd had that I could transcribe here. Or a letter she'd written me. But there's nothing. Only snatches of time, lyrics to songs on the radio when she'd pick me up from soccer practice at twilight, the crickets beginning to sound. The bell that jingled when our front door opened. The gum cracking in the other room while I slept. Her forearms. Her ring finger.

Dave and I went to another childbirth class, and I realized at some point that I was gripping the arms of the chair so tightly that my knuckles were white. They showed the baby coming out of the woman. My heart raced. Everyone was saying, "You'll be ready," but I became stricken with panic. I want more than anything to have Charlotte with us, but I wish Dave could just knock me out with a frying pan and wake me when it's over. What if I just have a heart attack? Could my heart actually explode? I'm also worried that I'll die of wanting my mother.

Then I sat on the floor between Dave's legs, just like they do in the movies, and nothing has ever felt so good. I melted into his warm chest as some Indiana homemaker cooed to us gently about a beach in Hawaii, and I could see us as we are now, twenty-nine and thirty, young and stupid, about to change our lives forever, and I could see us four years ago, younger and dumber still and unaware of all we'd experience together, and I could see the future, however uncertain, and I could feel—I almost wrote imagine, but that's not quite right, it was a sure feeling, as if I was experiencing both times at once—what it will be like to look back on this night when Charlotte is five, ten, twenty. I shouldn't forget it. I can't forget it.

In the company of the saints, I hope,

Jess

December 17, 2005

Dear Jess,

Dave called about an hour ago. I couldn't sleep after I heard the news. I got out of bed and lit a candle and prayed on my knees for you and Charlotte and Dave. Then I read everything I could about labor, trying to figure out how close you are to the end.

Oh, Jess! I am so overwhelmed by the knowledge that you are in labor, that the hour is upon you (the thief in the night has come). It seems an eternity before I will be in that state with all the expectation over and the actual moment come. But for you it is finally here! I can't wait to meet her in the flesh—no longer a visible wave under the belly skin or a grainy picture on the screen, but a real being.

Tomorrow night I will be one of three readers at "Advent Lessons, Lights and Carols." My part will be of Mary. As we read the nativity scene, I will say: "I am the handmaid of the Lord. Let it be done to me according to your word." I will say it for both of us. And when the next reader says, "And the word became flesh and dwelt among us," I will think of Charlotte, who is here now, or soon, and of the life that is growing in me and will arrive in the spring. "What a glorious thing our lives have become," you said to me after your baby shower. What a glorious thing. Now I feel, looking back, that we were hailing the start of this new age last Easter.

Charlotte, your little Advent baby. I long to see you and her. I will wait anxiously to hear from Dave. Until then, a candle burns for all three of you, and my heart and soul are with you.

With love,
Amy

December 18, 2005

Dear Amy,

Last night I was lying in my hospital bed, staring at the bassinet parked next to it. The nurses had just rolled it in, and Charlotte was fresh from a bath, swaddled like a burrito in her little blanket, a stripy cap on her perfectly round head. Dave was asleep on the foldout chair, and *Jerry Maguire* was on TV—that Bruce Springsteen song, "Secret Garden." I tried so hard to resist picking her up. For a moment we just lay there in our respective beds, staring at each other. I'm sure she couldn't see me, but it seemed that she could. She blinked once, slowly, sleepily, and I burst into tears. There was something indescribable about that moment. I think I suddenly understood the enormity of what has happened, of her life. My brain connected what was lying there in that blanket with the knocks I've felt in my belly for months. I've never felt such love.

I sprang from my bed to gather her in my arms, bury my face in her blanket, rub my cheek against her velvet head. I know I will remember that moment all my life. That little blink burned into my brain. Only I saw it. I wish you could have seen it, too.

With so much love,

Jess

Letters are among the most significant
memorial a person can leave behind them.
—Johann Wolfgang von Goethe

Lent 2006

How will I be able to develop (in the next four short months!) that steady, everyday cadence that mothers seem to have? You seem to have it with Charlotte. What if I can nurse only in bursts? Bathe in bursts? Love in bursts? It's the same feeling I often have with God. What if last Lent was just a burst of faith?

—Amy, March 8

• • • • • • •

Right now I feel that I'm living in a sort of dream state. The satisfaction I take in mothering my baby has overlaid my ache for God. In moments like this I feel it would be so easy to let faith just slip through my fingers.

—Jess, March 10

March 1, 2006
Ash Wednesday

Dear Jess,

Despite my best intentions, all that I managed to write before today were beginnings of letters. I should have sent some of them, but they were all unfinished and boring. I couldn't seem to get through the haze of work and morning sickness to actually sit down to the task of writing. So I must begin Lent by repenting.

Ever since I found out I was pregnant, I have been trying desperately to imagine the life growing within me. At first I would try to imagine my own interior, placing my womb somewhere between my belly button and pubic bone, somewhere midway between the outside skin of my lower stomach and the knobs of my spine, but as hard as I tried to picture it and care for it, nothing would come to mind. It felt like praying and being met with only silence and the rattle of my own thoughts and breath. I started examining the skin of my hands and face and realized that it is only this surface I associate with myself. What lies beneath is as alien to me as God.

Advent was the season of waiting. You felt that anticipation acutely as you waited to see your daughter's face. I was waiting, too, but for a more ambiguous encounter, for the mere feeling of a life within me, for some sign that would indicate something other than my own organs and bones. I would stare at my stomach and see the same familiar paunch. And even at Christmastime, when my belly was finally rounding out and I bought an armload of maternity clothes, I still couldn't fathom that anyone was really there.

Now, things are starting to change. About five weeks ago I started feeling the first slight taps from the interior. Initially, it was like bubbles bursting against the inside of my abdomen. Or maybe more like soft-headed mallets drumming. Or sometimes it felt simply like a shift of my muscles or organs, like something suspended had suddenly dropped or lifted. The first time I noticed it, I was sitting at my desk writing in my journal (one of the only times) and then, out of nowhere, came a little burst, a drum roll. I put my hands instinctively on either side of my abdomen, trying to caress what lay inside. For an instant I was overwhelmed with feeling. But even that sure sign—which only grows stronger by the day and now feels like full-body movements, like something turning over and rolling down—is not enough. I still stare in disbelief at the pregnancy test I saved and at the fuzzy ultrasound images on the fridge. Each day I work to believe in her. And what does she know of me? Nothing. Except that everything she knows is me.

The act of naming her is the only thing so far that has given me any sense of reality. Now when I put my hand on my belly, I call her by name: Clare Elizabeth. But still I struggle to connect her name to that strange interior knocking. I understand the amazement you felt in the hospital, seeing Charlotte and her body made whole.

Love,
Amy

March 1, 2006
Ash Wednesday

Dear Amy,
Sunday was Charlotte's baptism in the little log chapel. Have I ever smelled anything so divine as the holy oil on my infant's hair? Standing with Mark, as her godparents, you, pregnant with your own daughter, read from Psalm 139: "You knit me in my mother's womb." It was grave, intimate, and perfect.

After, the priest said to me, "I don't usually see so much emotion at baptisms." How can that be? I was so happy to see Charlotte welcomed into the church, clothed in white, sleeping in the arms of a priest as he called on her patron saints to guide and protect her. We were surrounded by family, but I could see her taking her place in a line much longer than ours. It felt like the most important gift I could give her.

The day was marred only by the absence of my mother. I still can't get over that you're due on her birthday. When you mentioned the date at the christening party, I saw a flicker of recognition cross my dad's face, and it comforted me to know that he hasn't forgotten.

Now it's Lent again, and today Notre Dame is a city of people wearing ashes in the shape of the cross on their foreheads, and I'm taking the same joy in this tradition that I felt on Sunday, the same gratitude for having something to hand on to my daughter.

Father Riley mentioned during the christening that those alleluias we said after blessing her would be the last we'd hear for forty days. Right on cue, we kicked off Lent with the news that Dave didn't get either of the jobs for which he interviewed. I suppose there was something not quite right about those schools. Maybe once the book comes out, everything will fall into place. (This is me trying to be hopeful.)

With love,
Jess

March 2, 2006

Dear Jess,
Last night at the Ash Wednesday Mass, I sang in the chant choir, so I wasn't able to walk up with everyone else to receive my ashes. When the Mass ended, the choir processed to the back of the church

singing "parce domine, Parce populo tuo" ("spare us Lord, spare us your people"). Maybe at that point I should have counted myself spared, having avoided the sentence of ashes, but I suddenly felt panicky. Where were the priests? Would they wait? I raced upstairs to the parish center to take off my robe and then back down to the church. I pushed my way through the crowd and found Father Brian standing at the front of the church holding a little bowl. "May I still receive ashes?" I asked, breathless. "Remember you are dust and to dust you shall return," he said, smudging my forehead.

I wondered later why I had been so desperate to receive that grim blessing, especially since I kept on thinking during Mass of the new mortal thing inside of me. How fearsome it seems to carry something mortal in my own mortal body.

This morning when I looked in the mirror, the ashes were still there, a sooty shadow under my bangs. I stood in the bathroom like a teenager who is hesitant to wash away a kiss. What does one do? Just let the ashes run down the drain like dirt? The ashes this year were made from the fronds from last year's Palm Sunday and mixed with the oil of catechumens, the oil that was crossed on my forehead when you named me Teresa. I continued to stare at my reflection for some time.

Lately, I spend more time than I should studying myself in the mirror. I guess it's an old, bad habit. Milan Kundera called this habit in his character, Teresa, her secret vice, but he was sympathetic. He said she had a "longing to be a body unlike other bodies, to find that the surface of her face reflected the crew of the soul charging up from below." But this suggests that she didn't fully identify with her surface. When I was younger, I stared in the mirror to determine if I was desirable; the face staring back at me was who I imagined myself to be. Now things are different. My body is changing so quickly that it is hard for my conception of myself to keep up. When

I look in the mirror, I am often surprised: a new pattern of blue veins on my chest, suddenly dark nipples, the linea nigra, like a penciled seam down the middle, becoming more visible every day. It is hard to imagine what my body will be like in the future. Up to now I've gained and lost a bit of weight, I've changed my hair a little, but it's been the same freckles across my nose, the same skin, the same basic shape. And even now with all the changes, my face seems much like it always has.

My mother tells me that when she looks in the mirror these days, she doesn't recognize her face. She says that how she looked at thirty is how she imagines herself to be, and when she sees her reflection, she is always startled. She worries that her children won't remember her as she was back then, only as she is growing older. I wonder if I am at that point right now. Is the face I have today, just before I have my first child, the face I will always consider mine? Next year or five years from now, will I have to work to accept each new wrinkle and gray hair as part of myself?

This worry over our reflections is largely private. Whatever my mother sees, I see beauty when I look at her. But it makes me think of that Sylvia Plath poem "Mirror." "A woman bends over me, searching my reaches for what she really is," says the mirror. "In me she has drowned a young girl, and in me an old woman rises toward her day after day, like a terrible fish." How sad it seems to be like that, flinching at your own face, but maybe it's not like that. Maybe instead of being horrified, you just turn away from the mirror and feel relieved that you are no longer so tied to that image.

I have started buying books of photography, mostly for the shots of old women. Young people seem so generic. When asked if one of his early girlfriends was beautiful, Steve Martin said, "I don't know. We were young. We were all beautiful." Young people live on the surface of their bodies, all deck. But when I look at one of those portraits of an old woman, she is so much herself, a body unlike other bodies, her fingers gnarled and face grooved into the shapes of her habits. And her eyes are deep, as if the crew of the soul is standing there lined up, one behind the other, stretching back to the beginning, looking through all her looks at once: young, middle aged, old.

Yet when I look at my mother, I don't see age. Her face is the very first face I looked up into, my original image of love; it's still what I see when I look at her.

Love,
Amy

March 2, 2006

Dear Amy,

I'm mourning the loss of my days as a stay-at-home mother. Next week, I go back to work. She's in the swing now, and my heart breaks to look at her, balled up in there, one sock dangling from her tiny foot, the other on the floor.

I'm trying to get back into a routine now, hoping it will help Dave and Charlotte when I go back to work. Every time I think about leaving her, my throat constricts. It hurts to go to the grocery store. Even now, I feel that I've abandoned her to this swing, and I'm only three feet away.

I've already begun to smother her. Sometimes she seems almost relieved to be with Dave. Can a baby so young feel relief? Maybe he should be the one to stay at home with her.

Anyway, it seems futile to pray for his job search anymore, saying the same words every night but filling in the blank with a different school: "Please, Lord, if it be your will, let Dave get this job at _____." When will I realize that this is our life? When will I stop peering around corners, awaiting what's next?

It has its own peculiar bliss, this domesticity, this life of diapers and laundry and the click, click, click of the baby swing. I'm not ready for this time to end. I've never been happier, or more boring (this letter is abysmal, forgive me). Is this what happens when you become a mother?

Love,
Jess

March 8, 2006

Dear Jess,

I fear that I operate in only two modes. I am either cramming for some deadline (teaching, writing, singing) or I am doing absolutely nothing, sitting around with that terrible, blank stare and feeling guilty about not cramming. Neither mode would be a good approach to motherhood. I think that is why I sometimes feel unready for the job. How will I be able to develop (in the next four short months!) that steady, everyday cadence that mothers seem to have? You seem to have it with Charlotte. What if I can nurse only in bursts? Bathe in bursts? Love in bursts? It's the same feeling I often have with God. What if last Lent was just a burst of faith?

Sometimes when I reflect on my life, it appears to me that there have never been any real changes, just escapes from what I have always been and still am. I fear that real change is impossible. Of course, there have been changes: childhood somehow gave way to adolescence, which somehow turned into adulthood. Partly, it's a problem of perspective. From the inside of history it is often difficult to see the revolutions taking place.

But I do remember once when I was about ten years old having a glimpse, almost a premonition, of what was coming. I was sitting on the concrete floor of our basement, near one of the steel poles supporting the house. My dolls and their world were spread out around me. I'm not sure what triggered it. Maybe my mother decided to go upstairs to make dinner or read for awhile instead of opting for yet another round of make-believe. I remember having a sudden flash of anger, not at her, but at the idea that I would ever be like her. I stared at my dolls in furious solidarity. "I will never be like that. I will never forget," I swore to them with all the serious intention my ten years could enlist. And yet by age twelve I had abandoned the basement, much preferring to spend my afternoons peering through binoculars at my neighbors' house, trying to catch a glimpse of my neighbors' son.

Back then I'm sure I couldn't have mustered an ounce of sympathy for my ten-year-old self. But now I feel for her. In some ways I am like her now, looking ahead to the next age, knowing it's coming but having none of the experience of what it will be like to tempt me into change.

I keep thinking about something you said the first time I met Charlotte. I think she was a week old and asleep upstairs. We sat together around your dining-room table eating Italian food, and you said the feeling you now have with Charlotte is the same feeling of home you had growing up. Without the presence of a child yet, I have started imagining the future in terms of my past.

What was it like? Now the presence of most things in my apartment is contingent upon utility, or at least appreciation. The chairs and tables and curtains stand in reserve for use or upgrade. But when

I was a child the objects of our home, and even the structure of our house itself, had the wild, inevitable feel of trees or boulders. Everything apparently given, not chosen, taking on the mysterious presence of inexorable reality. You often talk about the light from the hood over the range. The swish of the dishwasher. The junk drawer. For me it's the nap on the back of our velour couch, the worn green carpet on the basement steps, the curtain with pink daisies over my bed and the irregular swells in the window screen. Even more, I think of the murmuring of my parents' voices from the kitchen as I lay in bed, the occasional laugh, and calling down the hall, "Do you promise nothing will hurt us? Do you *guarantee* it?" Then asking for the moon song. The sound of my father searching around in the closet where we kept the turntable. The first, circling scratch of the needle, and the opening triplets of the Moonlight Sonata.

I've always thought it was my parents who made our house feel enchanted, but it is more reciprocal than that. When Clare arrives she will transform my world, and so hers, which for so long has felt like something temporary and unloved, into that kind of deep home that seems possible only when you are young and your parents keep watch in the night.

Today, out of the blue, I thought of the "Clair de Lune" by Debussy. I put the disc on repeat. Will Clare call out from her bed and mean this when she asks for the moon song? Will she lie there under the cracked plaster of her ceiling, as fixed and provocative as any night sky, survey the row of animals on her shelf, any of them at any moment ready to burst into speech, and listen to me and Mark talking in the kitchen? Will she at some point vow never to change and look at me as the thing she never wants to become?

Love,
Amy

March 10, 2006

Dear Amy,

It's 8:36 p.m., the second Friday in Lent, and Dave and I are already in bed. I pointed the time out to him, and he said, "So what? I'm perfectly happy." He's reading a book of conversations between Robert Coles and the Catholic worker Daniel Berrigan. For the first time, Charlotte is asleep in her bassinet. She jammed a fist in her mouth, rolled over, and drifted off like it was the most natural thing in the world.

I've longed for days like this my whole life—days of contentment. I have so many now that Charlotte is here. Today I spent twenty minutes chatting with our neighbor over the fence. We've lived here eighteen months, and I've never even seen her before. What a change this baby has wrought in me.

I remember you writing that the real test of our faith would come in the long middays, the stretches when nothing much happens. I think you called it the trials of good fortune. Right now I feel that I'm living in a sort of dream state. The satisfaction I take in mothering my baby has overlaid my ache for God. In moments like this I feel it would be so easy to let faith just slip through my fingers.

As I sat in Mass tonight, I stared at the Host and felt certain that it was just a piece of bread. *That's all it is*, I thought: bread and wine, and a little man waving his hands over the table. Suddenly the whole idea of what we were doing, and the fact that we'd been doing it for thousands of years, seemed terribly funny. The ridiculousness of it made me want to laugh.

The reason I was able to contemplate any doubts in the real presence was that Dave kept Charlotte at home so I could go to Mass alone. For the past three months I've been only half present at Mass;

n she's with me, it's difficult to pay attention, even when she's peaceful. I just sit there beaming like an idiot, full of pride in the way everyone smiles at us and dotes on her.

But tonight I was alone and in the first row, so as I knelt after communion, I watched everyone else process, bow their heads, cross themselves seriously. *They all think it's real,* I kept thinking to myself, incredulous, still near that nervous laughter. But as the long line crept by, I felt a measure of my faith returning. There is something so beautiful about other people in church, the leveling experience of coming before the Eucharist. The minister holds the bread up before us and says, "The Body of Christ," and each, no matter his or her age or station, must assent, "Amen"—yes, agreed—before taking the Host in the hand or on the tongue. I watched person after person, the whispered "amens," the bowed or upturned heads, the sign of the cross and the downcast eyes on the way back to the pew. Something about their willingness, and mine, to be humbled in such a way, week after week, stopped my laughter and made me long again to believe.

—Jess

March 12, 2006

Dear Jess,

In a recent letter, you spoke of always peering around corners awaiting the next step rather than actually living. That perfectly describes one of my biggest fears, that I will one day look back on my life and realize I have never really lived but have always been awaiting some vague future existence in which, as you put it, life would finally begin.

I think that is why I have often found myself longing to be taken hold of, so commanded by experience that I have no choice but to acknowledge the here and now.

I hear every day of this or that freak accident—a fourteen-year-old girl killed by a stray bullet, a blind woman hit by a car—and I become positively frantic to train myself to live here and now. Yet I seem not to have the requisite skills. Even the most trivial thing, such as what will I wear this weekend or how will I arrange the furniture, can become the central work of my mind if I am not vigilant. What if I am like that with Clare—always fretting over what I will do later that day, that week, next year? But in daily life, vigilance seems virtually impossible. Vigilance *is* a kind of prayer, and how exactly to commit myself to that is not yet clear.

More than anything else, this is why I am so attracted to the idea of natural childbirth. I see these pictures of women *in* birth, in "laborland" (as my childbirth teacher calls it), their mouths open, their heads slightly back. They are panting or moaning or yelling (not crying, ever), and they are totally, absolutely compelled by the experience of birth. In that moment, there could be nothing but the most peripheral distraction, the most fleeting self-conscious thought: *here I am, giving birth.* Pain and effort shut down all of that meta-living and force one into contention with the moment at hand. It's like that passage from the first letter to the Thessalonians: "Then sudden disaster comes upon them, like labor pains upon a pregnant woman, and they will not escape."

The Bernini sculpture *The Ecstasy of St. Teresa* shows St. Teresa swooning before an angel who is about to drive a burning sword into her entrails. But if you look only at her face—head back, mouth open—you wouldn't know if she were being tortured, seeing God, or about to give birth. It is the generic look of ecstasy. The self and all individual expression disappear into the experience.

But there is something that seems wrong to me about this pursuit of ecstasy. I think of Sylvia Plath pining away, even from a certain ironic distance, for that spasmodic trick of radiance. If ecstatic experience is the only real life, then most of our time *is* inconsequential, spent merely waiting for that rare, random descent of the angel. It's as grim as the life of distraction, always spent anticipating something other than life to come along.

Love,

Amy

March 12, 2006

Dear Amy,

Last night the moon came up, and it was so bright, it was brighter than the street lamps. The sky was navy blue. We turned off our night-light; the moon was so bright it almost hurt to look at it. I've never seen anything like it. I thought immediately of "Clair de Lune."

Spring is creeping in, and all I can think of is babies, and the cardinals, starlings, and wrens at our bird feeder, which I'm distractedly watching through the window. How long can such contentment last? It certainly isn't very Lenten.

Maybe it's just that I no longer have time to stare at the wall. How many of my days before Charlotte did I spend that way—gazing blankly, too exhausted by life, by myself, to think or move? The wall starer isn't so distant that she can't reclaim me. If I have a moment to myself, I begin to dwell on the idea that I've come to love life too much and that it would be unbearable to lose it. But stewing just isn't possible with a baby in the house, and I'm sure that's for the best.

Until reading your letter it hadn't occurred to me that this might be the home of Charlotte's childhood—or that she might feel for this place what I feel for my childhood home, the setting of all my dreams, even now, even last night. This seems like such a great responsibility. But it must be something like the way I thought of preparing myself for her arrival. I couldn't think of anything to do to make it imaginable, so I bought maternity clothes, baby furniture, and framed pictures for her walls. None of it worked. Even sitting in the rocking chair of the perfectly decorated nursery, crib painted but empty, onesies folded in the drawer, diapers stacked neatly on the changing table, I couldn't imagine a real baby in there. (In fact, she's still not spent the night in there—not a single one.) But now she is here, and with her, that feeling that she's been here all along. Still, it's hard to imagine that one day she may dream of the light in our kitchen window the way I still see the sun streaming through the sliding-glass doors on Meadowmoss Drive, the dust dancing in the rays. That this place, which to me is just a house, will be her emblem of home.

—Jess

March 13, 2006

Dear Jess,

I've been thinking more about my desire for ecstasy. In college I think it made me rather absurd. I considered "World Falls" by the Indigo Girls a kind of personal manifesto. They sing about being shaken by the beauty of the world, afraid it is too much to bear. I used to play the song for prospective boyfriends and gauge their response. Could they experience life with the same raw intensity that I could?

My mother used to tease me. "Passion," she'd say. "How did you get so obsessed with that?" But then she was the one who used to fantasize about John Wayne or Yul Brynner sweeping her up onto a horse with one muscled arm and racing off over the prairie.

Even now, I sometimes tend in that direction, so being married to Mark has been a helpful counter. I still remember the time he said to me, "I hope for a complacent life, a life of complacency." It was early in our relationship, so I think I briefly considered calling the whole thing off.

"You what?" I practically shrieked back at him. But he stuck to his guns, taking a slightly perverse pleasure in using a word with such a negative connotation. "It literally means *with pleasure*," he insisted. It does. We looked it up. "The state of being pleased. Tranquil pleasure. Delight." Mark saw the word as describing a life lived in harmony with reality, with the way things are. The desire for transcendent experience, he said, is the desire for everything to be more than it is, for life to be magnified and exaggerated, and for one's own psyche to be lifted out of and above the ordinary.

And it's not like I don't understand what he means. My own thinking has started to tend more in that direction. For example, in college I was an Annie Dillard fanatic, reveling in her beautifully wrought amazement. She is a self-proclaimed pilgrim in search of a vision, the lights flaming in the trees. But at least from her prose, it seems that, for her, that's all there is. You can see it in her metaphors. She rarely speaks of people but of things. And with a few exceptions, when she does write of people it falls flat. Christ himself is a creek. Where is love in this association? Where are the claims love makes on us? It may bring about contemplative ecstasy—"dancing at the feet of the Lord, all is bliss, all is bliss"—but again, where is compunction, pity, fellowship, charity?

Yet life has a certain built-in insufficiency, whether or not it is being compared to ecstatic experience. No matter how fulfilling our work or relationships, we continue to long for something more. It spurs us on to work harder, to seek greater love. And when we fail in work or love, it is easy to fall into despair. Even when we have moments of great fulfillment, they slip away before we've had the chance to respond with sufficient gratitude or wonder or love. Those transcendent moments give me faith that what I am seeking is actually there.

I'm not sure any of this makes sense. I feel scattered today, my belly huge and itching like crazy, my navel beginning to pucker out. The skin there is so soft, I guess from hiding in its depression all these years. I love to run my finger over it. I look at my belly button so differently now, knowing that just underneath Clare is living through me through this same place on her abdomen. I've actually been worried about her lately. I have imagined, at times, that her movements have slowed down (wait, she is kicking me like crazy right now!).

My childbirth class is tonight. I am sure I will have much to report.

Love,
Amy

March 16, 2006

Dear Amy,

Today I sank into my first real depression since the baby arrived. It wasn't quite the same as the staring-at-the-wall variety. I was just sitting on the sofa with her asleep in my arms, and suddenly I felt like crying.

The thought suddenly occurred to me: *I have no idea who I am anymore. I don't take pleasure in the things I used to. What pleases me now? Only her?*

Maybe I simply cried because my writing was interrupted. I felt the desire to write, which is rare these days, but soon as I gathered pen and paper and sat down near the sunny window, Charlotte became fussy. The warm sun that I was enjoying was too bright in her eyes, and suddenly we were both upset.

Today your letter was all about trying to hold onto brief moments of ecstatic joy and trying to live now instead of later. I'm afraid I grew even more depressed as I read it, as I was reminded of how we used to be, before the babies. Why did it make me sad? I don't want to go back there. I don't even like to imagine my life before Charlotte, and I don't doubt she's made me a better person. But I missed *us*, almost the same way as I miss being pregnant. It seemed awful at the time, but I envy that feeling of expectation you're experiencing now. I envy the passion I had for Lent last year, the attention, the devotion. I just can't get there now.

Who is this person I've become—who cries when she sees other babies, and chats with neighbors over fences, and is happy to watch birds in the backyard for hours on end?

Charlotte laughed at me today, in the midst of all this. I mean really laughed: a sound of pure delight, followed by a shriek. And it was at me, for me, only. She was lying in my lap, staring up at me, and I was making some silly face or other, and she was smiling and squinting her eyes, and then she laughed, this tiny creature, and it made my heart pound in my chest.

Somehow this feels different from my other existential crises. It's just so vivid: nothing can make me as happy as this baby. What a terrifying thought.

—Jess

March 17, 2006

Dear Jess,

I just read two letters from you and thought about the beautiful excess in our letter writing. There is a conversation that happens—I respond to this line, or you respond to that line—but so much of it seems to be sent out into the air. We can always imagine the other one reading our words, though, so maybe I should have said instead "sent out into the loving air."

Montaigne thought of all of his essays as letters, letters he imagined sending to his closest friend, even after his friend had died (the one who "led him, sustained him, and raised him up"). "For to talk to the winds, as others do," wrote Montaigne, "is beyond me, except in dreams." This is one of the things that makes writing letters to you feel like real prayer. Why can't prayer itself feel like real prayer? Writing to you erases self-consciousness, that terrible feeling of speaking to the wind for no clear purpose.

Prayer may still be an abstraction, or feel abstract, but I'll tell you what is real right now: birth. Since I have started taking this class, I can't stop thinking about this coming event in my life. The first class wasn't so overwhelming, because both of the videos we saw were of slightly surreal events: the first, an ecstatic birth in a small Mexican paradise (complete with a tiled, in-home hot tub built by the artisan husband; beautiful, naked children running about; and no blood or moaning), and the second, a hyperclinical hospital birth with a hyper-artificial-looking mother who actually yelled, "Take him away from me," when the baby emerged. I didn't see myself in either scenario, so my own labor and delivery remained entirely mysterious.

In the last class, however, we watched a home video. The goal was to show us the three stages of pre-pushing labor: early, active, and transition. In the first stage, the woman is at her kitchen table smiling, waving at the camera, eating cereal. At one point she winces, just a brief blink, and then she is back, waving again. Then, probably hours later, the movie cuts to the bedroom. Now the music is off, and she is kneeling on the floor, leaning her torso on the bed. Her eyes are closed, and she is breathing deliberately.

Cut again, and the room is now dark; she is naked, but still in the same position, slumped over the edge of the bed. Her husband is sprawled out in front of her on the bed, and she is grasping his hands. At first she seems collapsed and exhausted, but then a contraction starts and she starts to moan, throwing her head back and crying out as if she had just been whipped. Then she collapses again. The next contraction we "see" is obviously worse than the previous one, for this time her moans are irregular and a bit frantic, maybe as if she were afraid.

All night after the class, I felt odd. It seemed a combination of embarrassment, envy, and voyeuristic pleasure. Oh, yes, and dread. I was both captivated and repelled by that memory of her contorting, moaning body. The feeling, which I know I am absolutely failing to describe, is primal, and I think feels this way precisely because it has to do with the part of our humanity we have the most trouble grasping, our sheer existence and mortality. I think we tend to live and think of ourselves as if we were angels, endless, but in birth we face creation.

My first cousin just had her twin boys—the first vaginally, the second (because his arm was above his head in the birth canal) by C-section—and her e-mail was titled "They are here!" Isn't that the language we always use to describe birth? The baby arrives, as if from far away, as if from distant travels. Yet how very strange; the mother was all along *with child*, the baby was already *here*.

But I understand this language perfectly. My baby is Clare in my mind, Clare of the moon in my imagination. She is Clare in my arms—someday. But she is Clare only in these re-creations and projections. Inside of me she is a mysterious knocking. This is another reason I long for the actual sensation of birth—to feel, to see, to know what was hidden come to light. Is birth like that, Jess? I imagine that great anticipation, and then the realization that what you were waiting to see is moving through your very own body into the world. No! I just can't grasp it.

Yours,

Amy

March 19, 2006

Dear Amy,

On the way home from visiting Dave's parents in Toledo, we decided that we want to stay here in South Bend. My job provides for us, and Dave has time to write, which will increase his chances at a professorship later. We decided that we could be happy here. That we are, in fact, happy. What do we expect to find somewhere else?

I'm so used to scrambling and scheming. I can't seem to stop myself from doing it. But if I stop now and ask myself, "What am I chasing?" I can't find a good answer.

Reading your letter about Mark's "life of complacency," I remembered how disgusted we were when Ellen wrote to you that she was glad you'd found "peace" in the church. Peace! We screamed. We don't want peace! We made retching noises. We want intensity, ecstasy, passion, awe, consolation, eternity! Anything but *peace*.

We were like Dorothea Brooke in Eliot's *Middlemarch*, yearning for the radical passion of the saints. I imagine she would have responded to Ellen's remark with equivalent horror and disgust. As if God were nothing more than a balm for the neurotic. As if belief weren't a challenge to one's entire way of being.

I see the last lines of *Middlemarch* every day on the banner of one of my favorite blogs: "For the growing good of the world is partly dependent on unhistoric acts; and that things are not so ill with you and me as they might have been is half owing to the number who lived faithfully a hidden life, and the rest in unvisited tombs."

The word *faithfully* is the key to the passage, I think. Living faithfully may bring about goodness, but it doesn't guarantee peace, consolation, or personal gain. Living faithfully "a hidden life" seems to me especially hard. No one is watching but God. Nobody will ever know how you've spent your day—if you fold the laundry or wipe the baby's nose. Just like nobody sees your mother's gardens, the private acts of love and attention that bring about such beauty.

I want to content myself with those unhistoric acts, which Eliot saw were so necessary for the growing good of the world. If it's possible to knowingly and willingly embrace a life of complacency, I want to do it. Motherhood seems to offer the perfect opportunity.

—Jess

March 26, 2006

Dear Jess,

It was confirmation yesterday, and the bishop was there in his pink robes. "Be proud of your faith," he proclaimed, walking down the central aisle. "When you dream of your life to come, don't only dream of the world's dream of success and prosperity, but dream you are good, that you live with integrity, that you serve God." He was speaking to children, but it was a beautiful corrective to how I often find myself thinking about life.

I am so tired, sitting in this recliner with a heating pad on my rib cage, but I am going to attempt to keep writing this letter. I want to tell you about a strange recent episode. When my sister was here, I took her to my favorite new breakfast place. After we were seated, eating the pancakes, Katy asked me something about how I felt about Clare right now—if I felt close to her or was looking forward to being a mother. For some reason what immediately occurred to me was not my love but my fear, my irrational, sudden spasms of fear. "When I think of her," I said, "I see myself suddenly losing hold of her, her falling or flying out of a car, dashed by my hands. I see myself ruining everything, and Mark watching from a distance." I started laughing, in sharp bursts of laughter, and then I was almost crying, choked cries alternating with uncontrolled laughs. I became completely hysterical, holding my hands over my face, trying to push it back inside. Katy drew a picture of a dead kitten on her napkin with her eyeliner (a reference to the scene in the movie *All of Me* when Steve Martin's amorous mood is quieted by thinking about "very old nuns and dead kittens"). She held it up for me to look at, and, of course, this made it worse. I cried and laughed into the dead kitten on her napkin until I finally calmed down. See, I told you it was strange.

On Saturday, I went to my first prenatal yoga class. There must have been thirty-five pregnant women in the class. At first I thought I might hate seeing myself there, part of a mass happening. But as the class progressed, there was something beautiful about it. I kept thinking about the thirty-five hidden lives that were there with us, and that all seventy of us were careening toward birth. At some point we had to go around the room and each share something about either our anticipation of birth or an experience with postpartum. A woman directly across from me talked about how she felt when her daughter was first born. "All I could think about was, I've got to keep her alive," she said. "And not kill her." Her pediatrician told her, "Stop worrying! You are not going to drop her. You are not going to hurt her. You are not going to kill her." At least there is one other person who's as crazy as I am.

I hope you can actually read my handwriting in this letter. I have reclined the chair so far, I am almost flat on my back. You're not supposed to lie in that position during pregnancy, but I am still technically *sitting* in a chair, so it doesn't quite count. Anyway this letter is a mess, and come to think of it, it might be a good thing if you can't quite read it.

I am not diabetic, it turns out, but I do have anemia, so now I must take iron. I want to keep writing, but I am just dead, dead tired. More tomorrow when the iron kicks in.

Love,
Amy

March 27, 2006

Dear Amy,
Your diligence has sustained our letter-writing practice this Lent. I'm sorry I haven't been writing more. How will I muster the proper enthusiasm for Holy Week? This year I might kiss the feet of the cross in pure gratitude. Soon we'll be kneeling next to our daughters, and we'll hear their tiny voices in prayer. These fantasies of our two girls growing up together completely dominate my imagination.

We're just back from Pennsylvania. It was a strange weekend. Dave did a reading at Westminster College, and I met Rachael, an old friend from the journal, in Pittsburgh to go shopping. Her hair has grown so long it curls down her back, and I had a baby strapped to me. But otherwise we were so much the same, and I felt that I'd gone back in time and was dreaming the future.

At dinner with our old friends, I sat back and watched Dave chatting and interacting with everyone, and I had that weird disconnected feeling again. Has he changed? I felt I didn't recognize him. Maybe it was the two martinis, but he was talking slowly and saying odd things, and I grew impatient with him. I've felt so connected to Charlotte lately, and so disconnected from him. In the early days after her birth, we were all so close; it felt like a honeymoon. I felt a panic attack coming on, but it was about then that Charlotte's diaper leaked and I had to run to the bathroom with a huge load of crap on my new top.

I've been feeling so unlike myself, like a stranger. So much has changed in so short a time—new state, new job, new marriage, new baby, new friends, all in less than two years. In Pittsburgh I felt more recognizable. Still, I was grateful to get back home to Indiana. Charlotte looked happy to see her digs. She smiled and went right to sleep.

Today, Dave got the first good review of his book. Some hipster magazine said it was "impassioned" and "honest." He brought it upstairs to me and then just stood there with a genuine look of surprise. That memory of him standing there, speechless, makes me long for him. But he's in Valparaiso listening to Sister Helen Prejean talk about the death penalty.

—Jess

March 27, 2006

Dear Jess,

Last night I tried to write you a letter. It was rather pathetic, written in a shaky hand, but I will probably send it anyway. My rib cage still hurts, and some days it hurts all day long, and by the end of the day I am exhausted just from dealing with it. Clare is so high up in my belly that she's torquing my rib cage.

I am changing every day now, becoming more and more my body and less and less my mind. Now sometimes I just cry. I know I am being overtaken and my life is becoming subject to something else, but I can't know what this means, who I will be on the other side, or how I will possibly even get to the other side. What will be lost or gained? I am still on this side of my child's first breath.

I try to think about Clare. I picture a generic baby: soft down on the head, eyes closed, little fists up near the mouth, body relaxed and curled. Then I stare at my belly. Just under the skin lies that baby, I tell myself. There. I see a kick. There. But it never really helps. So instead I cry and feel the enormity of this transformation of my mind and body taking hold.

I am reading *Gilead* by Marilynne Robinson and just came across this line: "Every single one of us is a little civilization built on the ruins of any number of preceding civilizations." She means that we are each founded on the generations of people who have come before, but it made me think of something I wrote about to you, earlier in Lent. Even within the span of a single lifetime, there are marked ages, although we can usually make out their beginnings and ends only in retrospect. But through pregnancy, women are granted a more self-conscious passage from one civilization to the next. We can see the ruin coming in our own bodies. We can feel the new age forming in our bellies. And we know, give or take a week, the date of revolution. Birth faces us like approaching catastrophe, when the current order of things will be overturned.

Right now, I am beginning to feel the march of the tortoise. I want to dig my heels in and stay here a bit longer. I have so much to do. I must clean and prepare and finish everything I had ever imagined doing when my life was just my own, but I know I won't have time for any of that. Sometimes I imagine it will be like this to die, especially if I am old and the death is one I have some time to anticipate. I will try to wring meaning and magnificence out of my last days or year, and just as I feel now, all my attempts to look ahead will be vastly inadequate to what comes. "I am afraid of the future," wrote Teilhard de Chardin, "too heavy with mystery and too wholly new, toward which time is driving me." What is coming is coming, whether I'm ready or not.

Love,
Amy

March 29, 2006

Dear Amy,

I've found it so difficult to pray lately, it's all I can do to read the daily selection from the Magnificat while Charlotte sleeps on me. I try to leave it next to my nursing chair because if I forget, I end up just sitting there while she naps on me, waiting for her to wake up.

Today, I was impressed by this line from the book of Psalms: "The Lord does not treat us according to our sins." If I combine this phrase with the image of a God who loves us as a parent loves a child, I can begin to imagine a God who wants to give us good things out of love and a God who does not withhold goodness because we've underperformed. I can also imagine a God who knows better than I do what "goodness" is, and I can begin to conceive of how ultimate goodness can sometimes start with pain.

It's ridiculous to compare myself to God, but by way of analogy, I was thinking that if Charlotte did something terrible, I would be disappointed, even angry, but I'd still be there, pouring out my love for her, waiting eagerly for her to come to me, but loving her the same even if she never came. The parable of the prodigal son comes to mind. The father in that story loves both his sons, the faithful and the faithless, and rejoices in both their lives. "All that I have is yours," he says. It helps me to think of God this way, although I fear I'm being too pie in the sky.

Charlotte is stirring in her bassinet. I tried to sneak her in there so I could write you a letter, but she's gotten wise.

Love,
Jess

April 1, 2006

Dear Jess,

I am worried about Clare today. She has been so quiet, only the most occasional kick or turn. Sometimes I worry that the childbirth class I am taking is scaring me with too much information. We talk all the time about the tender cord that connects us, how it can be swept into the birth canal and compressed by the baby's head if your waters break too early. At my visit yesterday, the midwife said everything looked great. I heard the quick rhythm of Clare's heart.

I realized today that I do love Clare already. A vision of her came to me, all curled up inside. It was primarily her leg that I saw, most likely the right leg, bent at the knee and floating in front of her. I loved that little leg. A friend said to me the other night on the phone how odd it is to see a week-old infant and realize it could still be in the womb. It is the detail, she said, that surprises her most. I think she is right. When I think of Clare, she is always hazy: a turning shoulder, the profile of a nose, but never a real face, complete with all its own little curves and bumps.

I've been so obsessed with trying to picture her that I've been practically fetishizing her birth. Of course the moment she emerges will be wonderful, but it won't be enough to deliver *her* to me. In some ways I probably won't feel like I've really met her until years from now, when she starts to emerge from the physical demands of infancy into real personhood. I thought about my ongoing difficulty imagining Clare when I came across this passage in *Gilead*:

> I believe that the old man did indeed have far too narrow an idea of what a vision might be. He may have been too dazzled by the great light of his experience to realize that an impressive sun shines on us all. . . . Sometimes the visionary aspect of any particular day comes to you in the memory of it, or it opens to you over time.

This is an understanding of vision even Mark might accept. Instead of being an immediate and dramatic experience that amplifies or even takes you away from life, here a vision arises from daily living itself; it is composed from life over time, revealing eventually that God was speaking all along, even through the long, mundane stretches. And this would mean that visions increase as we acquire more life to look back on. But still, it's easy for me to get impatient. This is part of the appeal of witness accounts; I want to hear from someone who has already been to the far country what it is really like; I want to get the details.

That's one reason I found St. Teresa so seductive last Lent. She writes like someone with firsthand experience. I always remember the passage from *Interior Castle* in which she draws the distinction between spiritual sweetness and consolation in prayer. She's as precise and matter-of-fact as a botanist detailing the arrangement of petals on a bloom. She garners the trust a careful journalist might, so you're ready to believe her when she tells you about angels appearing with flaming swords and God bellowing in her ear. She must know.

I think it's this same hunger for testimony that drives me to read birth story after birth story. It's funny, but I seem to have as hard a time imagining Clare and imagining birth (both of which are imminent) as I do believing that I will ever die or that I will see God.

Father Bart's homily today was beautiful and I think related. He said ancient religions often used what is called a *templum* to discern divine will. They would lay a pattern—some sort of template—over animal entrails or up to the stars and read the image of the stars or entrails that shone through. For the Jews, he said, the Law was their *templum*. And now, for us, Jesus is our *templum*. We look to him as our pattern, our template, our temple.

Like my desire for testimony, this attempt to learn God's will is the need to glimpse what is beyond comprehension. I know I've been ridiculous about birth, building it into the ultimate experience of my life, when really it's the life of my child, which will open over time, that matters. But of course it's easier to anticipate a single day than the rest of my life and easier to imagine beauty and transcendence in something I haven't seen rather than in the details I see around me every day.

Oh, thank God, Clare is on the move again.

Love,
Amy

April 9, 2006
Palm Sunday

Dear Amy,

Anticipating the arrival of your daughter, I've been reading the *Little Flowers of St. Clare*, the book you gave me when you left Pittsburgh for Chicago two years ago. When I opened it, a picture of us in front of the Hotel Chelsea fell out. In your right hand, you are holding a white paper bag—inside was the copy of the book of Ruth we read aloud on the rooftop later that night. We are both in sunglasses we bought on the street and those mesh slippers that were all the rage that summer. I stared at the picture a long while, thinking how long ago it seemed.

The sun is shining at last. Yesterday I went swimming at Notre Dame and took Charlotte to the farmer's market. Everything interests her: a ripe red bell pepper, a pinwheel spinning in the yard. Through her, I have new eyes. Never in my life have I had such a desire for the natural world. I feel like I've been a hermit for the past twenty-nine years. Suddenly TV seems so deadening.

The days are getting longer now, which means that soon, Clare will be with us. You wrote recently that you have been looking for sacramental visions of her, the way the church gives us sacramental contact with God. Is it too much for me to think that Charlotte is one of those visions?

In fact, I think she's been sacramental for me too, making more real for me the unimaginable depth of divine love. Of course, it could all be a trick of the imagination. To me, all babies are Charlotte; I hear a baby crying in the store, and my milk charges in. But what if it's all part of a brilliant plan to open our hearts to humanity? If nothing else, loving her has enlarged my heart. I told Dave this, and he said, in his steady way, "I think you are just very sensitive,

Jess." And maybe he's right; I do feel so vulnerable now, like mother-hood is an open wound. I can't bear stories of children—or even animals—suffering or dying. Today, contemplating the Passion in Palm Sunday Mass, I thought of Jesus as Mary's son, and the agony was suddenly real and wrenching.

I wanted to tell you one more thing. Last night I lay in bed, smelling the chlorine in my hair, dozing peacefully with Dave and Charlotte beside me, *Saturday Night Live* flickering in the darkness, and I began to melt into a memory of sleeping in my parents' bed on summertime Saturday nights, so waterlogged from a day in the pool that I'd wake up splashing and kicking in my sleep. For a few miraculous moments, I existed in both times and could feel the love of my husband and child and the love of my mother pressed all around me. All that from a little chlorine. God is good.

Love,

Jess

April 10, 2006

Dear Jess,

Last night, Clare was thumping and drumming and turning like crazy. I put Mark's hand on my belly, and each time he felt a movement, he started pressing back. He was quiet for a while and then practically yelled, "I am communicating with her." Mark poked, Clare kicked, and I laughed until my laughter rocked her into a temporary stupor. I don't think they were communicating; how could she even conceive of a life outside her own? But maybe she was responding to the stimulus. Maybe there is some sort of prelingual curiosity that caused her to kick back.

I have been thinking about imagination since the talk we had when you were having a bad day with Charlotte, and she was demanding constant eye contact. You said that you imagine a person in the clouds with white robes when you pray to God. And that you imagined a cartoon baby when you thought of Charlotte, and now, thinking of Clare, you just imagine Charlotte inside of me. It's funny, but both Mark and I have slipped a couple of times and said, "I can't wait until Charlotte is here."

And this made me wonder about her name. Does it matter that Clare's name is Clare and not Charlotte? And what does it mean that I already call her Clare when she can't yet answer?

I wasn't quite two years old the first time I ever named something. It was a stuffed, black-and-tan spotted dog, Fergus. Soon after that, I named a doll Phyllis (the one whose sins I would recount to my mother each night). Then came a long line of appallingly dull names: Brown Car, White Bunny, Budgie, Gerbil, Owl Baby, Puffy. From where I lay in my bed at night, I could see the line of my animals and dolls arranged purposefully on a shelf so that certain personalities would not clash and other friendships might be allowed to flourish. The daisy curtain over my head would alternately billow out and lie flat with something that seemed quite like intention. And the air would ring with the bright syllables of crickets. I would fall asleep hoping to wake up in the night and catch my room in mid-dance—stuffed animals, dolls, the fairy moths I saw by the pine trees, the crickets, the chipmunk from the train tracks, even a few angels might all be there. And the prayers I made to God were part of this animation. Whether I fully believed in it or not, the whole world felt charged with the likelihood of response, as if I hadn't quite figured out I didn't live in paradise and didn't realize yet that people and animals and things had forgotten one another's languages.

This yearning for a real response must be part of what tempts a child out of childhood. When I was ten, just on the verge of leaving that enchanted world and not yet in full pursuit of boys (also a desire for response), I got my first dog. I wanted to take her through formal obedience training, so I gave her what is termed in training lingo a "call name." A call name should begin with a hard consonant, be short and punchy, capable of traveling and being heard over a crowd. I called her Bonnie. Now when I called, I finally got a real response, which was made more satisfying through the shared language of training. "Sit, stay, stand, come, heel" was a language we could both understand.

Mark has an odd little book by Vicki Hearne, a poet who was also an animal trainer. She says, "Deep in human beings is the impulse to perform Adam's task, to name people and animals . . . to return to Adam's divine condition." She imagines this condition as being one in which names are actions rather than labels, real calls, vocations rather than mere designations. "Not only did Adam name the animals," says Hearne, "but the moment he did, each recognized his or her name . . . and came when called."

When I first named Clare, I thought that choosing her name was the big deal, but I definitely treated it more like a label, always writing it out to see how it looked. But as soon as I had the name, it became something more. When I say "Clare," it feels as if I am somehow reaching her. Her name—arrived at after so much thought about tradition, religion, family, who Mark and I are now, who she will come to be, and what we hope for her in the future—gives me the sense of calling her into a world. She can't yet respond, but she will respond. Charlotte is already turning her head every time you say her name. In six months that will be Clare. Hearne says that we should "make names that give the soul room for expansion . . . and project the one named into more glorious contexts."

I once had a friend who thought dogs had secret names, which she could learn through some sort of deep, whispered communion. I remember feeling terribly irritated when she told me she would try to learn my dog's name, as if the name I had given him was not the real thing. This reflects such a different theology—that souls come to us from some other land, already with histories, already named. But as Christians we have such a radical belief, that God handed over to us the ability to create life and to call forth souls by naming. And it startles me to think that God will call us by the names we have given one another, for "the sheep hear his voice: and he calleth his own sheep by name, and leadeth them out."

Love,

Amy

April 10, 2006

Dear Amy,

I'm writing this with Charlotte in my arms, sleeping at my right breast. She's already so different, no longer newborn but settling into her babyhood, reaching for food off the table, pressing the buttons on the music cube, expecting the songs that come. Will this image of her replace the ones that came before? The weeks after her birth are all a blur. I remember being so sleep-deprived that I began to hallucinate. Everywhere I looked, I saw her round face: in Dave's face, but also in the bathroom tile, and on the inside of my eyelids when I closed my eyes as she nursed away. I couldn't stop kissing her. Her mouth, her velveteen head, the pads of her warm, soft feet.

I had the strangest dreams after she was born, scenes from my life before her. In one, I was riding my old BMX bike down Meadowmoss Drive with Charlotte in my arms, trying to balance her and steer at the same time. In the next, I was in Kelly's Bar in Pittsburgh with all our old friends, and I was trying to wash my hands in the bathroom so I could nurse her, but the sink was broken.

I think those dreams reflected more than just my anxiety as a new mother. They were about the jarring experience of that precise moment of birth—that instant when the baby is suddenly on the outside of your body, no longer hidden, abstract. In an instant, there is both body and being to attend. In an instant, my context was radically altered—everything must be reordered accordingly, even the dimmest of memories. In some moments it's as awkward as balancing a baby on the handlebars. It's also as unsurprising as if she had been here, somewhere, all along, on bikes and in barrooms, secret and waiting, but not really unknown. It's both things at once.

Madeleine L'Engle writes of *chronos* and *kairos*, the Greek words for time. *Chronos* is the measurable passage of time. It's chronology, the time "which changes things, makes them grow older, wears them out." *Kairos* is the immeasurable moment, an opening or a breakthrough, an intersection with eternity: God's time. L'Engle remembers an instance of rocking her grandchild, feeling no older than she had been when she rocked his mother, singing the same lullabies, but knowing all the same that *chronos* had done its work.

> I sit in the rocking chair with a baby in my arms, and I am in both kairos and chronos. In chronos, I may be nothing more than some cybernetic salad on the bottom left-hand corner of a check; or my social-security number; or my passport number. In kairos, I am known by my name: Madeleine.

She ends the section beautifully: "The baby doesn't know about chronos yet."

She describes perfectly how I felt the other night, lying in bed, smelling the chlorine of the pools of my childhood and the Rockne Gym at Notre Dame, suspended in both times at once. It seems that you and I have both sensed the tug of *kairos* against *chronos* our whole lives—maybe this tug, and not just a fear of death, is what has driven us to seek God. This obsession with time has become only more acute with motherhood. I can't experience a moment without mourning its passing. I try to burn each instance into memory, but it's impossible. Already I've forgotten how it felt to hold her when she was only eight pounds, unable to roll over in a flash and pop up on those pink arms. I shut my eyes and think as hard as I can, but it's just not there. Only Charlotte *now*, at five months, smiling with her mouth wide open, and growling.

You're nearing the end of your pregnancy now, and I envy you the coming the weeks. The time after Charlotte's birth passed so blissfully. I don't think we expected to feel so madly in love with her. I wanted to write it all down for you, again, to capture every moment, but then I didn't want to miss any of the sweetness of those first days, and I feel I've barely written to you at all. I guess I worried that in writing I would miss it. But that is never true in our letters. In writing to you, I have those moments restored to me.

With love,

Jess

April 13, 2006

Dear Jess,

Again I am exhausted, weak in the bones. Is the third trimester supposed to bring on such fatigue? It seems that the day is so long and that at the end of each day I have worked for a week. But I am aching to write you an epic. All day I think of things I must tell you, each thing its own world.

For example, this: It was wonderful seeing my mother this past weekend, yet the entire time I felt so sad that I never see her. She is getting older, now late sixties. Her brother died at about the age she is now. He had a sudden massive heart attack, and then an eighteen-wheeler smashed into his out-of-control car. He was gone with no warning, no preparation. I don't know how I would stand it if either of my parents died. I know that, like you, I would never get over it and the rest of my life would be sadder. The only thing that soothes me is trusting that God is good.

But I seem to have no zeal for God anymore. Do you remember how, during Lent of last year, I used to say that God lived at St. Gregory's? Well, now I think God lives in my belly. At least I treat my belly with so much reverence you'd think he did. Today the Mass readings kept mentioning the relationship of God to life in the womb. This time I noticed something new in Psalm 139. It says that God knits us together in our mother's womb but also that we are fashioned in the depths of the earth. The only commentary I could find said this is just figurative language for the womb, stressing the "mysterious and hidden operations that occur there." Since I can't even believe half the time that there is a baby inside, I certainly understand this interpretation. But if that is all the psalmist meant, he could have said simply "in the hidden depths" or "the hidden darkness" without using that strange reference to the earth, which makes our origin sound rather pagan—Prometheus molding humans out of clay—or strangely like a grave.

The Magnificat paired these readings with a meditation by Monsignor Benson. He interprets those lines of the psalm as being more about the pervasive presence of God than about the origin of life. His main idea is that Christ is everywhere, taking form around us and inside us all the time, "beneath the stone and in the heart of the wood . . . enwound in every fiber of our lives . . . deep buried in the depths of that heart of ours." He calls all the places we meet God *trysting-places*. So it seems that my notion that God lives in my belly is actually straight out of Scripture.

Benson also imagines God coming both through time or history and in the present moment. This made me think of your last letter on *chronos* and *kairos*. It's so helpful to think the two are dependent on each other: the slow, apparently dull movement of time, gradually opening our eyes, filling in a picture, until we have an intense moment when it all coheres. In pregnancy this is literally true, every day moving us closer to *the* day, every day filling in the face we will soon see. But usually this requires faith; usually, it's so hard to believe that time is purposeful, that it is really leading anywhere at all. Benson says it like this: we go through life expecting to find God dead and hoping to live on a memory. Wouldn't it be incredible to live all of life with that same hopeful expectancy I have right now? To really believe that every day is working to bring us closer not to death but to the life that will meet us at the end?

Sometimes I fear the return to everyday time when I am no longer pregnant. Your letters over Lent have been so comforting to me. You wrote all the time of the joy found in daily life with Charlotte. The most beautiful thing Benson says is that we meet God "in the common task and the daily round" and that "there is no garden path where he does not walk . . . no country road where our hearts cannot burn in his company."

I am so glad you'll be here tomorrow for Good Friday. After last year, it seems like we should always be together for Easter weekend.

Love,
Amy

May 8, 2006

Dear Amy,

You told me recently that you know your real life will begin with the birth of Clare. I think that's why the last few weeks of pregnancy are so treacherous. As you've said, there is a very definite feeling of one life ending and another beginning. The importance of every second weighs heavy. So you fold onesies and scrapbook; it's all you can do. I wonder if the feeling is the same with a second child, or third. One of the pro-life protesters I wrote about last year told me that every time his wife gives birth, she dies a little and God lives a little more. What a loon. Now, I fear I'll mourn the passing of every day for the rest of my life.

I do miss being pregnant. I find sometimes that I'm surprised by the difference between her body and my own—that when I reach for her hand, I can't feel my touch with her fingers. This often happens when I walk with her in the sling, which must be as close as we can get to the womb. I'll touch her little leg or head and be surprised by the feeling of otherness. Her body is her own now.

But this afternoon, as we sat nursing in the easy chair, she touched me so gently, rhythmically, as she drifted off to sleep; this difference was exquisite. She touched me as if I were something precious but also completely familiar. And I just sat there, resting my head on the back of the chair, trying to feel it as deeply as I could. Motherhood means days of a hundred little moments like this one, full of simultaneous joy and sadness. Too many to remember.

I'll never forget how warm and loving your house felt when we left Charlotte with you on Friday night. Clare is going to be so happy there.

Love,

Jess

May 9, 2006

Dear Jess,

Last night I dreamed that I could feel the bones of Clare's neck and shoulder perfectly. I pressed my finger gently into my belly and traced the outside of her skull, down the curve of her upper spine, and then out along the left collarbone. I realized, then, in my dream, that she was in breech position. In the morning I knew it was a dream only because in reality I can never feel that kind of detail on her body. I know the difference between a heel and buttock, but the head has so far been hidden from me, tucked down and in, away from the surface, and I can never feel individual bones or the clear shape of any body part.

The day before this dream, I lay in my bed begging Clare to move. In the past she has always answered these pleadings fairly promptly, but this time she was quiet. The light in the room, as always, was dim, and I lay naked in among the pillows and sheets I had made a mess of during the night. I flopped from one side to the other and stared at the clock. Ten minutes went by. Nothing. Twenty minutes. Still nothing. Finally, I felt the barest little blip of a motion. I decided then that she must be slowly losing oxygen and that these occasional blips were her last spasms of life. I became desperate, not even crying, just internally, silently panicking. I imagined her never arriving. I imagined the future without her, and I knew I would never get over it. How odd to spend the rest of your life mourning the loss of someone you never really met. I realized that I would still have to give birth to her, even though she was dead. Horrified, I jumped up and ran into the kitchen, still naked, and found two metal bowls and banged them together as loudly as I could about a foot away from my belly. I lay back down in the bed. Nothing. I banged them again, this time just inches from the surface, clanging, clanging. Silence. *Well, even if she isn't strangling in there, she is deaf,* I thought. I glared at my swollen belly and wished I could pummel it. But then, with twenty-five minutes on the clock, she began to move. Nothing spectacular, no real turns or kicks, but definite movement. And soon she racked up the required ten moves in an hour.

Today, as is often the case after a period of inactivity, she has been on the move since daybreak. I couldn't even sleep last night and spent the entire night on the couch. Every time I woke up, I could feel that hiccup sensation—almost like a rhythmic tic in my lower side. And she is moving even as I write this. I hope she doesn't shift around into a right-side-up position. I think her head is still down. God, Jess, I am just dying to see her, to get her out into the open so I can hold her and stare at her little stomach rising and falling with breath. I will never, ever let her out of my sight.

With love and panic,
Amy

III

Loss

Notes for Letters Never Sent

Jess

I dreamed that I found Clare in a basket on my doorstep—the side door, where we put the recycling bins. She was perfect and blonde and alive, and the basket was so beautiful—it seemed there was light all around it and her. I waved to whoever was dropping her off, as they drove away. I was so grateful. So grateful. I ran inside to call you, to tell you she was OK: "It's OK. She's here. I have her."

• • • • • • •

May 11, 2006

Last night ended like any other night. I was reading Francois Mauriac's *Life of Jesus* before I fell asleep, starring a passage that I wanted to remember for a future letter, something about Mary being the first to ponder the mysteries of the rosary, wondering if those visions had been true, after all, as she watched her son growing and living as other boys did.

I woke to Dave's cell phone vibrating on the nightstand. I thought it was the alarm, that it was morning. So I went back to sleep. When I woke again, Dave was saying, "Amy and Mark have been calling us," and I was so irritated in my sleepiness that I snapped, "Well, call them back!" and drifted off again. When I woke the third time he was holding the phone away from his face and saying what I knew he would say, had to say, no matter how badly he did not want to say it and I did not want to hear it: "It's Clare." "What?" I said, sitting upright. "Clare's not good," he tried again. "What?" I was panicked then. As if saying *what* could change it. "Clare's dead."

I grabbed the phone from him and heard you saying it, too. And all I could say was "What? What? What? What?" And think that this wasn't a dream. I couldn't believe it wasn't a dream, that I wouldn't wake up.

You said, "They're inducing me." I said, "Oh God." Then you whispered, "I'm going to have to deliver her." All day I've replayed these little snatches of dialogue, the pain in your voice. I cried and held Charlotte and drifted in and out of consciousness, although it seemed I never closed my eyes.

•••

I must have slept at some point, because I dreamed that I found Clare in a basket on my doorstep—the side door, where we put the recycling bins. She was perfect and blonde and alive, and the basket was so beautiful—it seemed there was light all around it and her. I waved to whoever was dropping her off, as they drove away. I was so grateful. So grateful. I ran inside to call you, to tell you she was OK: "It's OK. She's here. I have her."

This morning I called work to tell them, crying through the words, taking Libby's breath away. Then I showered and let the heat fill the bathroom, making it hotter than I could stand it.

• • •

You called and said that you felt so bad for bringing so much pain into so many people's lives. And my heart broke for you, and I didn't say what I should have said. What should I have said? I said, "Please don't think that again." I said, "I would do anything in the world for you and for Clare." I hope I said at least that.

Now you are in labor, and I'm keeping a vigil, rocking Charlotte with the cell phone in my hand, waiting for it to ring. Feeling helpless, wishing I could do something. I guess that's why I'm writing this, although I can't imagine why you would ever want to read it.

• • •

You are having contractions. You're trying to do this naturally. "It will be better for me if I want to do this again," you said. My heart filled with hope when you said this. You will do it again. But I wanted to beg you to have a C-section. To spare yourself. After we hung up, I looked up stillbirth on the Internet. One woman said she wanted to feel it—the pain. She wanted to scream.

• • •

May 12, 2006

Dave and I had milkshakes for dinner, and I fell asleep at 7 p.m. with Charlotte on my chest and the phone in my hand. It rang at 2 a.m. I was awake, watching *Leno*, Charlotte still on my chest. It was Mark. He sounded so far away. "Clare was born around midnight. Amy wanted me to call."

• • •

You sound relieved. There's something different in your voice. Still racked with pain and longing but comforted somehow by the sight of your baby. And proud. Clare. "She's absolutely perfect, Jess," you said. And I know because I read it online that she's soft and warm and seems like she's sleeping.

• • •

You asked if I wanted to come and see her. I should have said, "Yes, I want to see her and hold her and kiss her a thousand times." But I was scared. I was scared I would not be so strong. I said, "Why don't you call me in the morning?" and then I hung up and felt like a failure.

• • •

Your voice. We could have been talking about Clare alive. We might have said the same words: "She's absolutely perfect." You are a mother. The cruelty of it makes my throat close up.

• • •

All day I've looked at Charlotte's pictures. The day she was born. Her hand in mine. Her eyes open. Blinking. The feeling of relief.

• • •

The sun's up now, and you changed your mind about me coming. You saw her again, and she no longer seemed like a baby sleeping. I prayed all night for a miracle. I kept thinking of Jesus at the bedside of the little girl, saying, "She's only sleeping." But now, you are saying, "She's so cold." And my stomach is in a knot. Clare.

Someone is holding a sign on *The Today Show* that says "Hi, Clare," and I want to throw something.

• • •

You wanted to know what Catholics do. Cremate? Have a funeral? I told you I couldn't bear the thought of cremation. She needs a funeral, a grave. A place we can visit. You seemed relieved.

• • •

You're going to bury her in Pennsylvania. But first there will be a funeral at St. Gregory's. Today is my niece's third birthday. My sister is hosting a tea party, but she keeps having to duck into the bathroom, because she's crying, too.

• • •

Dave and I drove to Notre Dame, and I ran from the car to the grotto in the rain. I glanced at the notes people had left there, but I couldn't stand to see the pain of others. I lit a candle and said a Hail Mary. And I said her name: *Clare*. Pray for us.

• • •

I keep thinking of that baby bird I found on my doorstep last week—so tiny and pink and fleshy, I thought it was a petal, fallen from one of my plants. I kicked at it with the toe of my clog and realized, in horror, from the resistance of the flesh, the way it uncurled a bit at my touch, that it was a living creature, a baby. I gasped. I protested, out loud, to nobody—"Oh, no, no, no." I put Charlotte inside and then grabbed a Kleenex and tenderly picked the thing up and put it back in the nest. Then I sat on the porch and cried and prayed to St. Francis.

When I told you this, you laughed and said, "Oh, Jess," and laughed at how pitiful I sounded. But my heart had filled with so much inexplicable sadness at the discovery of this struggling creature. Life trying to live. I couldn't shake the feeling. Now it seems like a terrible omen.

• • •

The weatherman is pointing to a giant green patch on the radar screen. This storm isn't budging, he's saying. Rain and wind and black skies for the next five days. Tomorrow is Mother's Day.

• • •

Yesterday, while you were still contracting, we were on the phone, and the nurse came in, and you checked your tears, held the phone away, and said, "Good Morning." Good morning. When Mark answered the phone, he said, "Yello," like always.

• • •

I went to Target. I guess I was hoping I could buy something that would ease the pain. Of course there was nothing. I realized I was looking for something for Clare, and then, that I was looking *for* Clare. And then I got in the car and drove back home. I thought of how, when I visited you three weeks ago, we'd driven by St. Francis Hospital, where you were to deliver. We were saying, "Oh, we'll do such and such with the girls," meaning Charlotte and Clare. We said that with such joy, "the girls." I'm afraid that Charlotte, without Clare, will break your heart. She is breaking mine.

May 14, 2006

Today I received your last letter, dated May 10, the one you told me to burn before reading. In it, you were banging metal bowls over your belly, trying to wake Clare. You wrote hauntingly of a dream in which you could feel the bones of her body in your stomach. You wrote that you couldn't imagine mourning someone for the rest of your life who you'd never met. All this when Clare was still with us, moving, kicking. I'm going mad with grief. I want to go and get her! I just want to find her and restore her to you. It's infuriating, this feeling, this knowledge that she's out there, somewhere. That she isn't gone.

• • •

A week ago today we saw Sister Barbara in Starbucks on Clark Street. She blessed Clare in your womb while I drank my latte. You kept taking sips of it, and each time I'd take the lid off so you wouldn't catch my cold. Today, Sister Barbara told you that you now have a saint in your midst. You cried when you told me this. Thank God for her. Everything I say sounds awful and stupid. I will never send this to you. We're leaving now for Chicago.

• • •

May 14, 2006

When I walked into your house, you were sitting at the dining-room table. Mark held the door open, and I saw you. I don't think I will ever forget it. You looked so small. You were sitting with the purple box from the funeral home. In it, a lock of her hair, her footprints, the tiny clothes the hospital gave her. You had drawn the most perfect pencil image of her swaddled body, her little bud of a mouth, and written around it all you could remember of her. It was the most wonderful and terrible thing I've ever seen. "I'm afraid I'll forget her," you said.

I hugged you, and before I could stop myself, I put my hand on your belly. "I know," you said.

• • •

The funeral. It was raining. We went to St. Greg's early, and I paced. The music director was leading the choir through a quick rehearsal. He said, "Now, this is important," as he picked out the tune for the Litany of the Saints on his piano. "This is the only song Amy requested."

I saw Father Bart and asked if there was anything I could do. He didn't think so. But he must have seen the desperation in my eyes, because a few minutes later he came back and asked me to carry the crucifix in the processional. I was standing with it in the back of the church when you came in with that simple white box. I placed my hand on it. How I wish I had held her. Why didn't I come sooner?

I turned around, gripped the crucifix, and walked. Somehow, I felt fiercely proud. Scott's voice broke as he intoned the psalms.

I kissed the feet of Jesus when I hung the crucifix on the lectern. It seemed right. Jesus. Clare. After the funeral, we stood in your kitchen, and I found myself rubbing your mother's arm. All this uncontrolled affection. All this love with nowhere to go.

I'm back at work today, but I can't move. I just sit at my desk and fight to stay awake. I can't sleep at home; all I do is stare at Charlotte—her back, her tummy, waiting for the comforting rise and fall of her breath.

The rain keeps falling.

• • •

May 19, 2006

I went to the doctor today. They sent me to the nurse-practitioner, actually. She half listened to me and then wrote "postpartum depression" on my chart, in the square marked "diagnosis."

"Look on the bright side," she said, "and count your blessings." I think I must have smiled, but I wanted to scream. I left with a prescription for Zoloft and the business card of a psychologist. I made the appointment on the way back to work. I got lost somehow and ended up on the toll road to Chicago. "It's not your baby," the nurse said. "Be grateful."

• • •

I'm so afraid. I feel as if our friendship has died, too. I can't stop thinking of us as fools, these last eight months, planning our lives with these two little girls, never once really entertaining the thought that it might not happen. What else is in store for us? The beautiful life we anticipated now seems absurd.

• • •

Today you called me and said, "It's getting worse." The crushing, aching grief. You have returned from burying your child in Pennsylvania to your home on Berwyn Avenue, where she was to live. "I'm afraid I will forget her," you said. "You won't," I said. "You'll never forget the moment you held your firstborn." And you said, "But you have a living baby to remind you." I didn't know what to say. I can't imagine you will ever forget those few moments of holding your daughter. I know I will never forget your voice. *She's absolutely perfect.* I imagine how your body must long for the weight of her in your arms, and feel sick.

May 21, 2006

Today's Mass readings were all about love. Remain in my love. Love one another. *Thees is the call of Christianity*, said Father Ray in his thick Nigerian accent. You must have the courage to love. I leaned into Dave and sobbed.

All day I've thought about this long and hard. The love Jesus called for must be more than loving your neighbor and serving the poor, although it's those things, too. Why else would it require so much courage? I think he is calling us to love with intensity and depth, to love completely, as we love our children. Only when we know the stakes does it seem like more than a platitude. This radical love is how we come to know God.

And God, how I loved Clare! I love her still. The joy of these past few months was not absurd or naive; it was a sign pointing to heaven. And now, I've got to have the courage to persist in love, even in this pain. Courage. The determination to love despite the risk.

I feel so close to losing you. More than that, I'm afraid I will fail you, or that I already have. What if I don't have the strength? Where is my courage?

But what's the alternative? A shadow life. That is why I can't regret all we imagined for Clare and for Charlotte, for us. It was love that imagined Clare's life before she emerged from your womb, a life in our world, so real that it's hard to imagine she is no longer in it. But it wasn't merely imagined. In our love for her, we experienced the fullness of her being. Is that what radical, Christian love can do?

May 22, 2006

Dear Amy,

I've been going through our old letters, looking for something, anything, to comfort you. To bring back the feeling of life before May 10, and to take the weight from my chest.

I keep thinking of how I caressed your mother's arm after Clare's funeral. I miss my mother so much right now, and I realize now how much I depended on you during my own pregnancy. I didn't have a mother to look out for me, to care for me unconditionally, to love me even more than what I was growing in my belly. But you did those things for me.

You said on the phone that you were sorry to have brought so many people so much pain. But you have not brought this pain. Nevertheless, pain is upon us, and our worst fears are confirmed. But love will have to see us through. I have promised to go where you go, and I do it thankfully, even here.

I know that you may not be able to write to me for some time. I only want you to know that I am here, grieving with you.

With love,

Jess

Notes for Letters Never Sent

Amy

I was able to cry this morning, and I tried to cling to sorrow as long as I could. At all moments I felt it slipping away from me as finally as the image of Clare's face. I can't believe I am writing these words when I should still be anticipating her. Yet now it all seems inevitable. I think my guilt over losing her, the conviction that I somehow didn't will her into life or that I actually did something to cause her death, makes her death seem almost like something I planned. So, most of the time I am numb.

• • • • • • •

May 24, 2006

Slowly I remember my old body. My stomach deflates a little bit each day, but I can still see the linea nigra. It is even clearer now that I am not pregnant, probably because I can see its entire line. Today I can bear everything. I can think about anything, and it will not crush me. No wonder I have begun this letter today. Probably everything I write to you will be like this—the good days.

Yesterday I could barely move without weeping. I writhed around on my bed trying to escape. In the grocery store I could feel myself walking in the steps of my recently pregnant self, and my eyes stung with tears. I hate what I have been forced to become, this empty thing. I averted my eyes from all babies and small children, their lives seeming a terrible affront to the one I have lost. Birth and life so natural and easy for so many, and yet so effortlessly taken from Clare and from me. Never having a life outside of mine, sharing my life, she has taken part of me with her wherever she has gone.

• • •

I went to daily Mass again this morning. Sister Barbara told me she prays each morning for me and Mark. "Do you know who I pray to?" she said. "Clare Elizabeth." I try to pray, too, but usually I don't get any farther than her name.

When the pain subsides and I can breathe and think, the guilt sets in. The days I can forget are the days it seems I have truly lost her. Then I long for the pain to return. I won't drink tonight. I am worried that half a bottle of wine too many nights in a row has numbed me.

May 25, 2006

Daily Mass is not an obvious comfort. When I kneel there in the dark, all I can think of is her casket sitting on the low stool in front of the altar. And yet every day I go back.

I was able to cry this morning, and I tried to cling to sorrow as long as I could. At all moments I felt it slipping away from me as finally as the image of Clare's face. I can't believe I am writing these words when I should still be anticipating her. Yet now it all seems inevitable. I think my guilt over losing her, the conviction that I somehow didn't will her into life or that I actually did something to cause her death, makes her death seem almost like something I planned. So, most of the time I am numb.

But this morning I could grieve. It wasn't quite like some other days when it seemed that sorrow would define the rest of my life. This morning, sorrow and happiness hung in some sort of tenuous balance. I wanted to hold onto sorrow and fend off happiness. Sorrow keeps her close to me, but happiness will obliterate her. I even hate writing, rendering any of this in any way. I doubt I will ever send these letters. But just as much as I fear writing down my daily thoughts, I fear losing all of this—her—to time. And even though I fear happiness, it doesn't come.

Mark will be home soon. I look at him so differently these days, now that I have seen him as a father, holding the body of our child. More than anything else from those days in the hospital, I can remember the look on his face as he cradled her in his arms. He looked agonized and tender and even proud as the tears rolled down his cheeks and fell onto her forehead. I stroked both of their wet faces and kept whispering, "I'm sorry."

May 26, 2006

Yesterday Mark and I took a nap for several hours in the afternoon. I dreamed of my sister. I actually don't remember the dream anymore, just that she looked odd, with freckles and braids. I can't believe she doesn't know, but I still think it was the right decision to let her finish her band's tour in the Netherlands, such a long-awaited trip. In the dream, I had to tell her about Clare. I woke hearing one sudden, screaming sob. The first thing that occurred to me was that it was the sound of my voice, a cry of eternal agony and guilt.

• • •

The pain has taken hold. Today I am not afraid that the sorrow will vanish. Yesterday it started breaking into my consciousness in short bursts. I would sob out loud for a few seconds and then go back to thinking or talking or whatever I was doing.

The only relief was seeing Marilynne Robinson at the University of Chicago. We snuck into the room for the interview and tried to avoid looking at the beautiful, pregnant woman sitting just in front of us, stroking her belly in a loving way, as I so recently did, trying to discern Clare's being. I focused intently on Robinson's words. But as soon as the last question was answered, we ducked out and practically ran down the stairs. The pregnant woman seemed to be following us. At every turn I saw her ahead, caressing her belly. In the bathroom she came in just after me. And before the talk had even begun, when we were parking our car, Mark and I saw a beautiful baby. It was her feet we both separately remembered when we talked about it later. Images of feet seem to be especially painful. On the cover of a book given to us by the hospital (another guide to grief I refuse to open) is a pair of feet poking out from a blanket. The baby is like Clare, born still. I can tell because the baby's skin is puckered and loose in places, already pulling away from the body, kind of the way a blister might look. Clare's hands looked like that. Oh, and Clare's feet, how we can't bear to be parted from them. How carefully we peeled back the hospital blanket to examine her little body, her soft belly. How we timidly tried to part her lids, afraid she might tear, and see her eyes. The world is filled with the signs of new life—flowers, tiny green leaves, none of it indicating the horror that can arrive instead.

Mark and I talked for hours last night about sorrow and guilt. He is suffering so much. He is exhausted all the time and bumping into things, first the platters on the wooden shelf, then the decorative shelf in the foyer. Walking past, he completely knocked it off its nails. He sleeps long hours and longs for more. I try to fixate every so often on how it would be if Mark were gone. This morbid exercise helps almost more than anything else.

I just called the perinatal counselors to ask for the pictures of Clare. I ache to see her again. The woman said they will arrive by certified mail.

Happiness is not yet possible. What I perceived the other day as happiness and sorrow hanging in balance was not true. It was only sorrow and the absence of anything.

• • •

Today is hideous. Mark and I are zombies, trudging around. We seem to care very little about anything and are snapping at each other. I can't imagine caring about my life; it seems over. I have at least two glasses of wine every day. I want to disappear.

May 27, 2006

Last night I could barely breathe, another night of writhing and sobbing. I kept thinking about the day we found out she was a girl—how joyful we were, proudly showing her ultrasounds to the waitress over our celebratory brunch. My sobs are sometimes not even linked to physical tears, but more like muffled screams or moans. Nothing seems strong enough to alleviate the pain, and when I feel like this I know that there is nothing on earth that can stop it or change it. Always before in my life, crying or talking or working was toward the end of a remedy or moving forward. I never saw it as a symptom, plain and simple, of an unchangeable, rock-solid sadness. I know I feared death and talked about the awareness of death as my hot coal, which never allowed me to forget God. But that hot coal was somehow still a hypothesis. There seems to be this coal, so maybe there is God. But now Clare is my coal.

She lived in me for eight and a half months. She lived for that short period in me, and then she died in me. I lay in that hospital bed like a coffin, waiting for her to be born. When she was buried, I stayed to watch the four buckets of dirt poured on her little white casket and to hear the shovel tamping down the top grass. The day after her burial, I returned to the gravesite to lie on the ground beside her flowers, to stare at the copper plaque with her beautiful name: Clare E. Alznauer. The initial made it more unbearable. She could have been a person who had a middle initial. She was a person, but she never lived with us, with me in the world.

Yet, although she lived only inside of me, she was separate, because, as I read somewhere, my body didn't even know she had died. If it had, it wouldn't have brought in that flood of milk, squeezing out the most painful little white drops for me to weep over. The doctor told me to gently bind my chest and apply ice packs until the milk went away. But I held my breasts as if they were babies, like something separate from me, yet mine and in need of care. Oh, I ache for a little body to care for. So instead, I shampoo Mark's head and wash his feet. I stroke my belly and breasts so tenderly.

Today I got out my grading for DePaul. On a piece of paper that I had used to scribble down comments on student presentations, there were two names penciled at the bottom in pretty script: Clare and Claire. I had been trying out her name, yet again, wondering about the possible spellings. I stared at the names with a sudden shock of sadness. Mark winced looking at me look at the paper. "Cross them out," he said. I couldn't do it, so I left them but ripped the paper in two. What should I do with this? I said, holding out the names. Mark took it. "We can't save every little reference, every mention," he said. I think he threw the paper out.

There must be aversions. There must be times when I feel a thought coming and duck away or redirect my concentration. I can't perpetually engage in the memory of her, but every time I refuse, I feel I am killing her further. I must let her be as she is, a presence external to my own, but I don't trust her to still be there when I forget. And yet she burns so hot and painful; my thoughts jerk away from her all the time.

I have begun to notice that the only thing that actually helps is concentrating on some idea. I noticed this first with Marilynne Robinson's talk, and then this morning during a talk with Mark about the meaning of the Incarnation.

June 2, 2006

I had to look up the date again. My sister arrived yesterday, the day after she returned from Europe. I was the one to tell her when she called from the airport. She immediately starting sobbing. All else stopped. She canceled lessons, bought a ticket, and arrived the next day. She brought funny movies and vitamins. But it's hard for her, too. She cried this morning that she wishes she could have met Clare.

The oscillations of my mood have continued. When we went to visit you at St. Joseph's last weekend, I walked into a room full of children. I sat down on the floor and watched Charlotte try to crawl, moving sideways like a little crab. I braced my body and fought the tears until just a few came out, and I was able to get a hold of myself. The whole day was like that. At night, walking down to the beach, your nephew, who had been fascinated by Samwise all day, almost let him wander into a busy street. Mark grabbed Sammy's tail just before he stepped in front of a roaring pickup. I screamed, "No, no, *no!*" My voice crescendoed to a shriek. When Sammy was safe, the sobs rushed into my throat and eyes, and I walked away from the group, again to brace against the terror of it all and try to swallow it back.

Swinging on the beautiful arbor swing behind the little house, I felt that same alienation that has been occurring off and on. "You are a mother," your sister said. "A wonderful mother. I can't believe all the things you did for your daughter." I heard her words, yet I couldn't identify with the person on that swing hearing those things. They couldn't really be about my life. But then again, what do I think my life is? Some perfect part of heaven already?

Driving away from the little house, I looked up and saw the moon, its dark ball a visible bulk, highlighted on one side by a crescent of light. I thought of Clare of the Moon and started sobbing again. Again it was the horrible, heavy misery of knowing I could never have her, ever, ever, ever. I write this now and can write it without crying, and this is a horrible fact. I should never stop crying. But it seems physically and mentally impossible to bear it always.

One more thing. Did you notice on the wall of your beach house that there was that passage from Jeremiah? "For surely I know the plans I have for you, says the LORD, plans for your happiness and not for evil, to give you a future with hope" (Jeremiah 29:11). It was the same passage read at Clare's funeral.

•••

The day before yesterday, I got the initial autopsy report. The only visible sign of death was the cord stricture. My worst fears of being told it was my sugars or too many Rolos (I know it is absurd, but it was a serious terror) or dehydration were not confirmed. I took a shower after I got the call to ease my aching body, which seems wracked now by anxiety more than anything else. In the shower I leaned against the side and wept, and I felt for the first time that Clare really does love me. Before, I could barely meditate on this, because I felt I had killed her, and how could she love a mother who murdered her? "Do it for Clare," my mother said to me on the phone, referring to some aspect of getting on with my life. I wept in the shower for this new reality: Clare taking care of me, watching over me. How did we trade roles so quickly?

•••

Yesterday the pictures of Clare arrived. I signed for the package and tore it open. There was only one shot of her, both in color and in black and white. It was so disappointing to me at first. Her tongue is lolling out, and her head is sagging against her chest, rolling her chin in and pushing out the baby fat of her neck. It makes it impossible to see the delicate shape of her perfect little chin and mouth. I wish so desperately now that we had taken more photos. I can't bear for others to see this one image of her. Yet for my eyes, I am so grateful to have it. The image, together with my memory, remakes her in my mind and gives her more wholeness. I've been having that problem I had when I was pregnant: I can see only part of her: her nose, or the slant of her cheek in profile, or her pink, swollen eyelids, or the smooth surface of her brow. It is hard to put it all together into a face. But now with the photo I can do it. Yet the photo is not static for me, as it will be for other people. I can see her from different angles; I can feel her when I look at that photo. I can smell her head. The hands are not quite right either. They look heftier than they really were. In reality they were the most delicate beautiful little hands, her fingers long and very thin, so graceful.

I am glad my sister is here. She keeps worrying that her fresh anguish will somehow make it worse for me, but I am grateful.

•••

A woman from my childbirth class called today. I just cried and made choking attempts to speak, until she said she was sorry and hung up. Oh, the irrational fury at her is terrible. I can't imagine being her friend now. When I imagine her giving birth, that yell of ecstasy and pain that I so anticipated coming from someone else's mouth and mind, I can't bear it. I heard that birth yell from somewhere down the hospital hall as I lay on my back waiting to give birth to a baby who had already died. I lay there anticipating the silent birth of my daughter. No cry from her or me, nothing. One of these days, I should write down the story of her birth, so that I won't forget. Today is not the day. Today everything is heavy. I can't even cry. Today I barely want to live. Having my sister here is putting me back in the thick of it.

I am just sick, too, about that photograph of her. It should be perfect, but it's not. It is not at all perfect, and it is all I have. I can't ever see her again, and there's no escape.

June 4, 2006

Last night my sister and I were trying to watch one of the movies she brought and suddenly, without any obvious trigger, I started sobbing and sucking in my breath. My chest constricted. I found myself crawling, writhing on the couch, clutching pillows, gasping for breath. I was afraid and desperate. I couldn't get away.

I miss Clare all the time. I see babies and feel anger or sharp, stabbing resentment that they were somehow allowed to make it here and live while Clare was stopped short of life. But today I had a new thought. I would not take back her life. Even if someone told me that I could go back and erase her, do it a different way so that some other child would live and I would never have to bear the loss of Clare, I would not accept the offer. I love her. *Her.* I want her life the way I want the life of my sister. This thought gives me hope. Maybe someday I'll be able to think about her feet pressing up from inside my belly, how I used to stroke them and press back, and not immediately feel like collapsing.

I must write soon about God's will and how God didn't will Clare's death.

June 8, 2006

Yesterday was the lowest day so far. After driving my sister to the airport, I spent the morning researching cord problems online, trying to determine whether Clare died because of some extremely rare yet genetically caused cord stricture that would likely repeat. I stared at images of dead babies attached to cords that looked like Clare's, narrow and pale right at the belly. I felt a mounting fear. I left the house almost silently, barely managing good-bye to Mark, and drove down to the Container Store to buy a canvas box. I wanted to put all of her things in one place, out of obvious sight. When I got back in the car, I was moving slowly, numbly. I drove out of the parking lot, and just as I pulled onto Clybourn, I saw a glowing, pregnant woman. *That was me a month ago, should still be me*, I thought. I felt the whole of my body around me as a terrible burden. I began sobbing. The stuffed-animal bear on the dashboard stabbed its sad memory at me: a postmortem gift for her and the thing that kept vigil with her during her first night under the ground. I grabbed it and threw it into the bag with the canvas box, trying to banish its memory. But my body and its terrible emptiness shook me back to this reality: Clare and all of everything surrounding her death cannot be put away; there is no escape. I drove with tears streaming down my face and sobbed out chokes and screams. I focused on the road, recognizing through my agony a dumb, persistent will to live. But I wished I could die.

Every flicker of my thoughts away from the present encountered yet another image from which to recoil. Her body, her beautiful pink eyelids, my hopes for her, my lost body, my marriage, which dreamed and soon expected to encounter a physical image of its love, but saw, instead, death. I glared at my wedding ring and imagined yanking it off, dislocating my joint, and hurling the gold away. My whole life I longed to thrust away from myself. An angry man in an angry Jeep got frustrated with me and hugged my tail, honked, flipped me off. I responded with a relieved flood of anger. But it didn't help; I could still feel the horrible sadness in the weight of the air against my skin. I lugged the sadness collecting in my limbs to the house. I barely spoke to Mark and fell onto the bed. He tried to comfort me, lying beside me, placing a single hand on my back, but I felt fury rising. I didn't want this tenuous comfort that seemed incapable of rescuing me.

The room, its emptiness, the space I occupied, seemed unbearably heavy. I couldn't imagine having to continue to live, my body holding up all of this forever, my mind endlessly, tirelessly, either capitulating and quivering with remembrance or fending, fighting off all of it, interminably.

The rest of the day was horrible. Mark was equally miserable and couldn't begin to bear my extreme level of grief. He couldn't offer what I needed. But we somehow managed to end the day in bed, holding each other.

Today is better. Maybe today, later, I will be able to write down the good things I have been told recently—the good ways of thinking about Clare. But I never fear any longer that I didn't love her enough or that I will ever forget her. Instead, I am shocked I love her as much as I do. I can't believe that the moment of her birth was enough to confirm all of my anticipation and convert it into actual, intense, unflinching human love.

Letter writing is the only device for combining solitude with company.
—Lord Byron

Ordinary Time 2006

I am not sure what it means to eat much salt, but it doesn't sound pleasant. It makes me think of tears rolling down our faces into our mouths. And Lord knows that lately there have been many tears. The loss of Clare is our salt. I taste her loss every minute—in my mouth, in my arms, in my belly. I know that you, too, have cried long and hard for her, and for me, and for us. I know this, and I know that you have kindly hidden your tears from me. It makes me cry right now to think of you weeping in secret. So, let it be as it is: a time of eating much salt, alone and together.

—Amy, June 12

• • • • • • •

It's not that I want things to be just as they were. I recognize the impossibility of that, and anyway, it would be horrible to think the world hadn't changed, or that we hadn't, after Clare's death. But I hope that we can carry her with us and still be us, not shadows. That's what I am looking forward to, working toward, hoping for.

—Jess, June 14

June 12, 2006

Dear Jess,

Today is a good day, so I'm going to try to write the letter I've been meaning to write for weeks. I have been so afraid that our friendship will not survive Clare's death. I can sense this fear in your voice, too, when we talk. I think, all the time, of how I should be the one sharing new motherhood with you, discussing all the small trials and great joys of caring for our babies. But instead there is a building full of new mothers surrounding you and taking my place.

When I talk to Mark about this, he tries to console me with Aristotle (I hope you are smiling). Aristotle, he tells me, describes three types of friendship: friendship based on utility, on pleasure, and on virtue (or pursuit of the good). The third type is the highest and most stable form. Mark says that we pursue the good, and that sharing new motherhood alone could not possibly replace that.

Maybe right now we are confusing our friendship with a friendship of pleasure, since we have given each other so much of it (hilarity and clogs and dreams of Italy). And we are worried since these friendships fade when pleasure fades (and Clare has taken so much pleasure with her). But surely that's not all we've shared.

The highest friendships, Aristotle wrote, "require time and familiarity; for, as the proverb says, it is impossible for men to know each other well until they have consumed together much salt, nor can they accept each other and be friends till each has shown himself dear and trustworthy to the other." I guess we are now in the phase of eating much salt. But you have already shown yourself to be dear and trustworthy to me. I am reminded of this every time I take communion. Maybe you will remember this conversation we had over a year ago.

It was Holy Week, and we were walking somewhere, I think, or maybe we were just sitting on the couch in my old kitchen. I asked you casually how to take communion. You looked surprised and embarrassed.

"Do you really want to know?" you said, as if I had asked you to reveal a deep secret. I remember wondering why you seemed suddenly shy, but I said that I did really want to know.

You became serious and quiet as you explained how to cup your left hand in your right, how to take the Host with your right hand and, careful not to drop it, raise it to your mouth. But then you stopped and asked again, "Do you *really* want to know?" You looked at me intently, as if only a great need on my part would bring you to say the rest out loud.

I nodded.

"Well," you said, your voice straight and soft, "I place the Host on my tongue. Then, using my tongue, I crack it against the roof of my mouth, gently. I don't chew it; I let it dissolve there." Each word seemed to convey some sort of great intimacy. "I don't want to hurt it," you finished.

This last admission you said with a partial smile. It was almost funny; it almost could have made us laugh, your shy description of how to eat the Body of Christ. And I knew sitting there that we both understood the absurdity of this act, treating a cracker with such extreme tenderness. Yet I also knew, from the strange seriousness with which you described the act, that beneath any doubt or felt foolishness, you had earnest belief. And your belief helps me believe. Because now, when the apparent absurdity of taking communion crosses my mind, when my faith balks, I remember your huge, serious eyes that afternoon, and your shy voice—the only time, I think, I have ever seen you so timid—and I know that communion is not a mere symbol. I take the bread into my mouth and always crack it gently, as you taught me, against the roof of my mouth, and wait for it to dissolve.

Sometimes I do feel like laughing, but that laughter has much more love in it than doubt.

This memory contains all types of friendship. I can imagine someone telling me what I needed to know, or speaking in a way I enjoyed, or inspiring me to do the right thing, but you combined all three simply and naturally. There you were, detailing a practical how-to but at the same time leading me to God. And the way you spoke gave me so much pleasure that each time I remember it, it returns me to communion. Just think: isn't the liturgy of the Eucharist, all at once, useful, pleasurable, and intended for the good? And doesn't the fact that we both think this make us either raving lunatics or ideally suited friends? And how could a friendship such as this ever fade?

I am not sure what it means to eat much salt, but it doesn't sound pleasant. It makes me think of tears rolling down our faces into our mouths. And Lord knows that lately there have been many tears. The loss of Clare is our salt. I taste her loss every minute—in my mouth, in my arms, in my belly. I know that you, too, have cried long and hard for her, and for me, and for us. I know this, and I know that you have kindly hidden your tears from me. It makes me cry right now to think of you weeping in secret. So, let it be as it is: a time of eating much salt, alone and together.

Yet this time is not merely that. When I see you or read your letters, I am suddenly made happy. I see that I still love you, take pleasure in your ways, and yearn for your good and for mine. If this load of salt can't kill our pleasure or desire for the good, then I doubt anything can. And maybe this very salt will make us all the more dear and trustworthy to each other.

With much love and salt,
Amy

June 14, 2006

Dear Amy,

Yesterday was your anniversary. When I called, you sounded like you'd been kicked in the stomach, but when we hung up you were laughing and sounded brighter. Sometimes this is the only thing that lifts my own spirits, making you laugh.

But I wasn't trying to be funny when I said I've been praying for God to turn the world around. When I write it that way, it makes me think of what my dad and Mr. Sam used to do on Christmas mornings in the front yard of our house. They'd emerge into the morning light in their bathrobes, meet silently in the grass, turn toward the sun, extend their arms, and chant. My sister and I would watch from our doorway, enchanted, while they attempted to turn the world around so we could have Christmas again. I've always thought of Mr. Sam as having some special power, which is ridiculous. They were just two crazy old men standing in their front yards in their bathrobes. But I wish, wish, wish it were true. I want to turn back the clock. I guess that puts me firmly in the denial phase of grief. I'm still having dreams that everything is the way it should be, that you are still pregnant and we are anticipating June 25 with excitement, not dread.

It really wasn't until my wedding, when he read from St. Paul's Letter to the Corinthians, that I finally saw Mr. Sam as others might see him—I had fixed him in my imagination as a saint, or at least as a bishop (on special occasions, he used to wear a homemade miter decorated with a crawfish instead of a cross). But as he hobbled up to the altar with his large-print St. Joseph's Bible, I felt as if I were seeing him for the first time. He seemed so fragile.

The only other thing I remember clearly is when the priest blessed me and fixed me in a tradition with Sarah and Rebekah and Ruth and Naomi and Martha and Mary. I remember feeling exhilarated and horrified by this blessing, terrified by what it could mean. I anticipated then the suffering that was to come. I just didn't think it would come so quickly. Or even that it could hurt so much. I only anticipated some abstract suffering. The "in good times and bad" kind. Like when Dave didn't get the job at X University. That kind of bad. Not this rip-your-eyes-out-of-your-skull bad.

But then, there's the other side, the blessing part. God's love for us is as great as his love for those women. It's possible for a human being to have that kind of strength and faith. I don't know that this thought makes me happy, but it does make me proud. It makes me want to be strong for you, to deserve their company. I guess that's a start.

I'm counting the days until Dave has to go to Erie for the rest of the summer, dreading his departure. I wish I could go with him, but I have to work. I filled my prescription for Zoloft today and am sitting here, staring at the bottle on the dining-room table, considering taking one. It's hard to think of yourself as an Old Testament woman when you're holding a bottle of Zoloft.

It's not that I want things to be just as they were. I recognize the impossibility of that, and anyway, it would be horrible to think the world hadn't changed, or that we hadn't, after Clare's death. But I hope that we can carry her with us and still be us, not shadows. That's what I am looking forward to, working toward, hoping for.

Love,
Jess

June 19, 2006

Dear Jess,

My due date is in exactly one week. Now that Clare is gone, it's even harder to believe it falls on your mother's birthday. This is the week I would have been holding my breath as you did. I would have been wondering if each cramp or new pressure was the beginning of her arrival. Instead, I am lugging my collapsed body around. My stomach is crumpled and loose. The cramps I feel may signal a coming period, or maybe an illness—who knows? I am like a teenager, wondering what my body will do next. I hate this terrible return. I hate feeling "normal" again. I hate the return of all my time and the ability to sleep on my stomach. I guess in ways these things are nice, but I was through with nice. Mark and I both loathe careless fun right now. We avoid it at all costs and are miserable if we find ourselves suddenly in a position to "have fun." Instead, we prefer the schedule we have devised. Work in the mornings, exercise and do chores in the afternoons. The theme: work. We cook all our meals and shop at the discount Mexican market. We are planning to pare down our possessions to the things we need and care about, to junk the rest.

I wanted to write the story of Clare's birth today, but I still can't bring myself to do it. Her picture is starting to eclipse my memory of her face. God, I wish I could hold her. I still ache for that little body. I feel stunted and broken when I really try to think about her.

I am wondering now when my fertility will return and trying to lean on God for patience. It is easy to imagine patience when I picture my life from a distance, which is really only possible when thinking about the future. I try to predict what it will be like this fall when I attempt to get pregnant again. I imagine myself trusting God and knowing that whatever happens God will work for the good through it. I picture myself calm and holy. But that is only an image I wish were true, because now in the present moment I am filled with terror. What if that pain in my side is cancer, and I will never be pregnant again? What if Clare was our only hope to raise a child? What if cord stricture does repeat and the next baby dies? And the next? All of the cases of stricture in medical literature are of women who lost baby after baby. How long before I would be destroyed?

Mark and I talked this morning over breakfast about anger in the face of loss. I certainly have been angry at times, sick with fury, but I don't think I have ever asked, "Why me?" or "Why Clare?" Too quickly when such a thought occurs, a torrent of examples fills my head: the tsunami, Katrina, 9/11, the Holocaust, for God's sake. Either we can believe in a God who lets such things happen, or we can't believe at all.

But shouldn't I pray for the life of my next baby and not just for strength? I want to pray hard for it, but will that set me up for fury at God, or atheism, if something terrible happens again? (And speaking of intervention, I am still stunned by the discovery that the umbilical-cord specialist who might be able to help my next baby was your mother's ob-gyn. What in the world are we supposed to make of that?) So I try to yield control, imagine God holding my life, but it is hard.

Thinking about Clare in heaven has changed my thinking of heaven. The priest at her burial said that I will meet her there, recognize her with the eyes of my heart. I don't know what that means, but it can't mean just a meeting of two boring, bright lights. "Until the end when God is all in all," Pope Benedict said at the end of his encyclical, a union supposedly greater than any I could have hoped for here, by holding her. Yet that is still such an abstraction. Holding her is what I know. Nursing her and watching her live is what I long for.

—Amy

June 21, 2006

Dear Amy,

Dave is leaving for Erie next week. He wants me to go with him, but the thought fills me with dread. But then, the thought of staying here, alone, with Charlotte, is also terrifying. What if something goes wrong? It seems so likely that it will.

Why is it that grief feels so much like fear? It seems anything could happen now and will likely happen. God seems inscrutable and hidden. How could we ever understand or know him? How could he not have wanted us to have Clare? I never doubted for a second that she would be here this summer.

I want to write to you so much more, but I want my letters to be a comfort, or to make you laugh, or at least to be a distraction. But most days I have trouble thinking comforting, funny, or distracting thoughts. If I have moments when I'm not thinking of Clare, or you, or Mark, it almost makes it worse, because inevitably the knowledge comes flooding back, and I have to endure knowing it all over again.

But I do want to tell you about my meeting with Father Green. I told him that I worried you were abusing yourself, thinking you'd given Clare life only that she might die. He actually gasped, which impressed me—maybe because I've gotten so used to priests eyeing the clock during our meetings, and his reaction told me he was really listening, really understanding the gravity of what I was telling him. Then he said that what you and Mark did for Clare is the most loving and meaningful thing we can do as humans—you created her in love so that she could go to absolute goodness. My heart sank a little, and I said, "But it's so hard to be comforted by thoughts of heaven. I want Amy to have her here, now." He nodded. "I know, I know, it's too horrible," and the lines of age deepened on his face, and I believed that he did know my pain. "It's an incredible sadness," he said. He was quiet for a few moments before he spoke again. "It's an incredible sadness," he repeated, "but it wasn't for nothing."

He said we must remember that however much we miss her body, that you gave birth to a soul, too, and that soul is enduring in absolute goodness, for eternity, experiencing more joy than we can fathom, forever. "Remember it: the joy you felt during Amy's pregnancy. That's just a spark of the joy of heaven. Imagine the flame. This is the gift Amy gave to her child," he said. The greatest gift. Absolute goodness.

I just keep repeating the words to myself. Absolute goodness. It's the first thing I've heard so far that's really comforted me, the first thing about Clare's life that sounded reasonable and true and just.

Love,
Jess

June 22, 2006

Dear Jess,

One of the few things that give me happiness these days is sitting down with Mark and talking about something we have both read. Right now, it is the pope's first encyclical, *God Is Love*. Before I start reading, I always open the first page to look at the address: "A letter to the bishops, priests and deacons, men and women religious, and all the lay faithful on Christian love." There is something so beautiful and strange and antiquated about being part of an institution that regularly dispatches letters on such impractical matters as love or hope or the nobility of art. I have this fantasy of Roman heralds throwing open some upper window and calling out, "The letter is finished!" Then messengers setting out on horses or boats, mailbags stuffed, to distribute the letters around the world, and people rushing to their doorsteps to receive this urgent message on the nature of love. Can you tell I am living in my own little world these days?

Anyway, as Mark and I read and talk, I keep thinking about my parents' decision to convert. I shy away from telling other people, afraid they'll interpret this as a justification for Clare's death. Even though I know it would just be an attempt to see grace in tragedy, somehow I can't bear it. It makes me think of God as a sharpshooter, picking off people to gain a few more converts. But I do see my parents' conversion as grace, just a slower grace that began working a long time ago and is still playing out.

When I was growing up, our family felt like a little, isolated kiln of love. We were on the opposite coast from all extended family; we had no church or other community; we had few family friends—it was just us. But far from being lonely, it felt glorious. We all loved, truly and dearly loved, one another. And yet there was something else at work. Both sets of my grandparents lived through the Depression, labored in shipyards and construction, and grew their own food to make ends meet, and so instilled in their children a fierce ethic of self-reliance. Although it was no longer made grim and anxious by necessity, this self-reliance is one of the main things, I think, that caused my parents to resist religion.

This same pride came to me in the form of faith. It wasn't faith in God, but faith in my family. I could almost believe as a child that my parents were gods. I always think of them when I watch that final scene in *The Lion in Winter*. Peter O'Toole as King Henry stands on the banks of the river in Chinon watching Katharine Hepburn as Eleanor of Aquitaine drift away in her great, oared boat. "You know," O'Toole booms, "I hope we never die!"

"So do I," Hepburn thunders back.

"You think there's any chance of it?" says O'Toole, and both their arms rise and spread out. They throw their heads back and laugh, a great, regal, thunderous laugh, echoing through history, and for a minute you believe they will manage it—eternal life—holding it all up themselves.

I know this seems overblown, but to us as children it felt like that, that our parents could really do it—wipe away all tears, right all wrongs, lead us beside still waters and restore our souls. And yet since that wasn't true, we could feel, even before we understood, the insecurity of our faith. You once wrote that even before your mother died, you always knew the war was coming. We, too, always had the sense of some encroaching darkness; our heaven so small that to leave it we had only to open the front door.

And yet the love my parents gave us was real. Oh, if only I could convey the look on my father's face as he knelt by my bed in the hospital! My parents had driven all through the night and rain and arrived before Clare was born. He knelt there and looked into my eyes with such terrible, unwavering tenderness, such aching compassion. And how my mother gripped my hand in her hand in the hotel room just as she had kneeling beside me at the funeral. We were driving back to Pennsylvania, transporting Clare's body ourselves. We had a certificate allowing us to take her across state lines. Clare lay there on the hotel nightstand, hidden in her little, white box under a mound of wool blankets. I can't remember now why we had wrapped the casket up like that. To preserve her body? Shield it from view? Comfort her? "Always before I could do something," my mother said. I buried myself in her arms, away from that horrible swaddle of blankets. It was on this same drive across the country that my mother told me of their decision to convert.

The other day during one of our talks, Mark spoke of love as an argument for God. I've been thinking about this ever since. If it is an argument, the premise of the argument must be that love is eternal. In his letter, the pope says, "Love promises infinity, eternity . . . it seeks to become definitive . . . in the sense of being forever." But what could make sense of eternity but God? When Clare died, my family fell to its knees. What else could they do? The nature of love is forever, and here was death. No amount of mortal work or love could heal this, and yet love promises eternity. It's a proof by contradiction.

The day we arrived in Pennsylvania, we went straight to the funeral home before even stopping at my parents' house. They directed us to a small, privately kept cemetery dating back to the Civil War. We drove about twenty miles west, down the same road my parents live on. On the other side of a creek, and in the midst of tall trees, are a few green hills of tombstones. We walked around looking for a good plot and decided to buy enough space for four graves: for Clare, my parents, maybe someone else. And shockingly, even as I stood there imagining the day when I would come to tend three graves instead of one, this wasn't one of the terrible moments. The love that had always made me tremble for fear of its disappearance was still there; but I was no longer looking to my parents as love's source. It seemed to have been released into the air around us.

"Love is indeed ecstasy," writes the pope, "not in the sense of a moment of intoxication, but rather as a journey, an ongoing exodus out of the closed inward-looking self toward its liberation . . . and the discovery of God."

Thank you for being there to receive my letters. It helps so much to write them. I wish I could send this one by horse or carrier pigeon: a letter to Jessica on Christian love.

Love,
Amy

July 6, 2006

Dear Amy,

Last night I had a very strange dream about my mother. Mourning Clare has opened that wound anew, but I haven't dreamed about her for a long time. In the dream I got very close to her so that I could get a good look, and I remember thinking, *It's so nice to see her.* She was young, in her twenties, with her long hair and shimmering pale eye shadow and lots of mascara. Smooth skin. The dream was like watching a movie; she and my dad were arguing about something, and occasionally the camera would cut to me as a baby, except it wasn't me at all. I had very dark curly hair and pale skin. I kept saying, to whom, I'm not sure, "See—Charlotte really does look like me." Something about the dream was unsettling, but I was still happy to see her. When I woke up, I tried to close my eyes and hold the image in my brain. I can still see her, smiling, still so familiar. I suddenly remember her face in such detail. And there was a moment in the dream when I was staring at her bare leg—she was wearing shorts and Dr. Scholl's sandals, of course—and I thought, *That's not what her leg looks like.* It was not the right shape at all. But I wanted this to be my mother so badly that I decided I didn't care. I wasn't going to be picky.

I thought about the dream for a long time this morning, lingering on the details of her face, trying to conjure other memories of her expressions. It has put me in a mood.

I'm back in South Bend, working, arranging babysitters, trying to hold it together for these four weeks without Dave. The apartment building that was supposed to be such a comfort—full of young families and pregnant women and new mothers—has become a curse. They know I'm here alone and graciously check in on me all the time, but I can barely stand to see them. I fear for them, and I envy them for what I feel you should have.

This summer has been a nightmare. Dave's absence is horrible and feels like a betrayal, an abandonment, even though I know we need the money and had no other choice. Charlotte has had illness after illness: stomach bugs, respiratory infections, teething, sleepless nights. Every day I mark the calendar with a big red *X*, waiting for it to end.

I keep searching for comfort in books. Sometimes this backfires. Today I read that pointless love is the only point of life: we are called to love wholly and completely that which can only die. I let the book drop to the floor and sat rocking Charlotte through the rest of her nap.

Today you came to help me, in all your pain. You came to my rescue. You installed a window-unit air conditioner in my bedroom, where I've been sleeping with Charlotte every night. You took pictures of Charlotte. And then you had to sit at my dining-room table with my pregnant neighbor and listen to her modest complaints about the trials of pregnancy, and only I saw the lines grief in your face, and I wanted to cover her mouth, and I couldn't change the subject fast enough. I am so sorry.

—Jess

July 8, 2006

Dear Jess,

I just finished *Gilead* and am sitting in a coffee shop at a table near two pregnant women. They are chattering away about sonograms and breast size and what they should or shouldn't eat. There is a tinge of anxiety that they are trying to quell through conversation. I look at their bellies and imagine their babies curled up inside. Alive. I hear their conversation, and it seems so strange and familiar. I feel that clench in my stomach and sharp turning away. But I have the calmness of mind right now for some reason (some days I certainly don't) to sit here and take it.

There is a lag in my self-concept from the fact of losing Clare. I sometimes still feel myself as the person I was before all this came to pass. I don't even consciously imagine myself that person, I just feel it, and then with a start I notice that I am on the outside of this pregnant women's chatter. Never will I sit so glibly and discuss the life of my baby and the fate of my body. Well, maybe I will be overheard doing that, but it won't at all reflect what is taking place inside of me. Lately I've started feeling that Clare is a stranger. My own daughter, a stranger.

Finally, those two women are gone, and that's a relief. Last night, out of the blue, I got out that CD you once made for me; I think you called it a soundtrack for our letters. One of the first songs is by Nick Cave. I don't think I ever really listened to the lyrics before, but today I was suddenly riveted and realized it's an example of love working as an argument for God.

The song begins with a declaration of disbelief, one I have said a thousand times. "I don't believe in an interventionist God," sings Cave, "but I know that you do." He is talking to a woman. And then, since he's not a believer, the rest of the first verse is posed as a hypothetical. "But if I did," he says, "I would ask God not to intervene when it came to you, not to touch a hair on your head."

In the next verse, his disbelief has lessened into doubt. "I don't believe in the existence of angels, but looking at you I wonder if that's true." But still the rest of the verse is conditional. If I did believe, he sings, I would ask them "to watch over you, to each burn a candle for you . . . and walk, like Christ, in grace and love and guide you into my arms."

Finally, the last verse starts with faith. "I believe in Love." And now he is no longer talking to the woman but to the angels. It's no longer hypothetical. "Keep your candles burning," he prays. "And make her journey bright and pure that she will keep returning, always and evermore." His love for her and his desire for it never to end (again the nature of love being eternity) brings about his conversion. He can't sustain doubt. His words turn slowly into prayer.

It reminds me of the conversion scene in *Brideshead Revisited*. Charles Ryder kneels by the bedside of the dying father of Julia (the woman he loves). At first his prayers are prefaced with doubt, "O God, if there is a God . . ." But soon he is truly praying with no qualification, "O God." You have the sense of doubt capitulating under the pressure of love.

The chorus is simply "Into my arms, O Lord, into my arms," over and over. All day it is the prayer I've been repeating.

Love,
Amy

July 27, 2006

Dear Amy,

It's nearly over: Dave will be home day after tomorrow, and the new semester is just around the corner. I'll be so happy to see this season go.

I had to call Dave's mom after Charlotte fell on Monday. My nerves were fried; I couldn't stop shaking. I just lay on the sofa and cried hysterically. I called Dave, but what could he do? I wanted my mother. Not just in that moment; it was as if I was feeling the pain of all the absences from the time I was thirteen on, the scenes flashing before my eyes in rapid succession—from Charlotte falling off the bed, to Clare's funeral, Clare's birth, Charlotte's birth, my pregnancy, my marriage, my engagement, my graduation from college, my first night in the dorms at LSU, the day I left home, my first breakup, my fourteenth birthday. Every major life event, rite of passage, and milestone collapsing into one another, and I endured her terrible absence in each moment all over again.

"Please call my mom," Dave said. But how could I? Could you imagine calling someone else, anyone else, when all you want is your mother?

So, Dave called her. She came on Monday night and took me and Charlotte out to dinner. She even encouraged me to have a drink and didn't make a sarcastic crack when I had two. She rubbed my feet. She did the laundry. She went grocery shopping. She said she didn't know how I was doing this—working full-time and raising a baby and supporting a husband—not to mention the trials of my past. It sounds more than pathetic when I write it, because my lot in life has really not been so bad. I've had more than my share of blessings and consolations—that husband I'm supporting, for starters, and Charlotte, and you, and on and on. But it did feel good to have someone—well, especially Lois—praise me. Sometimes all I want or need is someone to tell me I'm strong. Somehow it makes me strong just to hear it.

But there was something else. When we were walking into the restaurant, I said, "I wish you could have known my mother." And she said, "But I do." This seemed like the nicest thing anyone could have said to me in that moment. I actually smiled at the pure niceness of it. I remembered how she had so carefully sewed my mother's name into the christening gown she made for Charlotte. Sometimes Lois just really nails it.

With love,
Jess

July 28, 2006

Dear Jess,

Lately I have been wondering what the consolation of faith really is. From the outside it's so often ridiculed as a crutch, but now that I am grieving myself it is hard for me to understand this. I've had so many days when I've felt crushed by grief. Faith clearly does not erase suffering, and yet it changes it. It is like the difference you would imagine between lying on your deathbed alone and lying on your deathbed with someone you love holding your hand. It would be rather absurd to say that holding hands at that moment is a crutch or a balm or a distraction; you still have to die. But it makes all the difference in the world to die one way rather than the other.

Ever since May 10, it has felt something like that to me, that faith has accompanied suffering, walked by its side. At Clare's funeral, this accompaniment took physical form. During most of the Mass, I wasn't conscious of the crowd of people because I was sitting in the front pew. But at the end, Mark and I stood together, as we did at our wedding, and one by one we received the words and embraces of everyone who had come to the funeral. One man came up, hugged me tightly, and said, "Every heart in this parish is broken." I remember feeling that Christ was there, in this body of believers who had come to suffer with me and bear my burden.

Another time like this was Clare's burial. Two of Mark's aunts, who had already flown from Akron to Chicago for the funeral, drove ten hours straight to make it to Pennsylvania for the ten-minute graveside service. When Mark had told me of their plans to come, I asked, "Did you tell them it is going to be a very short service?" "I told them," he said. "Did you tell them we will see them in Ohio in just a week?" I asked. "I told them," he said. They came anyway, against our advice, and brought a beautiful blanket of flowers—pink sweetheart roses shaped into a *C* and complete with a little stuffed bear. They drove up in Mary's pickup and were there for less than thirty minutes. They stood with us on that hill for the brief prayers and interment—small Pat and large Mary, side by side, and wept and prayed and hugged me and left. Again, the consolation was of not of relief but accompaniment.

Alone, it is easy for me to believe in emptiness, in nothing. But in the presence—the physical, surprising presence of loved ones, fellow mourners—I can believe in the Resurrection, in that great declaration that love is more powerful than death and that our absent friends and family members stand before us, just as I saw Mary and Pat standing on that grassy slope even though I had imagined the distance too great. Their presence turns heaven into something that is already here, not just at some end point. It's like how Lois stood there with you and saw your mother in your face and motions. It's the consolation of communion.

And yet, even today, I have spent hours crying and couldn't bring myself to open the box from the hospital to get out a clipping of Clare's hair. I wanted to put a few strands in the locket my best friend from math grad school gave me, the one I had engraved with Clare's name, to keep a relic of her close. So I am still wearing the locket, but it remains empty.

—Amy

August 2, 2006

Dear Amy,

I've been thinking about your last letter and how grieving with believers changes grief, makes it endurable, even hopeful. I almost wrote "grieving in a community," but I remember how that grief counselor in the hospital made you so angry. There's something different about holding the hand of someone who believes in a suffering God. It's one of the things that drew me back to Catholicism, this acknowledgment of the pain of human life. My dad used to complain about the morbidity, the memento mori of looming crucifixes and somber rituals that felt, to him, funereal. But I always liked the feeling that we were standing there together in church, staring death in the face.

At the Vespers we prayed for Clare on the eve of your due date, I read from Paul's letter to the Corinthians: "O Death, where is thy sting?" I practiced many times before the service, trying to get the cadence, the emphasis, just right. I wanted to convey to you my defiance in the face of death. I stood at the lectern and made the mistake of looking away from the little slip of paper printed with the readings, looking up at you and Mark. When I said the words, they came out all wrong, a little too loud and too fast, and despite all my practice, with the stress on all the wrong syllables. I hoped, walking back to my seat, that you hadn't perceived my bravado. Where is thy sting? "It's right here," I wanted to say. "In my heart, in hers."

The note in my study Bible says that Paul imagined these words on the lips of the church triumphant, chanting in victory upon the return of Christ at the apocalypse. He was being encouraging. He ends the passage, "Your labor is not in vain." But anticipating some later victory over death is cold comfort.

And yet we were comforted. It was enough that night to be among those who mourn her, not only as your daughter but as "our sister, Clare." It was enough to hear Scott's voice breaking as he sang. To see Dan, a stranger to me, pressing his hand into yours, telling you with tears in his eyes that watching you and Mark, still standing, still here, still praying and letting others pray for you, has restored his faith.

I think we all were looking at you with a sort of incredulity, as if we were having a collective vision. Death had struck his fiercest blow, and yet you remained. You had become, like your Pat and Mary standing on the grassy slope of Clare's grave, an image of heaven here, now, and death, conquered.

Thank God for these little glimpses. They make the hard days, here alone, more bearable.

Love,
Jess

August 18, 2006

Dear Jess,

I dreamed last night that my sister got pregnant by mistake. I was furious with her—hot, quick fury. When I woke this morning, I was covered in blood.

I feel haunted. I go about the day; the day ticks along; I perform the motions of the schedule we have devised. But always I feel something like a ceiling above my head, and walls all around. The events of May 10, the day I discovered that Clare had died, come to me as still images, as if spans of time were condensed and forced into single expressions and scenes. Most of the time I don't focus on them, so they hang there at the periphery like an invisible crowd.

The first thing I see is what happened before I knew. I am stopped at the end of a lap, breathless, leaning on the rough concrete of the pool, my hand resting flat on the top of my belly, laid over the new sensation of something buoyed up from the inside and hard. The way it must feel near the end, I tell myself.

Then nothing, until night.

I must have been too busy all day to pay attention. But now I am squeezed into a desk chair, watching students do their final presentations. The screen at the front glows, and the students are dark shapes in front of it. I barely see or hear them. The nothing that has been with me all day has finally risen above the clamber, and now it is all I notice.

I am on my side, on our dingy, yellow couch, waiting. I lie there, wait for two hours without moving. The entire day of stillness finally registers, blotting out everything else. The unresponsive mound at the roof of my abdomen refuses to stop its dull pressure, and my mind, as if it has fists, tries to beat out a response.

The midwife tells us to come to labor and delivery. "She probably shifted—it's probably nothing," she says over the phone. I make Mark change his shirt. I don't pack a bag or shave my legs.

We drive up Ravenswood. The network of lines of rain on the windshield are spread like a pattern of hollow veins, slightly blue in the dark.

We are taken to a room, which I now remember as one of those vast, endless chambers from a dream, stretching out and far away in distorted lines from where we are clustered at one end. A small African nurse, who doesn't speak English, puts the Doppler on my belly. Nothing. She moves the cold disk from spot to spot and then gives up, flustered, and walks away without saying a word. I grab the black end of the Doppler and start moving it rapidly, over and over and over the hard swell of what must be the baby's back. A resident is suddenly there lugging a portable ultrasound. She takes the Doppler gently from my racing hand and clips a monitor on my finger which immediately picks up my heart, rushing at over a hundred beats per minute and soon keeping perfect time with the one on my belly. She clicks on the fuzzy gray monitor, and for a minute I cling to the familiar narration as she moves the sensor over my abdomen. "That is her skull. Her leg. The spine." She stops moving the wand, and the image on the screen halts over a dark, four-holed, stationary lattice. "There is no easy way to say this," she says, letting the sensor slide off my belly. "Your daughter's heart has stopped."

I turn to Mark. It is the only thing I remember clearly from the next few hours, the way his face looked and how hard I looked into it. Our faces must have been perfect copies of each other, because when I think of it, I see his expression and feel mine. An open mouth like awe, twisted at the corners; clenched, almost surprised eyes, as if startled by physical pain.

We decide not to leave the hospital, to begin the induction immediately. They give me something for sleep and start the Pitocin drip. It is midnight, exactly twenty-four hours before Clare will emerge.

Mark climbs over the rail into the hospital bed with me, threads his arms through the plastic IV tubes, and collects me close, holds me like a child. I lie with my back curled hard against his abdomen and chest all night, trying to press the life of his body into mine.

I think I told you the rest before. I don't know why this came out today. But maybe having written some of it down will ease the haunting. The last thing I remember from the hospital is Mark steering us through the parking garage, winding down floor after floor and finally turning out into the light. The rain was still steady, the clouds a low, white ceiling, everything thoroughly soaked. We drove back down Ravenswood, into the terrible return of life.

Sorry.

Amy

August 19, 2006

Dear Amy,

I just returned from my sister's house in Oklahoma. My dad flew in—alone—for my thirtieth birthday. We finally got our wish, to have him all to ourselves again.

I think we were both surprised to find him diminished without my stepmother and brother and not, as we'd hoped, more himself. I realized, with terrible sadness, that our version of the past has probably never existed. It's a fiction we've created out of longing for our mother.

My sister has carefully decorated her house in New Orleans fashion, with wrought iron and fleur-de-lis, and the same *Cooking with Jazz* poster we had in our kitchen growing up. Sitting there, I had a vision of myself as Miss Havisham in *Great Expectations*—wearing my wedding dress as time marches on and my house crumbles around me. I felt the despair of clinging to memories. Unreliable, untrustworthy, faithless memory.

I felt desperate to be free of it all—the deep homesickness, the longing to be back there. Back where? I kept thinking. The place no longer exists. My mother is dead. My father is a new man—maybe even more fully himself than he was with us. We should love him as he is, or admit that the defect is our own lack of love or forgiveness, not his.

Everything in my sister's house seemed to be screaming at me to move on. *Talitha koum.* Arise, little girl. Live now, and love what is here. Childhood is over, wiped out by Katrina—as if the very hand of God came down and swept it back into the marsh. It's time to put away childish things.

I hoped that I'd return to Indiana with some new courage, the strength to set aside this romance of the past and live the life in front of me. But now I'm back and faced with stacks of work, and I remember why I prefer the romance to reality.

—Jess

September 1, 2006

Dear Jess,

I have had so many ideas for letters come. I think what stops me from writing lately is the worry that you don't want to hear this right now. You said in your last letter that you want to move on, live now. That makes sense. For me it is a little different. If I lose my sorrow over Clare, I will lose almost everything. But I have been trying to move forward and begin anticipating the next pregnancy.

Last night I couldn't sleep, so I got up and started packing for our trip. And then I found myself, like so many other nights, in front of the computer researching cord stricture, sorting through all the links to medical articles, trying to make sure I hadn't over-looked some crucial bit of research. The doctor in Slidell is really the only one who has devoted himself to studying umbilical-cord accidents, yet stricture is not what he typically sees. It seems conceivable that stricture is a rarely occurring but lethal genetic disorder, which will always repeat in afflicted women. The only hope in such a case would be to take the baby out early, before the cord inevitably folds at the weak spot, like a kinked hose, and cuts off the blood supply. But with only a few scattered cases to go on, every article stops short of this conclusion. I am so grateful you are going with us.

Invariably, when I start clicking through the same grim websites, I come across photographs of babies who have died, their long, pinched cords trailing away from them like withered tails. And I begin to wonder, maybe the way any person would who has survived a gruesome war, if I will ever be normal again. I walk around and imagine that there is some residue, some impression from these gory images and the birth of Clare, visible in my face, causing people to flinch in my presence. In one of the pieces on stillbirth I was given (all of which I can read only in bits), a father said that if this had happened to him two hundred years ago, there would have been no one around to tell him it was a tragedy; everyone lost babies back then. He was reacting to the same sense of social alienation I feel, but I don't think it is quite right to say it wouldn't have been tragic. In countries where whole crowds and villages die from starvation, disease, war, natural disaster, I imagine sorrow just expands to take in more and more; the shadow version of love expanding, rather than being parceled out and diminished, in order to encompass any number of lives.

To escape this sense of alienation, this same writer and his wife went to an exhibit on the human body and wandered for hours through the rooms of pickled fetuses in jars and tiny, preserved body parts. I understand this perfectly. It was this same desire to be in a world that acknowledges death that took me to the Art Institute last week. I went there to find the *Ayala Altarpiece*, the inspiration for one of the paintings in the Consolation Chapel at St. Gregory's, but when I got to the museum I couldn't remember its name. So I went to the second floor, past the rain-soaked street in the first gallery, into the smaller rooms of mostly religious works.

I moved from one image to another of the Madonna, some of adoration, some with her bare nipple squirting milk at a happy baby on her lap. But then I came to the *Mater Dolorosa* and stopped. Draped folds of white and black fabric shield everything but her face and hands. Her palms cup together in prayer, but look weak. The skin of her hands is blotchy, the rinds and tips of her nails dark, a visible residue from how she must have just been kneeling on the ground, raking up and clenching fistfuls of dirt. There are tears on her cheeks, but this is not an image of fading sorrow, drying tears, and the movement to resignation, for she is still crying, fresh drops forming at the red, swollen rims of her eyes. And her eyes are wet and bloodshot, unfocused. You can almost make out what she is seeing, a remembered scene, burning, wracking her vision. For a long time, I couldn't take my eyes away from hers but was still aware of her hands at the periphery. It seemed like they might at any minute fall limply apart or fly up to cover her face. I finally walked away and saw other people, staring intently at other paintings. For a moment, it felt like I was in a church. If someone had fallen to her knees or crossed herself, it wouldn't have seemed out of place.

Through a passageway of stoic Buddhas, in a hall along a courtyard, I finally found the *Ayala Altarpiece*. Running from left to right, bottom to top, are the pivotal scenes from the life of Jesus and Mary. I passed over them all, even the Crucifixion at the center, to the last image in the upper-right-hand corner. It's an image of reunion, Mary coming into heaven to meet her son, and the angels and apostles rejoicing. I sat on the white marble ledge across from the altarpiece for at least half an hour, staring and crying before this portrait of heaven.

Before I left, I went back upstairs to look at *A Sunday Afternoon on the Island of La Grande Jatte.* In the center of that painting, there is a little girl, seemingly made from light, the only one apparently drawn from memory rather than from a model. I have a tender sketch Seurat did of her, "Child in White," four bright shapes: shoes, the skirt and top of a dress, and the crown of a hat. The girl's face disappears under the shadowed brim of her hat. There is just a hint of her arms, one straight beside her dress, the other lifted up, where in the final canvas it will meet the hand of the woman with the red parasol. But even on the final canvas her hand doesn't clearly reach the woman's; they aren't definitively joined. The other ghostly presence on La Grande Jatte is the few shadows from absent trees. You get the sense of two worlds—one of flesh and blood, water and grass, and another, just coming into view, filling in the missing forms.

—Amy

September 15, 2006

Dear Amy,

I'm writing quickly before I lose the nerve. I was just dancing in the living room with Charlotte. The sun is shining outside, a beautiful fall Indiana day. I hung the Notre Dame flag on the porch, standing on tiptoe on the rickety white bench. I wanted to surprise Dave. It's a football weekend, and the whole city is excited; I can feel it even inside our apartment.

I'm unpacking from our trip to New Orleans—our pilgrimage, at last, although it was nothing like what we'd imagined. I'm still marveling that the only doctor in the country who might be able to help you is my hometown obstetrician. God may not be an interventionist, but it seems that every so often he likes to remind us, with a flourish, of his existence.

My last letter was all about wanting to be free from that desire to return home, but going back to Louisiana with you, the longing for the place became so real again, I wanted to eat the ground.

Dave doesn't understand. "What's there for you?" He keeps asking. I ask the same question. And all I can say is, "The land."

But that's just a cliché. When Mr. Sam took me to the house on Meadowmoss to see the hurricane damage, we walked through the hole where our French doors had been, and I touched the doorknob to our back door, concentrating hard, trying to feel my mother's hand on the door seventeen years ago, trying to make some connection through time and space and the thick layer of dirt and rust the flood waters left behind. Mr. Sam looked around, teary eyed, remembering us in those rooms, seeing our shadows. But I felt nothing, just a doorknob.

Still, I do want to go back. I think it's got something to do with that mural of the resurrection in St. Joseph's Abbey, and something you said about Clare—how meditating on the Resurrection, the reality of it, is the only true comfort.

Yesterday, I was walking across campus, very slowly, to waste as much time as possible on my way to a meeting. Watching the leaves float from the trees, signaling the arrival of fall, I became unbearably sad, thinking about Clare and how the seasons are passing without her, and at the same time, about how I have to get out of South Bend. I realized that the thoughts were related. *If we stay here*, I thought, *losing Clare will always be happening. I'll go on enduring her death in the present tense.*

I've never been comforted by the hope of our resurrection, something that seems so distant and unimaginable. But in Louisiana, I didn't have to work so hard to imagine my mother resurrected; it seemed like a given. She was all around: in the accent of that lady in Lee's Hamburgers; in that Dumbo cloud we saw on the lake; in the heartbeat thump of the car wheels on the bridge to New Orleans; in the baptismal font of Our Lady of Lourdes, the only bit of the church that survived Katrina, standing alone on the bare foundation, as if it were the very font of life. Here, in Indiana, those things exist only in my imagination, and it all starts to seem so impossible. Louisiana is a dream, and resurrection an even more bizarre wish.

Love,

Jess

IV

Providence

A letter always seemed to me like
immortality
because it is the mind alone without
corporeal friend.

—Emily Dickinson

Lent 2007

*This is the first concept of heaven that has filled me with
anticipation rather than dread. That I may remember and
know my life and its loves in the next life, but that all the
pain of existence will be made whole at last. We will not
forget or long for the past; we will have it, perfected.*

—Jess, March 17

• • • • • • •

*Heaven is some consolation in thinking about Clare, since
she is already gone, but John is here with me, and now
heaven seems more like a menace. I want to fend off
heaven and keep John for myself. . . . I can't shake that old
desire to fall down on my knees beside my bed and beg God
to give me what I want as long as I swear to be good.*

—Amy, February 21

February 21, 2007
Ash Wednesday

Dear Amy,

The first day of another Lent, our third to endure together. I barely made it to Mass for ashes. After dropping off Dave at the airport, Charlotte and I came home for dinner, and it was all I could do to boil spaghetti and change her diaper without collapsing into hysterical tears. *Why do I need ashes?* I kept thinking. *It's all I ever think about: mortality, this finite existence.* But we went anyway. Late, we walked through the doors of St. Hedwig's just in time to line up for ashes. Charlotte did not stop babbling and squirming and trying to break free to run down the aisle. She doesn't get solemnity. It pained me to see her with the ashes on her head. So happy and curious. She stared at the mess on my forehead and touched it with her fingers. I remember thinking I would be proud to see my child wearing ashes, but how can this be so? How could I have been eager to see any reminder that she is mortal? Sometimes I am amazed at how naive I've been about life, and about faith. We left after getting our blessing and walked the block home to our apartment. I made cookies, and we ate them with cold milk. Not exactly a fast. But we fasted in spirit, as it seems we have since last May. It's hard to muster enthusiasm for penitence and sacrifice when they seem to be such a part of life, our daily existence.

Last night, on the phone with my dad, I broke down in hysterical, gasping tears and begged him to prove to me that there really is a God. He told me a story about the time after my mom died. He said he would cry and beg God for an answer to his pain. Why her? Why now? Why this way? And all he ever heard back was a question: "Am

I sovereign?" I imagined God standing like a gladiator over my broken dad, a foot on his back, demanding allegiance and assent. I cried more than I have in weeks.

You're afraid to love this new baby in your womb. I am too. And yet we do love, already. And with that love comes hope; even the worst fear can't take it all away—I can hear it in your voice. Still, this pregnancy has already been a long and terrifying road. I'm praying for you constantly, as so many are, on earth and in heaven: please, God, give us the grace to bear our love, no matter what.

Dave just called from the Atlanta airport, en route to Charlottesville, Virginia, and then to Sweet Briar for his job interview. It seems that we've been through this routine so many times, and I just don't have the energy to panic.

Love,
Jess

February 21, 2007

Dearest Jess,
It feels like such a relief to sit down and finally write a letter to you. The sun is shining this morning, and I know my relatively good mood is because of its rare appearance. I feel ashamed that I haven't written in so long, but you know all that has been keeping me. Last summer, when I anticipated being pregnant again, I knew it would be hard, yet I somehow hadn't imagined the relentless nature of it.

At the very beginning, the moment I realized I was pregnant, I was joyful. Mark and I were with my parents on a tour boat, winding through the rivers of Chicago. It was cold, and my hands were wrapped around a hot cup, and I was huddled under layers of coats looking up at those odd honeycomb buildings at the river's edge. Right then, there was a deep twinge in my lower abdomen, and my hand instinctively flew down to my side. It was too early to take a test, but I was sure. I remember smiling to myself and telling no one. For this brief time, the secret made it seem safe, a tiny flame cupped in a hand. But then the endless wait for movement began. And now that I can feel movement and call the baby John, I am terrified whenever my belly is silent.

I just got off the phone with you, and you worried at the end that you weren't being cheerful enough. But talking to you, even while we laugh about the temptation of atheism, restores my faith. Anyway, our conversation reminded me of something I recently read by Marilynne Robinson on why so many of us these days are filled with anxiety. She thinks that we have lost the ability to talk about God and the seriousness of human life, although we still believe in both. And at the same time, we have this new portrait of ourselves as either fortunate or unfortunate instances of statistical studies: "creatures too minor, we may somehow hope for great Death to pause over us." You and I talk about God all the time, but when it comes to this pregnancy I think I have shifted into that other way of being. I read countless medical articles, I make spreadsheets, I calculate this baby's chances for life as if I could outwit all coming calamity with science. But all of this seeking leaves me chewing my nails, wondering if I will be the next unlucky statistic, identified in a journal article by total pregnancies and live births: *gravida* 2, *para* 0.

Robinson cries out against this image of ourselves as patients and case studies. "This being human," she writes, "people have loved it through plague and famine and siege. And Dante, who knew the world about suffering, had a place in hell for people who were grave when they might have rejoiced." I keep thinking about that phrase, "people who were grave when they might have rejoiced," for here I am with a cause for rejoicing in my belly, but most days I am filled with dread. The thing that keeps plaguing me is the question of

divine providence, the action of God in our lives. Every day someone tells me to pray or have faith, and I always think, *Why? God
doesn't intervene.* Before, it was so much easier to believe in that
action—God leading me to conversion, deepening my faith through
pregnancy, consoling me in grief. I imagined God's action like some
vague force, always drawing me toward the good. But now that I
want something specific and the outcome is undecided, I wonder
how God really acts.

I've become rather obsessed with the problem of providence. I
have stacks of books on my nightstand. I follow Mark around the
house, forcing him to read and comment on various passages. Really,
the problem is not just about God but the unthinkable combination of God's supposedly loving care and human suffering. Strangely,
or maybe not so strangely, one of the books sums up this apparent
impasse with a simple question: "How could a good, all-knowing,
all-powerful God let a mother's baby die?" So I guess I am living the
classic case in point of the oldest problem in the book.

I want to trade my recent gravity for rejoicing, but on what
grounds? That God will eventually make all things right? Heaven is
some consolation in thinking about Clare, since she is already gone,
but John is here with me, and now heaven seems more like a menace. I want to fend off heaven and keep John for myself. And on
what grounds do I pray? Should I pray like the monks: "God, come
to my assistance, make haste to help me"? When I say *help* now, I no
longer mean strength and inspiration; I mean John. I mean a miracle, if that's what it takes. I can't shake that old desire to fall down
on my knees beside my bed and beg God to give me what I want as
long as I swear to be good.

Pray for me.

Amy

February 22, 2007

Dear Amy,

Day 2. Charlotte refused her afternoon nap and then decided to go to bed at 6:30. If she wakes up again, she will never go back to sleep. It could be another long night here.

I still have ashes ground into my hairline from yesterday's Mass. No shower today. No dinner either. I can't bring myself to eat anything. Except cookies.

How long can this feeling last? I've got to snap out of it eventually, right? When will faith return? I feel so apart from God.

So far the job search has taught me at least one lesson: I have no idea what is best for me or for my family. After talking to Dave, Sweet Briar sounds every bit as destined as Memphis did three weeks ago, and as San Diego and Washington and Ohio and Notre Dame did before that. I'm desperate for permanence and the opportunity to make a home. In that desperation, I could see our destiny waiting for us any old place.

I long especially for the South, for warmth, for green, for a place that will seem familiar, so that I'll seem familiar again. Is that all just delusion? Will it really bring me happiness? This is why I have to trust in God's providence. If it were up to me, how badly would I screw up this decision?

I've never been able to shake the feeling that our move to South Bend was a mistake, a rash decision made easy by the lure of a regular paycheck and health insurance, and by the desire to have a definitive end to my adolescence. We were no longer students; we were getting married. I wanted real life to begin.

I guess there is some comfort in thinking that no matter which way we choose, God corrects the course. I don't believe that our lives turn out the same no matter the choices we make, but I do believe that God can work even our bad choices for good—like the old Bible story of Joseph and his brothers. When they sold him, in their jealousy, for twenty pieces of silver, they imagined his death or at least a life of slavery. Instead, he became Pharaoh's chief steward, the ruler of Egypt. When famine came, the fate of his family was in his hands. "Do not reproach yourselves for having sold me here," he tells them when they come begging for food. "It was not really you, but God, who sent me here."

The story of Joseph offers an example of how God's providence can work through our free will even when we choose wrong. I don't know if God sent me here, but I must believe that he'll bring good from this time, for both of us.

Love,

Jess

February 22, 2007

Dear Jess,

After yesterday's attempt at setting myself on a joyous course, I spent today panicking, imagining the worst, panicking some more, and trying to avoid actually losing it. Last night at Ash Wednesday Mass, I kept thinking of the way you once wrote about Mary, looking in some portrayals as if she might take her child and run, hide him away from all the angels and men who would pursue him. I wonder if you were thinking in particular of Raphael's *Sistine Madonna*. One of the more out-there parenting books I read recently, one of the Waldorf ones I think, recommended hanging this print beside your bed to meditate on the meaning of motherhood. So I looked it up, expecting to find a serene, wise Mary. But what I found instead was a young mother looking distressed, her arms wrapped tightly around her baby, fingers digging into his chest.

Most of the commentary online is actually about her mysterious expression. I guess the painting had been removed from its original context and so for years everyone was puzzled. But at some point it was discovered that Raphael had created this work to be an altar-piece and to hang directly opposite a crucifix. So he had painted Mary and Jesus and the kneeling pope reacting to this vision of what was coming: the cross. Somehow I doubt this is what the Waldorf author had in mind.

Anyway, at Mass I watched everyone processing up and then returning with those sooty crosses on their brows. One man walked by holding a little girl against his side with a bent arm. She had a high forehead and blue eyes like Mark, blond hair like we both had when we were small. She must have been four or five. I watched her go up to the altar with all the others, and then I saw the two of them returning down the far aisle. Her brow wasn't marked. For a second I thought I was having a vision, that she was Clare, but then I saw other children who were also unmarked. Maybe their parents at the last minute had jerked them back. I wrapped both my arms around my belly as I stood in the queue for ashes.

I prayed for you and Dave many times during Mass. I know what you are going through now is terrible. Any minute, one phone call could lift it all and give you the future you have been working toward for years. Or the phone might not ring and the days continue to drag on. I know you worry that your plight right now is small compared to mine, but that is not true. Finding a place to live and work and carry out your vocation is huge. We are both facing daily the possibility that our futures will be vastly different from what we had hoped. I am not going to try to be theologically uplifting tonight. "They think faith is a big electric blanket," Flannery O'Connor said, "when of course it is the cross." Of course. Yes. And so here we are.

In solidarity,
Amy

February 23, 2007

Dear Amy,

Yesterday as I sat by the phone waiting to hear how Dave's interviews went, you sent me an e-mail about surrendering to hope, saying that if it all goes badly with this pregnancy, then God will just have to stage a rescue mission and that's that. I thought about it all night—surrendering to hope.

It seems like the right word, *surrender*. Because hope feels like a threat sometimes, doesn't it? Just when you think that you've got the world figured out and that you've closed the door on any future goodness (wrongly thinking that a strong lock will also keep out disappointment and sadness), light starts to shine around the edges. It's almost painful to see it, because you've gotten used to its absence, and after all that pain of adjustment you don't want to see it for fear of it fading again. And so you try to stay the door, or at least I do, with fear and doubt and memories of what's come before. What a mistake! If only we would surrender to hope, throw open the door, and hold God to his promise to save us no matter what waits on the other side.

The phone rang after I'd fallen asleep on the sofa with Charlotte. The interviews went well, and Dave is full of confidence. It's already warm and green in Virginia, he says. No snow, only a long springlike rain. Tomorrow he'll teach classes and read from his book and meet with the students. Then he'll fly home and begin another long wait for the phone to ring. But he sounds different this time, somehow at

ease. Maybe it's just that he's mastered this horrible process and gotten very good at job interviews. But maybe I see some light creeping
around the edges of the door. If so, I surrender!

Love,

Jess

February 24, 2007

Dear Jess,

I was up half the night last night and so discovered John's secret. He
never stops moving between midnight and five. How have I been
sleeping through it? Is another nocturnal baby like Charlotte on the
way? Well, bring him on.

When I was lying in bed trying to sleep, my mind reverted to
its old standard: imagining myself giving birth. Usually, ever since
Clare died, it has been her birth that has played over and over. And
then sometimes it has been John's, but the same as hers, soundless. I
remember how unnaturally quiet everything was: the room dim, the
clock hands clasped together at midnight, Clare emerging, silent as
a doll, and all of us—the nurse, me, Mark, my mother—speechless.
But last night when I lost conscious control of my thoughts and
yet wasn't quite asleep, I found myself playing out his live birth. I
remember watching the hospital monitor, not to measure my own
heartbeat or to time my contractions, but to watch *his* heart beating.

It is so odd now. My life is running over the same tracks as last
year, only two weeks behind schedule. I teach the same classes, live
in the same house, go to the same church, and lie in the same bed
feeling that same strange inner turning, inching forward to some
unknown end. If I lose John, it will feel so much more ground in,
indelible this time. I will have to reimagine my life as one without
my own children in it, and that little hillside in Pennsylvania will

hold the bones of two of my children. That hillside kills me, Jess. In some ways, even though I have hesitated to say it, Clare is being returned to me by my parents' conversion. At least I take some comfort in that and can imagine I see God working for good. But how could John's death accomplish anything like what hers did? Well, now I'm back to the question of providence.

These days I shy away from attributing any action to God, not wanting to mix God up in any sort of evil. So I am tempted by deism, imagining God as the first cause, a distant creator who set the world in motion in such a way that he would never have to tamper with it again, never have to halt a single storm or even influence a single thought. In this sense, God is the Alpha and the Omega, the beginning and the end points of creation. I guess I worry that if we start attributing the good things to God (a certain person rescued from a flood), then the bad will soon follow (all the others he let drown). Annie Dillard once wrote that when God prays, he prays for his love to overcome his wrath. So instead of believing in this dubious God, I imagine God as the Watcher, the Eventual-Bringer-about-of-Goodness, but not the Intervener.

Yet there is one way in which this view of God allows for intervention. God in every millisecond chooses to preserve the world as it is, as it is currently unfolding. So, in a sense, no matter how you look at it, God is fully culpable in all acts, because all acts are held up at their base by God's choice to permit their existence.

Thinking of God like this makes my days seem precarious. What will God allow today? This morning I read a poem by Billy Collins in which he likens our days to delicate gifts that we receive each morning when we arise. It's like that for me. Every day I wake up and immediately hold myself perfectly still and wait for the first kick. Sometimes I wait for ten interminable minutes before I feel anything. Then it comes, and I get up, assuming I have at least this day.

Collins pictures our days being stacked up like an impossible tower of plates and cups, each one balancing on the one before it. And then he imagines himself perched on a ladder trying silently to set one more cup on the very top. Each day feels like a fragile achievement, and I walk around as if in a china shop, no quick movements, hoping to prevent the cord from twisting, never letting my focus break, continually aware of the position and motion of my torso.

So should this be my prayer—Please, God, allow another day?

Love,
Amy

February 25, 2007

Dear Amy,

It took me twelve hours, but I've finally cleaned the house. After hearing Dave's good news about Sweet Briar, I felt as if we needed to scrub the place free of all the dust and crumbs and stains that have accumulated during all this anxiety and waiting. Hope has returned, and our home reflects it. It is sparkling.

Dave's in bed; I think the exhaustion of the past six months has finally caught up with him. He's trying hard not to let me see that he's still nervous that the job won't come through. But we have surrendered to hope, even if only for today.

Still, every time Dave leaves the house, I make him promise to be extra careful, imagining that he'll be struck by lightning or hit by a bus. I can't stop myself from imagining some tragedy that will prevent us from ever making it to Virginia.

In between moments of panic and elation, I've been reading *Moby Dick*, thinking it epic enough to distract me. But Melville is not exactly comforting. Early on, Queequeg and Ishmael are weaving a sword mat. I have no idea what such a thing is, but Melville likens it, beautifully, to the loom of time. He imagines the threads stretched across the loom as "the straight warp of necessity," all that we cannot alter. Ishmael plies the "shuttle between the given threads," and so exercises his free will. And Queequeg occasionally brings his "impulsive, indifferent sword" down against the threads, altering them in some way that I can't quite picture. Queequeg's sword is chance. "Chance, free will, and necessity—no wise incompatible—all interweavingly working together." The passage ends with this: "Chance by turns rules either, and has the last featuring blow at events."

It's my greatest fear that chance, not God, rules all. That Queequeg's sword will sunder my dreams.

Love,

Jess

February 25, 2007

Dear Jess,

In the last day or two I've been worried that at my core I really have no faith. Do you remember our friend, a self-proclaimed atheist, who used to repeatedly kiss a little wooden box before he left his house? If that box promised to ward off cord stricture, I think I might kiss it, too. I would be the first one in line at the witches' hovel, begging for a spell, running around in the glen or forest glade searching for frog legs and newt tongues. Abracadabra—John lives. It seems I wouldn't bother with God if there were other, more surefire routes to John's safety. And since I have little inclination to turn to God, I am starting to wonder if I believe in God at all.

Last night I was at the big cathedral downtown for the rite of election. Mark ended up going with me because it was so icy outside he was afraid I might fall or crash the car. We squeezed into the end of a pew almost behind one of the marble columns. Two years ago, when I was there with you waiting to go up to the altar with the other catechumens, I remember feeling overcome with mystery. The cathedral with its mismatched parts, the abstract bronze art and six-ton granite altar, seemed like an appropriately strange vessel for miracles. But last night, when I looked up and saw the risen Christ punching through a huge suspended cross over the altar, I couldn't help thinking of Fred Flintstone and the Kool-Aid Man. The whole thing seemed absurd.

As the Mass progressed, I felt more and more distant from the ritual. I glanced around at the people near me—their faces looked blank and bored—and I thought about telling Mark that I needed some fresh air and walking out. I imagined what it would feel like to exit the church mid-service, open one of the enormous bronze doors and immediately be out on the street, the intricately carved door swinging shut behind me and leaving me there with the lamp-posts and the tall glassy buildings, the night and the horns and the sound of tires on the ice. And then would I go back in, or would the air be too bracing and real? I imagined standing there and accepting it—*I no longer believe*—and feeling relieved.

I once saw a video installation in which the camera moved horizontally back and forth, slowly in and out of a garage. It began at one side of the room, moving past a few speakers and electrical cords, past the junk and tools hanging on the walls, past a few guys sitting on milk crates and another standing up and playing the guitar we'd been hearing the whole time. He was playing the same knock-off Nirvana riff over and over. Then the camera seemingly passed through the wall and into the night. The room moved off to the left as the dark yard overcame the screen. The guitar was still audible, still cycling through the same notes, but no longer commanding. Now it was the dark sky, the crickets, a barking dog, the sense of being alone and outside it all, until the camera reversed its path and headed back in, the sound of the dog fading. Back and forth the camera moved, through the world of the garage and the guitar, and then into the night and the crickets. It was somehow more comfortable to be out in the night, to hear the music from a distance and yet not have to be there in the thick of it. It made me think about how much faith it takes to remain inside any house, any little arena that we find ourselves part of, when always just beyond it is the open air.

Instead of feeling relieved, though, when I imagined giving up my belief in God, I felt that same quick reversal I always have at such moments. I look around and think, *Really? All of this—all these people and buildings and sky and cars going by—and no God?* Somehow I can never convince myself that God isn't there. So I didn't get up and leave the church. I sat there and made it through the service and walked out with the crowd at the end.

But does this really constitute faith? I can't seem to get rid of my belief in God, but lately it gives me little comfort. A couple of years ago, maybe when I was trying to pick a patron, I read a book on the saints, which told a disturbing story about Mother Teresa. It seems that after her first dramatic encounter with God, she spent much of her life in darkness, with the sense that God was absent. Every action, every word was in service of the faith she proclaimed, but in her own quiet nights, praying in her bed or her pew, she felt nothing, ever.

Without the feeling of God with me, I don't know what else to do but turn to the books I have by my bed, to theology, and read and read and try to make sense of a God who apparently behaves like this, allowing innocent deaths and saints left in darkness. I want to have some sort of understanding or imaginative grasp on why things might have been set up like this so that I can get beyond my skepticism and actually pray a real prayer. Lately, all the books seem to be saying the same frustrating thing: it's a paradox. We are free, and

God is in control and that is that. "There is an inner principle that makes forward movement possible, but how that is done we do not know," was one take.

Right now all I want to pray is, "God, please protect John." But how can I pray this prayer and mean it when I truly, truly don't believe God has any intention of guarding anyone in such an explicit way? So most nights I just hold my belly and stare at the ceiling and wait for time to pass.

Pray for me.

Amy

P.S. I am so sorry. I managed to get through this entire letter without saying a word about Dave's job offer. It is truly thrilling.

February 28, 2007

Dear Amy,

Going back to work has reminded me that we're not quite ready to take the new road. The weight of the next three months—your due date, my last day here—has settled upon me. Will I look back on this time with anything but relief for its being over?

I know we're not supposed to reject suffering, and that we should, as you said, know that it is the soil from which real joy grows, but it seems impossible to live fully while enduring it. The temptation is to keep my head down, shut out the world, and distract myself from feeling anything at all. But which is more torturous? To miss opportunities for joy, so that life is one long plane, each day indistinguishable from the next? Or to feel that joy and later have only its memory?

It's blasphemy as a Catholic writer to say so, but I'm relieved to be done with O'Connor. Reading her entire collected works in one shot was a grinding chore and perhaps not even the best preparation for the conference, as now I feel rather fed up with her whole world-view. I wonder how she managed to write so much when she was in so much physical pain, and even when she was anticipating her own death. Imagining her in that little bedroom in Milledgeville, crutches propped beside her bed, typing page after page of her grim visions of God's grace, I think she must be a saint. But Flannery's God seems to me the gladiator God of my dad's visions.

In one of her letters, she explained that she used distortions and the grotesque because it was the only way to make people see. Sometimes, we do need an O'Connor to shake us awake. But we can't remain forever in that heightened state. We'd be lunatics.

I remember Dorothy Day, in *The Long Loneliness*, related a charming story of how good old St. Teresa shocked some old nuns by dancing with castanets at recreation time. When they questioned her, she answered simply, "One must do things sometimes to make life more bearable."

I hope this absolves me for enjoying *Little House in the Big Woods* so much more than *The Violent Bear It Away*.

Love,
Jess

March 1, 2007

Dear Jess,

I am proctoring an exam, so I thought I would try to squeeze my Thursday letter in now. Yesterday, I had a terrible moment of longing for Clare. I was shopping in Target, and I walked past the racks of spring clothes for little girls. Lately, such sights haven't caught my eye, probably because I'm now anticipating a boy instead. But the particularity of her, my own little girl, suddenly struck me. I could have dressed her in this, or this. My fingers inadvertently brushed over a line of dresses. And again, it wasn't at all a longing for girl things, but for *her*, her body and skin and hair and thoughts. I had to rush out of the store and back to my car. I cried the whole way home.

For the rest of the day I was haunted by the memory of the last time I saw her. We were called to the funeral home to identify her body. Right before we entered the room where they had laid her out, I looked through an open door across the hall. In a huge vacant space with rows of chairs set up, there was an open casket on a table. I could just see the profile of an old man's face over the edge, staring straight up at the ceiling. His skin was the color of newspaper. He was only the third corpse I had ever seen. The first was in India. Walking down the street to find breakfast, we passed a horse-drawn wagon covered with orange and pink garlands. People walked all around it, some playing flutes and bells. I watched for a long time and even snapped a photo before I realized that in the center of the blooms there was a little, pale-brown shriveled man lying perfectly still. Later, looking through my pictures, I came across that one and recoiled. How dare I, who never loved him, look upon the details of his naked face, no longer softened by his soul.

Clare's room was the same as the old man's: rows of empty chairs. She lay at the front, wrapped in what looked like a little yellow hand towel. I knelt there and stared. I don't think I touched her. I kept choking on the words I tried to pray. I don't know how I long I stayed there, kneeling and choking, but I remember that leaving seemed impossible. What was the right moment to get up and walk away? Mark must have done it for me, hauled me up and taken me out.

Needless to say, I couldn't sleep last night. I dozed off around midnight but woke up again at 1:30 with my stomach growling, and then I was just up. I lay there and listened to the hailstorm spattering against the sidewalk. There was a strange rumbling in the background, which I finally realized was thunder. It was so odd to hear this intrusion of summer sounds in a winter storm.

Eventually I picked up a book, O'Connor's *The Habit of Being*. I was on the last several letters, dated mid-July 1964, less than a month before she died. She was thirty-nine. In one of her final letters, she included a prayer to St. Raphael. I read it over and over. It begins:

> O Raphael, lead us toward those we are waiting for, those who are waiting for us. Raphael, Angel of happy meeting, lead us by the hand toward those we are looking for. May all our movements be guided by your Light and transfigured with your joy.

I thought of both John and Clare. But the prayer doesn't stay at that same pitch of hopefulness:

> Lonely and tired, crushed by the separations and sorrows of life, we feel the need of calling you and of pleading for the protection of your wings, so that we may not be as strangers in the province of joy . . . you whose home lies beyond the region of thunder.

I closed the book and lay still. John moved virtually all night, every few minutes or so, and I imagined it would be something like that if I actually had him with me, a combination of desire for sleep and pleasure at being in his presence. I lay there and listened to the rumbling and spattering of the storm, and I prayed, not to Raphael, but to O'Connor (is that wrong?).

In just a few hours, you will be here, and we will be on our way to Atlanta. I am overwhelmed by the idea of travel, but I can't wait to spend time with you and journey out to Milledgeville to see O'Connor's place. Another pilgrimage. I wonder if they'll have peacocks.

Love,
Amy

March 1, 2007

Dear Amy,

It's after midnight, and I'm up late packing for our trip to Atlanta. In addition to our letter-writing penance, I intended to give up shopping this Lent, but I must confess, I couldn't resist the urge to buy something new for the conference. Silly vanity.

My dad has always told me that all feelings of peace come from the Lord and all anxiety from the enemy. I think I might alter that statement slightly to say that peace comes from abandonment to providence, while anxiety comes from my determination to wrench providence according to my own desires. I've been thinking of my dad's theory since I heard Dave's good news.

On the last night of Dave's stay in Virginia, I woke in the night, feeling certain he'd gotten the job; it was as if I were having a dream and in the dream he was already working there. Only I wasn't dreaming; I was awake and sitting up in bed, and it was as if someone was telling me this, assuring me, although there was no audible voice. When I woke up the next morning, I remembered it so clearly, this feeling of peace, that it gave me comfort even before Dave called—in the middle of Charlotte's adorable music class with Miss Paulina—to say, with his voice full of happiness, "How do you feel about moving to Virginia?" He said that he felt something similar the same night, a moment of deep and thorough assurance that all would be well.

The thing that troubles me about this is that for the first time in a long time, I hadn't prayed at all that night—I'd been too exhausted to wrestle with providence. I remember thinking only, *What will be, will be.* Then I watched a marathon of *Little House on the Prairie.* I felt beaten. No, that's not quite right, because the feeling was not unpleasant. I felt somehow relieved. I had surrendered.

Prayer throws an extra piece into our providential puzzle. Just when I think I've figured out a workable understanding of providence, chance, and free will, I remember that as Christians we're supposed to pray, and then I wonder how this can be, how our prayers could have any purpose in that drama. I'm not thinking of the "listening" prayer of Gethsemane or of *lectio divina*. We're taught to petition God, too. How does that fit with providence?

I was reading the article you recommended by Pope Benedict. In it he says something striking about being ready to engage in a particular service that God requires from us in history: "We cannot always think through in detail why this service has to be done by me, now, in this way." I couldn't help but think of Tolkien, of Frodo and his ring. Frodo is told again and again that it's his burden to carry the ring, but even the wise don't know why. He simply must continue his task, carrying his burden alone (although he's accompanied by a stouthearted friend, your beloved Samwise Gamgee).

It's too bad so many people dismiss Tolkien's trilogy as pure fantasy; really, it's imaginative theology. There's no God to speak of in *The Lord of the Rings*, but there does seem to be "an inner principle that makes forward movement possible." That principle works through all the characters of the tale, the little Hobbits and the wise elves and wizards, the trees of the forest, even the shriveled Gollum. None of those characters knows what good or evil their choices will bring about, or even that they play a role in this greater drama. But Frodo must rely on them nonetheless.

Maybe that is a model we could accept—that a petitioning prayer is like a horn blown in the forest. We don't expect God to come down from heaven and change our path or to take the burden from us, but we can ask for him to move, like that "inner principle," through the hands and choices of others, to help us fulfill our purpose. Sometimes, the help that comes is only the light of a new day—it seems that whenever things got really grim for the Hobbits and all was surely lost, they'd look up and see the sky brightening with dawn, and hope would return.

The other night when I begged my dad to prove the existence of God, he made a list of Scriptures for my benefit. One of them was Lamentations 3:26–29:

> It is good to hope in silence
> For the saving help of the Lord
> Let him sit alone in silence
> Let him put his mouth to the dust
> There may yet be hope

I didn't look it up until tonight, and I immediately thought of you, waking in the dark to monitor John's heart, alone, prostrate, unsure of how to pray, or what to pray, or if you could bear to pray at all, or if you can even believe, and yet believing and praying nonetheless.

There may yet be hope.

Maybe after all, we are more like Frodo and Sam than Ruth and Naomi (they seem like more attainable role models, and we *do* like to eat). God will not let us walk in darkness forever.

Love and hope,

Jess

March 9, 2007

Dear Jess,

I was finally unpacking from our trip to Atlanta, and I came across your last letter, which I had tucked in among my socks. I am glad you gave it to me by hand so I would be able to read it on the trip, but I remember feeling a little embarrassed when I took it from you, almost like I was coming face-to-face with my secret correspondent for the first time. It's so odd how our letters have become this other thing that quietly shadows our out-in-the-open friendship. I remember that in our hotel room I looked over at your bed to make sure you were asleep before I took out the letter. As I read, I kept glancing over to make sure you hadn't woken up. It was actually sweet to see you lying there, propped up on pillows, with Charlotte flung over your chest, both of you open mouthed.

Anyway, it was a beautiful letter. I put it on my nightstand next to the stack of theology books. It seems like a helpful counter—faith being worked out in a story instead of an argument. I also came across that postcard I bought at Flannery O'Connor's home: "Don't expect faith to clear things up for you; it is trust, not certainty." I put it above my desk.

But somehow the search for a sympathetic God in theology still compels me. I feel driven to it, the way I felt driven to search the medical journals for statistics. In both cases it seems I have been trying to crack some technical problem to make my way clear. Well, earlier today I came across what the books call "the process model of God." It imagines God as having two poles, a pole of constancy and a pole of changeability. The eternal God with a fixed nature is most clearly seen in the far pole. This is the distant God of the philosophers, the one I've been imagining. But the close-up God, the God of the near pole, the one we feel by our sides, is a God who is in process.

Father Brian came over to our house last night for dinner. I hoped the entire time he didn't feel cornered, as if we had lured him there with a roast in order to ply him with questions about God, but I plied him nonetheless. He said a few helpful things, as I knew he would. He said that the workings of God can be discerned only in retrospect and that he is always skeptical of people who speculate on God's will for the future, either the future of the world or of an individual life. He said also that providence can usually be discerned only from inside a given life.

All of this—thinking of God in stories, in process, inside a given life—seems to be leading to the same point: I should stop pursuing the God of theology and turn instead to a God who lives in time with us, the God of scriptural and traditional witness.

I want to tell you one more thing, which is actually related. Recently, I've been developing a friendship with this woman, Siobhan, from St. Greg's. Well, it's not quite a friendship yet, but I have started to realize that she is praying for me in a significant way. So many people say, "I'll pray for you," and I know this means they will say my name in a list before they go to bed at night or during the intentions at Mass. I don't mean to downplay this, but with Siobhan it's different. I can tell she sets aside a few moments every day to really think about me, to imagine what it must be like to be me right now waiting for John to be born, and to hold up these thoughts before God. I know that you and my family members are doing that, but it's striking that Siobhan is, because she is virtually a stranger.

I met her years ago, long before I was Catholic, when I was living in Rogers Park. The only people I knew during those first weeks in Chicago, before I'd even met Mark, were the ones I ran into early in the morning while walking Samwise on that long stretch of beach that runs from Albion to Touhy. Anyway, through those chance encounters I was invited to a party and met Siobhan there. I remember her because of her British accent. She is also rather striking, tall and quite lean with unusually dark, green eyes. Anyway, I didn't see her again for years, five at least, until she suddenly appeared up at the lectern after Mass, giving a short talk on stewardship. I recognized her accent at once. But still we didn't become friends. It was only after Clare died, and I started bumping into her in the aisle, that I became increasingly aware of how she had taken on my plight in her prayers.

Siobhan has actually started to stand in imaginatively for me for the whole St. Greg's congregation and even sometimes for Christ—this presence that has been there all along, even when I didn't take notice. And this is part of why I wanted to mention her in this letter. She has become a witness for me, a real, lived example of faith and the meaningfulness of prayer. Even though I can't seem to pray, I am glad she is praying.

The other day Siobhan gave me a card in which she had copied out a prayer titled "Patient Trust" by Teilhard de Chardin. The prayer begins, "Above all, trust in the slow work of God." The whole prayer—and this was the other reason I wanted to mention Siobhan—talks about our experience of God in time. Chardin actually defines time as "grace and circumstances working on our own good will," that same mysterious trilogy you and I keep going over and over. The prayer ends with this:

> Only God could say what this new spirit gradually forming within you will be . . . Accept the anxiety of feeling yourself in suspense and incomplete.

Accept. Trust. Everything seems to be urging the same thing. The reminders are posted around my house and by my bed, but I know I am failing resoundingly to do either. Tomorrow I have another ultrasound. I am filled with both urgency and dread. I can't tell you what it's like, those first few moments after the monitor clicks on, the fuzzy gray screen, the slow movement of the sensor over my belly, until I finally see the black ball of John's heart rapidly pumping away.

Love,
Amy

March 11, 2007

Dear Amy,

Tonight we went to Vespers at our parish, and afterward, everyone shared a simple meal of soup and bread. The older ladies made the soup, and Dave made wheat bread. Charlotte charmed the men and women who visited from the Hope Rescue Mission. Each of them gave a brief talk after supper about how they'd become homeless and what they were planning to do about it. I was afraid that hearing their stories would push me over the brink, into the yawning depression that always seems to be waiting hungrily for me. Instead, each of these men and women told stories of faith being restored, of looking forward to the future. *There may yet be hope.*

When I came home, I read your letter, in which you decided to seek the God of scriptural and traditional witness. The God of story. A long time ago, you wrote me that one of the reasons you wanted to enter the church was that you wanted to enter the story; you knew it was the only way to understanding. (Incidentally, that was the same letter in which you quoted Tolkien's "On Fairy Stories," which, being inspired by my recent revelation that we're Frodo and Sam, I've finally found in its entirety. More on that later.)

With each of your meditations on providence, I return to my dad's horrifying vision of God—the gladiator who crushed him beneath his sandal and asked, "Am I sovereign?" I can't accept it, though I know there is biblical truth in it, and the truth of tradition too, and even some of my favorite books, like O'Connor's. It's the truth of Job, of the crisis of faith, and while it's good reading, there's little comfort to be found there.

But Job is not the whole story, only the beginning. Job paves the way for Christianity, for the theology of the cross: the believer must accept that death, sickness, and suffering are not punishments for sins. Neither do they constitute isolation from God (as Judaism describes hell). Suffering waits on the path of all mankind, but it's not meaningless, for it unites us with God, who will also suffer. The God of Abraham suffers the death of his own son. Being fully human, he suffers on the cross. But we can't know any of this until the end of the story.

And it's still so abstract. I doubt it would comfort one who is actively suffering.

Maybe I'm wrong, and the whole story ends not with Christ but with us. We are living the story now and can understand providence only from the other side, the end.

I did not get back to the Tolkien, and now Charlotte is awake. That will have to be my next letter.

Love,

Jess

March 13, 2007

Dear Jess,

Last night I truly panicked. I was watching *Dolores Claiborne* with Mark and Harry, the guy from our parish who's becoming a monk, and I became increasingly aware of the silence in my belly. I went over the day in my head; John had been moving some, but not vigorously or for prolonged periods of time. Maybe it was because I had been up and about most of the day. But now I was settled down, watching a movie. An hour went by, and another hour. Silence except for what seemed a few feeble kicks. I watched the movie in a daze. A familiar numb calm came over me. As soon as the movie ended, I went into the bedroom with Mark and pulled up my shirt to stare at my belly. I knew he was alive, but I kept thinking, tonight is the night.

"Maybe we should go to the hospital," I said flatly.

"No, it is still too early. The baby isn't viable," Mark said. "At this point we just have to trust God."

"Trust God? Why? What would God do?"

"I just mean, it is in God's hands."

"No, it's in nature's hands. And I know you don't believe God will intervene."

Mark turned away from me and picked up a book. Furious that he wasn't in crisis mode too, I turned my back on him and grabbed a book off my nightstand. It was something by Simone Weil. The first paragraph started with affliction, which Weil said puts one at the greatest possible distance from God. I stared at the word *affliction* and tried to stifle my fury at Mark. I glared at my belly. No movement. Nothing. And then it was too much. I turned to Mark and screamed something hideous at him. I started sobbing and slid off the bed onto the floor, trying to cover my sobs with my hair and hands, hoping Harry wouldn't hear me in the next room.

Mark got me back into bed somehow, and I apologized, and then we both just stared blankly at my belly until it started moving. We must have watched that surface of skin, no longer really seeming like me, for another thirty minutes. Every time it stopped, Mark would gently push on this or that side of my abdomen, until another little bulge or kick would shake the surface.

In the morning I checked again. "Still alive" is his current status. I watch my belly as if it were one of these green-screened heart monitors hooked up to a critical-care patient. I watch it, waiting for the flat line. Maybe he is thriving, or maybe he is struggling. I have no way of knowing, and God seems farther away than ever.

You mentioned the book of Job in your last letter, so I started reading through it. You're right; it's hardly comforting. Job asks the same question I've been asking: "Where is the place of understanding?" And the only answer he comes up with is:

God understands the way to it,
and he knows its place.
For he looks to the ends of the earth
and sees everything under the heavens.
He made a decree for the rain
and a way for the lightning of the thunder.

That God made a way for the thunder is all too clear, but where is *our* way?

Right now I am staring at the postcard above my desk, about faith being trust, not certainty. It was taken from a letter O'Connor wrote to her friend, Louise Abbot. It seems Louise was struggling with providence too. In that same letter O'Connor writes, "You arrive at enough certainty to be able to make your way, but it is making it in darkness."

—Amy

March 13, 2007

Dear Amy,

Charlotte and I have another terrible stomach bug and are laid up. In your last letter you were convinced that God would not save John, that he was not coming to your rescue. This fear plagues me, too, that we can't dare hope for happiness in this life, only the next. Worse, it blinds me to happiness when it does arrive. Even when needs are met and prayers answered, that fear hovers and drives away peace.

I don't know if I told you about this, but I want to tell it again now anyway. The last time I went to church with you at St. Gregory's, we were feeling lost and pathetic. I remember sitting next to you in the pew, helpless. The hymn was one of those I usually can't stand, but the words were St. Paul's: "Eye has not seen nor ear heard what God has ready for those who love Him." I clung to it as thought it were a raft in the ocean. Then I remembered that Mr. Sam whispered those same words into my mother's ear as she lay dying. He said she thanked him, but I wonder if his words were any comfort to her at all. Anyway, St. Paul wasn't making any promises about this life, only the next. Or was he?

We've settled that it will never do to wait on an incomprehensible heaven. How can we desire something we can't imagine?

With this in mind, I've been reading the pope's *Eschatology* (figured I might as well go right to the top). But instead of offering a clear vision of heaven, he chips at the barrier between our present and future. He emphasizes the blurred edges between the kingdom of God that has come, is now, and is still to come, and of God's promises in this life and the next. It seems that we really are supposed to see life after death as a continuation—not a resurrection of a totally new self but a seamlessness. God's promises do matter here, Benedict says, in this mortal life, precisely because of God's timelessness. God is not blocked by the same barrier we face between here and heaven. God, instead, regards us in our totality, even as we are being perfected. In fact, we're not blocked by the barrier either—is that what we mean when we talk of Christ's victory over death?

When I think of it this way, there's no reason we can't believe in happiness in this life. In fact, there's every reason to claim it. I once told a friend, a Methodist minister, that I couldn't imagine why anyone would want to convert to Christianity because it's such a terrifying religion. He looked at me, full of genuine concern. "No," he said emphatically. "As Christians we should be full of joy, because death has no power over us."

So fine, death has no sting. Suffering still hurts. Even if I can imagine a desirable eternity, there is no cure for the human fear and avoidance of pain. In your quest to understand providence, it seems to me like you want to stare down the darkness and come away with some understanding that will help you to believe. But what you're finding, while it might satisfy your intellect, doesn't give you strength. No matter what we believe is waiting for us at the end, we still need courage to go on.

Maybe that is why we desperately need stories—other stories, not just the Scriptures. Which brings me back, finally, to Tolkien.

There is an entire section in "On Fairy Stories" titled "Recovery, Escape, and Consolation." More than anything, I feel that this is what you need now—not philosophy, or Simone Weil or even the grim humor of O'Connor, but consolation. Maybe there is a kinder road, the road that brought you to the church in the first place.

Tolkien talks of recovery as the "regaining of a clear view . . . I do not say 'seeing things as they are' and involve myself with the philosophers, though I might say 'seeing things as we are (and were) meant to see them.'" Escape here is "the Great Escape: the Escape from Death," which we desire now more than ever. And then there is the consolation, "the Consolation of the Happy Ending," the "suddenly joyous turn (for there is no true end to any fairy tale)." And here I want to quote at length:

> This joy, which is one of the things which fairy stories can produce supremely well, is not essentially "escapist" nor "fugitive." In its fairy tale—otherworld—setting, it is a sudden and miraculous grace: never to be counted on to recur. It does not deny the existence . . . of sorrow and failure: the possibility of these is necessary to the joy of

deliverance; it denies (in the face of much evidence, if you will) the final defeat and in so far is *evangelium*, giving a fleeting glimpse of joy, joy beyond the walls of the world, poignant as grief . . . joy . . . for a moment passes outside the frame, rends indeed the very web of story, and lets a gleam come through.

At the end of the *Lord of the Rings*, Gandalf leads the men into a battle that they know they will lose. Only after they have charged, and because they have charged—for their charge draws the dark forces away from Frodo and Sam—does the miracle happen and the turn come. But how did they summon the courage to rush toward their doom? There was faith—that all hope was not lost, even if they could not imagine how help would come—and there was love, love for Frodo, love of goodness. They raised their banners and charged.

Does it help at all to remember your love of that story, of the nobility of those men and the unexpected courage of the Hobbits? Somehow I think it might. You are there, facing the darkness. And you will need the courage it takes to fight against death for the sake of goodness—John—no matter what waits on the other side. Maybe it is sorrow. But there may yet be hope.

Love,
Jess

March 15, 2007

Dear Jess,

I haven't decided yet what I want to write today, a gloomy treatment of delicate themes or a delicate treatment of gloomy themes. They are both so perfectly appealing! Your letters tend on the side of the latter, but I think mine would be better described as a gloomy treatment of gloomy themes. Maybe I'll try for delicate today.

I have started accumulating a little stack of your letters on my nightstand. I actually think I have all of them from this Lent. It somehow helps me to see them there. Occasionally, I take one out and read it again and try to let your words sink in. You've been writing about light and hope, and I seem to be able to respond only with darkness.

In your last letter, you talked about clinging to a line from a psalm as though it were a raft in the ocean. Although it's not quite related, it made me think of that image Pope Benedict draws of the plight of the contemporary believer: "Only a loose plank bobbing over the void seems to hold him up." And he imagines the believer and the nonbeliever in the same boat, both surrounded by an ocean of doubt, what he calls the "perhaps" and the "perhaps not" of faith.

Although I'm sure I'll always struggle with doubt, the "perhaps" and "perhaps not" of faith are really not what's at issue for me right now. At the start of Lent, I did worry that faith was my problem, but no matter what happens with this pregnancy, I don't see myself turning away. It's the immediate "perhaps" and "perhaps not" of John that I can't handle. It's here that my prayers fall apart. That's why I keep reading your last letter. You weren't really focused on faith but on courage. What a beautiful shift. Faith is always straining to see what lies beyond. Courage is not like that. It is a stance, a rally, a charge as you said. "It is good to hope in silence for the saving help of the Lord," said the Lamentation. Reading this from the point of view of faith, I focus on the second part: Will the Lord really save? From the point of view of courage, I hear instead: It is good to hope in silence.

I say this, and yet I seem to have no courage. Mark takes the brunt of it, hauling me up from the floor, from a chair, from the bed. My fear for John's life permeates everything. I can't tell you how completely an awareness of my belly dominates my life. These days even when I sleep I think about John. I dreamed last night that my student Rose (the one who made me the dress) was pregnant and someone shot her in the belly. I actually watched the bullet in slow motion penetrate her skin and sever the cord. I know, I'm sorry; it is so gruesome. And last week when my mother was visiting, we went to see a concert at the Old Town School of Folk Music, and I had to leave halfway through. John hadn't moved for a while. I sat in my car in the parking lot with the little handheld monitor I keep in my purse and listened to John's heart until I felt calm enough to drive.

Nothing really seems to help. But please don't take that to mean that you should stop writing. I need your letters. I need to have them sitting there on my nightstand. I've actually been thinking a lot lately about companionship in times of trial. Siobhan praying for me. You writing to me. My mother and father converting.

One of the most beautiful portrayals of spiritual companionship I've ever seen is a painting Meltem did of Joan of Arc (do you remember Meltem, the artist who brought a glorious bouquet to the prayer service and made Charlotte laugh?). She has it hanging in her living room. I first saw it last summer. She had invited me over to talk about the painting she might do of Clare and also to look through the sketches she had done in preparation for the huge murals in the Consolation Chapel. While I was there, she gave me a tour of the house. When I came to the Joan of Arc painting, I just stopped and stared. Meltem left me alone for a while so I could just sit there in front of it.

An angel and Joan of Arc face each other, kneeling, separated by a thin seam, actually two separate panels, almost touching. The landscape around them looks like St. Raphael's region beyond thunder, but just barely beyond. A dark storm draws away to the edges. The trees are scorched spindles against the clearing sky, and the rocky ground is still hot. Flames run over the top of Joan's head like a halo, or like the fire from the stake.

But the most striking aspect of the painting is the hands. The angel, who is supposed to be St. Michael, his sword lying beside him on the ground, holds up the palms of his three hands in a gesture of blessing. The Father, the Son, and the Holy Spirit. Joan's hands mirror his; just a little closer and she could press her palms into the angel's. One of her hands is connected to her body, but the other just floats there, apparently severed, already crossing over into this new realm. And if you look closely at her eyes, you can see that they aren't quite closed, but at half-mast, as if she can dimly make out the angel kneeling before her.

I know this sounds so grandiose, picturing myself as Joan of Arc, no less. But I am thinking more of the angel, help coming like that, not in miracle cures and dramatic interventions but in companionship. A humbler example is how I felt as a child when I was crying from some sickness. My mother would sit by my bed, and after a while, thinking it was doing no good since I kept crying, would get up to leave, hoping to let me sleep. And then I would cry harder, and she would sit back down. I can still remember the sensation of finally drifting off with my mother's hand lightly touching my forehead. It's the closest I can get to courage these days, imagining someone else's courage beside me.

Love,
Amy

P.S. OK, so I failed to do anything in the ballpark of delicate. No surprise there, I guess.

March 16, 2007

Dear Amy,

Charlotte is recovering from her illness, sleeping fitfully beside me in bed. Her little body is so warm with fever, her skin pink with the heat of it. I can't keep from imagining the details or the dangers of such a tiny form fighting off an illness like the one I've had. So I sit here and stare. Watching every breath, every twitch of her limbs, every smack of her dry lips.

Charlotte has been so insistently active for most of her days that I might have enjoyed the softness of her limp body, conformed to my own for the past forty-eight hours, her hot face nestled into my neck, if it weren't for the fear that she might slip away from me at any moment. How will we overcome such a fear?

I just finished *Audubon's Watch*. All of John Gregory Brown's books treat grief and suffering, both physical and psychic, but here he seems especially interested in the problem of the body, the desires of a physical being, and the improbability of existence.

The watch of the book's title is a broken timepiece that John James Audubon gives to a doctor the night his wife dies. As the doctor carries her body to the gravesite, he looks at the watch and sees that it has begun to keep time again. And in that moment, he becomes convinced that God does not exist. For why would he choose to perform such a paltry miracle, yet not intercede to save the life of one so adored? It seems like the same problem we have been turning over and over since Clare died.

Audubon seeks some deeper meaning in his cataloging of the birds of America, his rigorous attention to their particularities, habits, songs, and plumage. What does he seek, ultimately? Truth, he says at one point. But this is too pat. He says elsewhere that birds would have no majesty at all without belief in God, without the hope that their flight brings them closer to the divine.

But what brings humans closer to the divine is memory—the only indication we have of eternity, the ability to suspend time. It's painful to remember those concrete details of what and who we've lost, but it's also comforting. Grief can become its own comfort, and Brown attends to this too—the moment when grief itself overtakes the one grieved. When they become one and the same, so that we fear grief's retreat as much as we feared the beloved's passing.

On the last page, there is a beautiful line that sang out to me of our friendship: "The laden heart's burden is eased, not made weightier, by meeting another heart sick with the same bruise."

Right now I am in love with the idea of Audubon's birds and the thunderous beating of thousands of wings.

Love,
Jess

March 17, 2007

Dear Jess,

Today is a good day. I even managed to go to morning Mass, and John has been moving fairly consistently, just little kicks that signal ongoing life. When I got home from Mass, after walking through one of those light, focused rains, the sun still shining across the street and on the next block up, I sat down with Simone Weil's *Waiting for God*. I think this book speaks to me more than many things because it is a collection of letters and journal entries, so it is driven by her own obsessions and spiritual longings.

She begins with physical affliction. But affliction itself, even on a grand scale, gives her no trouble, since she takes it as given that people and nature are free to perform atrocities. What disturbs her is the power affliction has to put our souls in darkness. You can see why she has me from the start.

With better spiritual intuition that I have, she turns immediately to love to find an answer. For love to be love, she thinks, it has to be infinite, capable of reaching into every dark corner, every agony, every unthinkable loss. The ultimate example of this—what she calls love crossing the greatest possible distance, the infinite distance—is God being torn from God, or, the crucifixion. If love can cross even this distance, then there is nowhere it cannot reach. And then she puts the two together: affliction and love. The only way to know the extremity of love is to be thrown, as she says, at the foot of the cross, in a state of affliction. She imagines the afflicted soul, without leaving the body to which it is united, being "nailed to the very center of the universe." And this center is "the point of intersection of the arms of the cross."

This might have seemed abstract or fantastical to me if I hadn't experienced something like it at Clare's funeral. Losing Clare wasn't anything like the atrocities some have undergone, but it is the greatest tragedy so far in my life. I have wanted to describe that moment to you before, but have always stopped short, afraid I wouldn't get it right.

I remember kneeling in that front pew staring at the little white box with Clare inside. At that moment it seemed that all my hopes had died. My hopes for my marriage, my parents' hopes for me, my hopes for my daughter's life and my own. I kept trying to imagine what my life would be like from then on. I couldn't picture it. And then this feeling came over me, almost a physical sensation of movement even though I remained still and kneeling. Maybe it was my intense urge to collapse that caused it. I felt myself stretched out, face down, my arms spread to either side, as if I were lying across a bed. And again, it wasn't that I was consciously picturing myself like this, I just could feel that posture in my body, as if my thoughts were temporarily located less in my mind but in my limbs, thinking in motion and space rather than in words. I would almost say that I was feeling the action of my soul. It seems possible to me that at times of great distress or joy we might actually be able to perceive our soul's movements. Anyway, even though I was having this strange experience of internal collapse, I didn't feel disconnected from the world around me. Instead, everything seemed more vivid. My groin still ached from giving birth. My kneecaps ached against the red rubber kneelers. My left hand gripped my mother's hand, and my whole right side pressed into Mark's ribs and hip and thigh. I pressed my bones into theirs as if to force some sort of greater communion out of our separate bodies. And so many moments from the funeral are still crystal clear. You carrying the processional cross as though it were the only thing on earth that mattered. Scott's voice breaking in the psalm. Listening with desperate attention for Clare's name sung out in the Litany of the Saints.

The odd thing is that, somewhere in the midst of that experience, I suddenly felt buoyed up, as if I had to hang on to whatever it was that was sustaining me, the way a child might wrap herself around her mother's body and cling even though she is being carried. Grief came in waves, almost physical swells, but it was at those moments most acutely that I felt somehow conveyed over the swells. The desire to collapse no longer felt like a reaction to grief but to the pressure of God's presence. Do you remember that monk at Gethsemani saying to me, "Christ is real!" I can still see him glaring across his desk, the light of truth seemingly in his eyes. Usually for me,

Christ has been a beautiful idea presented in churches and books, but at that moment the actual form and person of the cross seemed to lift up from the story and fill the church, bearing all bone and air.

Amazingly, I look back on those moments with something like envy. Maybe awe would be a better way to say it, yet there is an element of longing. I once tried to describe that moment to Mark, and the only word I could come up with was *ecstasy*. Maybe I should have said joy. But I mean the piercing, suffering joy of love. The revelation of that moment for me was that in the center of the greatest tragedy of my life, I felt the presence of God, more intensely than ever before or since. And I have to be careful here. I am not saying that the shock was that God comforted me. Nor am I saying that it was the knowledge that God had suffered, too. The revelation was God himself, the visceral feeling that Christ, the source of love, is real.

"It does not mean that God's Providence is lacking," Weil says. "It is in his Providence that God has willed that necessity should be like a blind mechanism . . . anonymous before all things. Affliction would not have this power"—and here she means the power to throw us into the arms of God—"without the element of chance contained in it."

Right now, with John kicking away, and out my window rain falling to the left, sunshine to the right, this seems like a vision of providence I can accept.

Love,
Amy

March 17, 2007

Dear Amy,

It's beautiful today, clear and cold, blue skies and sunshine. But I sit here alone, in a fog, dreaming of June.

In our letters, we seem to overlap our thoughts. You seem to be longing for a God who comes to us in time. I was also thinking that a God outside of time would be abhorrent, as I finished *Audubon's Watch*, and the narrators talked of memory as divinity, as a way to suspend time, or to experience a world unbound by time.

Is that what eternity really is? The experience of the past, present, and future at once? At first this seemed equally distasteful. But then, I thought, *No*. Imagining you in heaven, experiencing the joy of your pregnancy with Clare, the agony of losing her cut with the joy of holding her in your arms—all those events, experienced simultaneously, would reveal God's design. As you wrote, quoting Father Brian, providence will be discerned only in retrospect. Maybe this is a rudimentary way of understanding how heaven will not be an undesirable, unrecognizable, timeless other, but rather, the fullness of our lives, all we have experienced—but fulfilled, not cut short. All our love for Mark, Dave, our children, brought to its completion in God's embrace.

This is the first concept of heaven that has filled me with anticipation rather than dread. That I may remember and know my life and its loves in the next life, but that all the pain of existence will be made whole at last. We will not forget or long for the past; we will have it, perfected.

Love,

Jess

March 19, 2007

Dear Jess,

Last night I dreamed again about other pregnant women, this time about an entire group of large-bellied women. "Mine has a good twenty-minute hiccup period every night," said one woman. "Is that good?" I asked. Later in the dream, it became a two-hour period. "That is not good," I told her, and thought of my own baby. *Does he do that?* I wondered. *Is he doing that now as I sleep?*

I never know if these dreams are when I am asleep or partially awake. There always seems to be some consciousness of John. In the morning I immediately reached for the monitor. The first heartbeat I found was too fast to be mine and too slow to be his. I could hear Mark stop making coffee in the kitchen. We listened from our different rooms to this unfamiliar beat. I put more jelly on my skin and moved the probe around a bit more, and then there it was, the rapid, swooshing pulse. What was that other beat? Maybe mine mixed with his, one slow, one fast, making a third.

Last night, Mark finally lost his mind, too. He found me lying on the couch and crying. Instead of his usual words of comfort that sound a little like he isn't really thinking about the situation, or that he is tossing it off from his position of relative distance, he said, "We can get through anything." And then he put his head in his hands and said, "But I just couldn't take it, not again." Then he just sat there for a while. "You have to let me hold him as much as you do," he said. He told me how anxious he is, how every time he sees my worry surface that his own heart moves up into his throat. I guess I have noticed how Mark has started listening, wherever he is in the house, when the static of the monitor flips on. Could we be doing something differently to ease the tension? I don't know, really. Now John is officially viable, and I feel it is what I must be doing to watch him, to patrol my belly. Actually, speaking of monitoring John, I have to stop writing so that I can get ready for my ultrasound appointment. More soon.

Love,
Amy

March 20, 2007

Dear Jess,

I fell apart yesterday after the ultrasound. The ultrasound itself was so reassuring, seeing John all curled up and perfect in there, but then when I talked to the specialist, he told me these horrifying stories. I really can't figure out why he mentioned them: one woman with four losses in a row, another who knew something was wrong but didn't make it to the doctor in time. Anyway, while Mark was away teaching, I spent the afternoon on the couch doing kick counts, filling my little brown book with hash marks. Mark called between classes, and I just cried into the phone.

When he came home last night, he was practically breathless. "We got good news today," he said. "Today was a good day." Shocked that he was ignoring the terror I had been going through for the past several hours, I opened my mouth to yell at him. He saw my about-to-pounce glare and said, "Sweetheart, please." He was begging me. "I need this as much as you do," he said, "to believe it was a good day." I realized he had also been panicking. He'd spent an hour or so researching kick counts online. "You only need to get ten in two hours," he told me. "All the sites said ten in *two*, not one."

The room became quiet. I saw how he looked standing there in the middle of the kitchen, his cheeks flushed and tears in his eyes, and had a terrible rush of sympathy for him. I thought also of how

I had counted eight kicks in one hour, maybe even twelve, on the day before Clare died, but I said nothing. We ate in silence and then agreed to play cards.

While we sat across the table from each other, dealing and shuffling, I remembered how I felt about him last summer after losing Clare. He became both my husband and my child. I loved him with that fierce, protective, wrenching love mothers have for their babies. His head and cheeks and eyelashes became so sweet and tender to me. Playing 500 last night, I felt that way again. His voice and gestures and his unconscious expressions while he studied the cards in his hand filled me with love and wretched sadness. It was as if we were already at the last station, he with a good nula hand, and me with only a few aces and tens to my name, and both of us silent, pretending the game mattered, as we sat there, in desperate solidarity.

"It would be OK," he said finally.

"I know," I said.

"But it oddly makes death less undesirable. To just think of that whole desert of life left to be lived without children. . . . If we lose this baby, we will have lost a whole family."

We went to bed and lay there in each other's arms watching my belly. It complied. Bulges and ripples came at regular-enough intervals that we were able to sleep.

I woke at 5:00 a.m. and waited. Within a minute the first kick came, and then another. I stayed awake with him, in a state of almost bliss, until it was time to get up.

Love,

Amy

March 20, 2007

Dear Amy,

I feel so helpless. All I can do for you right now is write letters. I want the time to pass, and recording it will somehow make it seem as if it were behind us.

Last night I had another dream about my mother. Or it was somehow about her, even though she did not appear in it. It was more like she was a presence in the dream, if that makes sense. Or maybe it was just my grief for her that was present. In the dream, I was listening to the old Christopher Cross song "Sailing"—maybe you remember it from the seventies. This is a really cheesy song, but I buckle when I hear it. I remember so clearly driving along the Gulf Coast with my parents when I was probably no more than seven or eight years old, listening to that song, and my mom saying what a perfect song this was for this night, or something similar, and me thinking to myself, *Yes, it really is perfect*, but at the same time feeling some intense sadness. I don't think that I projected the sadness back on the moment. I think I really felt it and was aware even then that this perfection could not last, and that maybe I loved my mother too much for my own good. I remember trying to look back through the rear windshield, keeping the shoreline and the sunset and the road in sight, trying to stretch time and make the moment last.

In the dream, I listened to the whole song on the radio, but I was in the house my dad and stepmother lived in when I was in high school, the house that makes my chest constrict when I think of it. And my stepmother was standing behind me, watching me as I listened to the song and cried. I woke up overwhelmed by sadness and longing. I had a hard time clearing my head of the dream, and so I just lay there with my eyes closed for a long while and let Dave wake with Charlotte and feed her breakfast.

Something about this week has put me in this fog. The hands on the clock are moving more slowly than ever. I suppose it's no surprise, and we knew it would be this way as we await John's arrival in this world. He seems to be bearing so much on his tiny shoulders. Yesterday I bought my neighbor, Kirsten, a St. Christopher's prayer card for her journey to Washington. St. Christopher is the patron of travelers, and the story goes that he carried an infant across a raging stream, and the infant became so heavy that Christopher realized that the infant was carrying the world, and he knew then that the infant was Jesus. Looking at this card, I thought of John, carrying so much for all of us who love you. And I felt so guilty about this, about me needing him so much.

All around me it is clear that this time is ending. My last day at Notre Dame, our move to Virginia, Kirsten and Nathan leaving for Washington. The world of the past two years is ending, and this summer it will start again, and we'll all be something new and different. It's a welcome ending in so many ways, and it should be exciting, but instead it's unnerving. For I want the new world to be perfect, and I know it can't be, and I'm afraid.

I heard fear in your voice when we talked on the phone last night. I want so badly to keep this vigil with you, to bear some of that fear, to share your burden even if I can't ease it. I pray every night for your peace, especially when I wake in the night and think of you waking to check John's heart.

I will continue to pray, and write, and anticipate.

With love,

Jess

March 21, 2007

Dear Jess,

The other day, I went for a walk with Samwise in the sunshine, that damn sunshine that seems to control our moods more than anything else. Think of our delirious conversations lately after just a few days of sun. Anyway, I started thinking about angels and why I always picture them dark. Part of it, I think, is how I feel about sunshine. Didn't you once write about the mean sun on the grass when your mother was diagnosed with cancer? Lately, I have looked around at beautiful things and wondered how I would see them if John dies. We have these purple flowers on our dining-room table that look like fireworks, a hundred skinny petals tipped with orange shooting out from a hidden center. They are glorious. But if John dies, I think I would hurl those flowers against the wall. *How dare the sun rise*, your sister thought after your mother died. And so to think of heaven as some sort of perfectly happy place, all sunshine and bliss—it's enough to make you turn away from God.

This recoiling before sunshine and happiness seems a bit perverse, like darkness shrinking back from the light. And that may very well be the problem. But I don't think that is the whole story. Rilke writes, "Every angel is terrifying" and recalls the days of Tobias, "when one of you, veiling his radiance, stood at the front door slightly disguised for the journey, no longer appalling." And Ford Madox Ford imagines God coming to a couple in heaven, "Yet he never looked at us, knowing that would be such a joy as must be over-great for hearts that needed quiet; such a riot and tumult of joy as quiet hearts are not able to taste in full."

But even more than showing restraint, the darkness of angels signals to me a kind of beauty that is lacking in the images of perfect light and happiness we often see. Think of how Simone

Weil describes the heart of God and of the universe: "This tearing apart [God from God], over which supreme love places the bond of supreme union, echoes perpetually across the universe in the midst of the silence." This is not a truth that can be conveyed merely through the language of light.

The silence Weil speaks of here I imagine is something like what Dillard heard from those fields of angels she once witnessed. Dillard says that the silence was as if God had said, "This is loneliness unendurable; it too has always been mine, and now will be yours." Weil has a fuller vision, for it is more paradoxical; Dillard only gets at the lonely side of it. But it is this lonely silence that I think must also accompany angels. How could a perfectly happy angel, some sheltered resident of heaven, dare to come to us in our hour of need, or at the hour of our death, as the Hail Mary says? It would be like that well-meaning friend we wish to strangle, extending a hand to our elbow and saying, "It's all going to be all right; look on the bright side."

So the angels I imagine, now, are always dark. Once I saw such angels, or what could have been angels. I was walking down the street at late dusk, everything just barely illuminated by the last lights of the sky. The street lamps were already coming on. It must have been fall, for there were black, wet leaves on the sidewalks, and the trees were almost bare. I walked on, staring at my feet, avoiding places where the concrete was heaved and broken and where the leaves lay in dark pools. And then something caused me to pause. Alone on the sidewalk, standing beside a few naked oaks, I looked up. There they were, perched in lines, on the high branches of a tree. There must have been twenty large crows. They were utterly, flawlessly silent, like twenty sentinels, or twenty nuns. Their heads were turned in different directions, a few gazing down at me, but most out across the tops of things, into some distance I couldn't see from the ground. They had an eternal air about them, as if they had been stationed there for centuries.

It was the combination of my oblivion and their presence that struck me. I could have walked by easily without noticing them. I could have passed unknowing, and probably had a hundred times before, beneath their patient roost. But whether I had glanced up or not, they would have been there, cloaked in darkness, their blacks eyes and wings invisible against their black bodies. They would have been there, like praying monks are perpetually there in their pews at vigils, like guards standing watch at midnight. These hidden presences, gentle in their silence and darkness, seem to come from that center where the two notes ring out both infinite distance and love, where silence speaks of loneliness unendurable but God endured. These are the sounds they muffle in their dark wings and heads. Eventually, I walked on. I must have, for I am no longer there. But I remember those birds as if they were angels. And I think of angels by imagining those dark, silent bodies that roost just above our heads and wait, whether we notice or not.

With love,
Amy

March 24, 2007

Dear Amy,

I'm in Toledo with Charlotte. She's out back now with her grandfather, swinging in a plastic swing they hung from a high limb in the yard, near the creek that runs behind their house. Her grandparents love her so much. I could never in a million years imagine my own mother as a grandmother, frozen in time as she is, at age thirty-six. Dave's parents seem to have been born grandparents.

We went to the zoo today. When's the last time you went to the zoo? It's horrifying. At every exhibit, I felt like Hazel Motes staring at the monkey/creature/shrunken head man in O'Connor's *Wise Blood*. One in particular, a colobus monkey, I think, and her baby, made me feel totally depressed. It looked so much like me and Charlotte, this mother with her baby clinging to her, swinging from her neck, occasionally nursing. She guarded him from us, from our eyes, and looked at us suspiciously, and for a moment I thought, *There is no God*. My heart broke for her and her baby, in captivity. I even felt some sort of ridiculous kinship. I wanted to tell her, "It's OK, I'm not coming anywhere near your baby, and you're much safer here than in the wild. And by the way, I've seen suffering in a mother like you could never imagine." Pure foolishness, but I felt it all the same. And with the awareness of the foolishness came the conviction that there is no God. And I am no different from this monkey. It was the same at every exhibit: the baby elephant, the baby wallaby. It all seemed so absurd. Charlotte liked it, though, and made quacking sounds and the sign for duck regardless of which animal we passed. Anyway, I've recovered now, and I believe in God, and I'm more than a monkey mother. We may share the same primal instinct to shield our babies, but I doubt she could spin off into that sort of existential crisis at the zoo.

Your beautiful vision of the angels roosting in the trees reminded me of Audubon's birds. As I read your letter, I was conscious of the world going on around me: Charlotte babbling, Lois's sewing machine clacking, the hum of the riding mower outside the window, all the ordinary noise of life at my in-laws' house. I often think that heaven will be like a spring afternoon here, full of happy industry, with flowers blooming in the garden and sheets snapping in the breeze on the clothesline. I've had many afternoons here that I would like to imprint on my brain, just in case we get to choose our heavens. This is another one I want to remember, sitting in the sunlight of the open window, reading your letter, the family bustling around me.

I'm so grateful for our letters. They keep at least some of our time from passing unobserved.

Love,
Jess

We are like a batch of letters that someone
has sent. We are no longer in the passing, we
have arrived.
—Knut Hamsun

Easter 2007

*Pope Benedict says that death is a confrontation with the
basic situation of human existence. Clare's death
intensified this confrontation by bringing the moment of
death so close to birth. The utter gift and dependency of life
was revealed, and revealed again. Benedict goes on to say
that death places before us a choice, and we can either
"keep ourselves trustingly open to the future, in confidence
that the Power which has so determined us will not deceive
us," or we can try to stanch the pain and move on.*

—Amy, March 29

• • • • • • •

*I believe your daughter has revealed the communion of
saints to me . . . For I know she is with us, and in us, and
with God, all at once. And this makes God, too, a reality
for me. Your daughter has done so much for so many of us.
Somehow she's made eternity make sense. The pain and
love I feel for her simultaneously, the enduring of all she
has given to us along with all we never had with her—all
this coexists within me when I think of her and look to the
time when she'll be restored to you.*

—Jess, May 10

March 29, 2007

Dear Jess,

Next weekend is Easter, and my parents will join the church. My mother sent me a photograph today of her and my father standing in front of their house wearing the medals I sent. Hers is of St. Clare, whom she has taken as her patron.

So I have been thinking about my mother's conversion and also something I read in the book you sent by the pope, *Eschatology*. At the beginning of the book, Benedict tries to understand how people come to a belief in immortality. It's really a story of conversion. He pinpoints the moment in the Old Testament that he says breaks with "truly explosive power . . . out of everything that came before." This moment is the end of Psalm 73, when the psalmist writes:

> Whom have I in heaven but thee? My flesh and my heart may fail,
> but God is the strength of my heart and my portion for ever.

I don't know enough about Jewish thought to evaluate whether this was the actual moment of revelation, but what struck me is how the psalmist finds the answer he is seeking. He finds it not in reflection but in "the certitude of experience . . . in all its profound originality." My father's conversion is definitely the result of years of reflection, a long, intellectual journey from his days of atheism and socialism to an eventual suspicion that God is there. But my mother's conversion is more dramatic and has that same feel of breaking from what came before.

I remember so clearly the moment she told me. We were sitting together in the backseat of my parents' van, stopped at a gas station, on our way to bury Clare in Pennsylvania. Mark and my father were standing outside in the rain waiting for the tank to fill. At some point, out of the blue, my mother turned to me and said, almost like she was confessing, trying to make it more real by saying it out loud, that she wanted to convert. She said that when she was kneeling beside me at the funeral, holding my hand and praying, that she suddenly felt the overwhelming desire, almost a directive, to continue to pray for me in exactly that way.

I've sometimes worried since that she is not converting out of conviction but just out of love for me. When I told this to Mark, he looked bewildered. "But love is a powerful reason to convert," he said. There's another story my mother told me around the same time, which helps me make sense of her experience. I am not sure she connected this story explicitly to her conversion, or if I've just made that association. It's actually a story she has told me many times throughout my life.

The day after I was born, she was holding me, all swaddled up, in the hospital rocking chair, trying to take in every detail, when she was suddenly overcome with a fierce urge to protect me from all harm. I never fully grasped the significance of this story until I held my own child. I'd never had the improbability of existence, something so easy to take for granted, suddenly lying stark and lonely and real in my arms. Mark said that the moment he saw Clare he believed in the reality of the human soul. When my mother looked down at me, the new soul in her arms, she tried to convert her whole being into a shield.

She told me later that she couldn't shake this memory as she cradled Clare in the hospital. I remember watching her pace with Clare around the room as the doctors pressed on my abdomen trying to dislodge the placenta. She bounced her arms ever so slightly as if there was still a reason to soothe and bent her head close to the blankets. I heard her whispering sweet things. I sometimes think her agony was greater than mine, having the whole life of her child to imagine losing before it had begun. When we knelt together at the funeral, our hands clasped, it was our shared weakness, more than anything else, that made us feel so connected. We had both failed to protect our daughter.

Pope Benedict says that death is a confrontation with the basic situation of human existence. Clare's death intensified this confrontation by bringing the moment of death so close to birth. The utter gift and dependency of life was revealed, and revealed again. Benedict goes on to say that death places before us a choice, and we can either "keep ourselves trustingly open to the future, in confidence that the Power which has so determined us will not deceive us," or we can try to stanch the pain and move on.

I remember that feeling at the funeral, of not being able to see my future or how I would go forward. My mother must have been feeling something similar. And I try to picture what it would have been like for her, or for me for that matter, if she hadn't found a way to stay trustingly open. I try to imagine her back in Pennsylvania in her garden, dragging the hose across her lawn, forgetting and then remembering and mustering the energy to walk back to turn it on, walk back again and clamp her thumb over the nozzle, leaning to avoid the spray. I try to imagine it but at some point it seems the burden of hauling water, the burden of growth, the whole sprawl of her garden would be too much, and she would just turn off the tap and go back inside. Or maybe not, but every day would be an act of will rather than an act of love.

And actually it's difficult for me to imagine my mother going on like that. It would be too counter to her nature, so full of vigor and fiery optimism. I could feel that vigor in her hand as she gripped mine at the funeral. Every once in a while she even shook our clasped hands, as if in protest or trying to urge us on. So I imagine her conversion something like this. She knelt beside me, remembering the moment she first held me and the moment she held Clare, and she shook with the ongoing desire to protect us. And at some point the power she had tried to marshal in her own being gave way to prayer. Instead of offering herself as a shelter, she began to offer those she loved into the shelter of Another.

She called yesterday to tell me she had been out to visit Clare. She tried to explain how she feels peace, even joy sometimes, sitting there in the grass next to the grave. The headstone reads, "Clare Elizabeth Alznauer, daughter of Mark and Amy." I like to imagine her sitting there beside our names. Please pray for her and my father this week.

Love,
Amy

May 10, 2007

Dear Amy,

I think this has been the longest year of my life. It seems like ten years since last May, and I only hope that the next four weeks don't stretch out like another eternity.

It seems that I shouldn't dwell on Clare's death at this time, when we are working so intently toward John's birth. Honestly, I don't know what is best. I want to commemorate her, but it doesn't seem quite right. Maybe that's because it would be right to memorialize only something that is definitively past, and Clare seems to be so much with us, even now. Especially now. I believe your daughter has revealed the communion of saints to me, even more than my mother has. For I know she is with us, and in us, and with God, all at once. And this makes God, too, a reality for me. Your daughter has done so much for so many of us. Somehow she's made eternity make sense. The pain and love I feel for her simultaneously, the enduring of all she has given to us along with all we never had with her—all this coexists within me when I think of her and look to the time when she'll be restored to you.

I don't want to go on too much for fear I've already spoken badly. I only want you to know that I'm thinking of her this week, one year after her birth, and that I, too, am keeping the vigil for John.

—Jess

May 13, 2007

Dear Jess,

Yesterday, the anniversary of Clare's birth was unreal. It began with a call from the specialist telling us to go straight to labor and delivery. He had seen troubling patterns on the heart strip we had sent early that morning. Mark called the hospital; I got dressed and packed a bag, but I couldn't seem to remember how buttons work or how to fold clothes. Everything was stuffed and barely fastened. We drove down Lakeshore Drive in stunned silence.

When I was finally in a room, hooked up to a monitor, I still couldn't calm down. My heart raced, and I was having contractions. The place seemed too familiar—the monitor, the hospital bed, the worried frowns. The nurse kept giving me cups of water, and eventually my body settled. John looked fine through all of it, so they sent me home.

Later that day, wanting to honor Clare in some way, we went to the Saturday vigil. At the end of Mass they called all the mothers up to the altar for a blessing, and I suddenly remembered that it was Mother's Day weekend and thought about running out, but someone beside me, imagining she was being kind and hopeful, was already pushing me up. It felt that everyone was watching, so I walked to the altar with the others and hid at the back of the crowd.

I was embarrassed and jealous and sick to be up there with them, all mothers of actual children. And then I started sobbing, silent heaving sobs, and pushed out the side door. I found Mark halfway home, looking for me, and I just stood there on the sidewalk and wept on his chest.

Tonight I am doing what I do most nights: sitting in front of the television watching reruns of *Little House on the Prairie*, and knitting. Every week or so I go to the yarn store around the corner and buy six more skeins and another pattern. I've already made a huge baby blanket and sweater. Before this pregnancy, I couldn't even knit a stitch.

These days I can almost feel each tick of time. Everything I do seems like a way to tally minutes and convince myself I am moving closer to the end. I count the stitches on the needle and watch the finished rows slowly accumulate. I listen to John's heart on the monitor, and the readout scrolls by on the tiny screen, creating a record of swells and dips over the top of the faint grid, every vertical line another ten seconds. I fill notebooks with kick counts, page after page cluttered with five-bar gates. I rock in my chair and make my way through the seasons of *Little House*. And even though the upbeat seventies jingle of the opening credits is getting almost unbearable, it gives me that same sense of keeping time. I knit another few rows, count another block of kicks, and there are the Ingalls girls again at the top of the hill.

Mark and I are also watching *Deadwood*, the HBO take on frontier life. I'm addicted to both shows. They are chock full of affliction, which seems to be the common draw for me, but unlike *Little House*, *Deadwood* includes all the sex and dirt and realistic gore. Actually, after watching the first gruesome episode of *Deadwood*, I thought I wouldn't stay with it, but I keep going back for more. It has a seductive beauty. A haunting mandolin jangles over scenes of squalor. Iambic pentameter turns the foul soliloquies of Swearengen into poetry. The camera makes even mud and bruises artful. But the pleasure I take in it sometimes seems a little perverse. It makes me think of Kundera's theory of beauty. He writes: "Lives are composed like music. Guided by his sense of beauty, an individual transforms a fortuitous occurrence into a motif, which then assumes a permanent place in the composition of the individual's life." And he says we deprive our lives of a dimension of beauty if we don't attend to these fortuities, gather them up as they flutter down "like birds to Francis of Assisi's shoulders." I don't think I would have noticed how unsatisfying this theory is if he hadn't offered the example of Anna Karenina to flesh it out. When she met Vronsky she happened to be at a railway station just as someone had been run over by a train. So in her hour of despair, as Kundera says, she later was seduced by the dark beauty of this theme and threw herself on the tracks. He somehow sees redemption in this (this is Kundera's take, not Tolstoy's). But the problem—and the thing that makes Kundera's view seem so perverse to me—is that redemption is only for the reader. We find her death beautiful, but Anna herself is dead. It's the same with *Deadwood*; the beauty is almost entirely for the viewers.

On the other hand, no matter how Hollywoodish the rendering, redemption in *Little House* is intrinsic to the lives of the characters. Whether or not we can respond as viewers to the scenes of Laura running across fields into the arms of her Pa (which I confess get me every time), it is this love, a relationship that is within the story, that grounds the whole show. And actually, if we don't respond and write it off as sentimentalism, it underscores my point. It is almost impossible to enter into other people's love. From the perspective of a distant acquaintance, the emotion of a wedding or funeral always seems overdone.

Kundera's theory of beauty is really his theory of chance. That is why I keep returning to him. He writes about all the important things, just with the eye of an atheist. "Chance and chance alone has a message for us," he says. "Everything that occurs out of necessity, everything expected, repeated day in and day out, is mute. Only chance can speak to us. We read its message much as gypsies read the images made by coffee grounds at the bottom of a cup." I agree with Kundera that chance rules our world. But he thinks that only we have the power to glean chance occurrences and make something of them. I believe we are not alone in this work.

But I *am* like a gypsy these days, glaring down into my coffee cup, reading my little book of tallies, reading the printouts from the monitor, looking for patterns and clues. Only in writing to you am I able to get away from this endless fortune-telling. Somehow in this letter I managed to make it all the way from labor and delivery to the prairie. Thank God for our letters.

Love,
Amy

May 21, 2007

Dear Amy,

I've written you dozens of letters in my head over the weekend. I've been reading two wonderful books: the pope's new *Jesus of Nazareth* and *A Severe Mercy* by Sheldon Vanauken. I came—providentially, I'm convinced—across the latter title in my random blogging last week and went to our wonderful used bookstore to find it in the stacks. It's about two pagan intellectuals who marry and develop a friendship with C. S. Lewis while studying at Oxford, converting to

Christianity in the process. It's a spiritual autobiography, not of a person, but of a love. But it's also, like Lewis's *A Grief Observed*, a meditation on providence and grief.

The woman, Davy, dies in her thirties after a short illness. I marked many passages that I'd like to return to, but there are two in particular that I wanted to write to you about: one discusses the reality of the soul and the other the doctrine of substitution.

I wrote in my letter to you near Clare's birthday that I still felt her presence with intensity, and we have spoken many times of her *reality*. When Davy dies, Van is fully aware of the death of her body, but her reality remains. He feels her with him, not in a superficial way—"in spirit" has become such a cliché, but as in all clichés, there is truth there at the core, right?—he feels her in a way that is nearly tangible, in that he might speak aloud to her and not feel foolish, might write her a letter and address her as if she were reading it over his shoulder. This presence is detectable for a year or more, and then, he senses just as clearly that it has departed. He remembers Davy, he loves Davy, he longs for Davy, but she is no longer a reality in this world. He calls this feeling the second death. The death of grief.

I've written before of the second death, without calling it such. I know from experience that it can be worse than the first because of the emptiness, the hole where the reality of the person once was. And there really is a physical hole, it seems, where my mother once was, which will never be filled again. But it seemed that way from the start with her—that she departed immediately and did not remain with us, or at least with me, in the days after her death, even "in spirit."

Certainly the reality of a soul can and is psychologized away in grief counseling, the freshness and shock of a new death leading us to feel as if we are still in contact with a person. But as Christians with a mystical worldview, why should we dismiss this feeling as a trick of the brain?

Lewis and Vanauken wonder if, maybe, there is a time after death when the departed soul is permitted by God to mourn—to miss those still living. (Why does it give me such comfort to think of mourning in heaven!) Or maybe, permitted to help the living to mourn. Perhaps the closeness of Clare, the *reality* of Clare, has been permitted by God to remain with us in this time. Is she, too, waiting for the arrival of her brother, keeping vigil by your side?

Clare's reality to me is not that of a baby. I do not see her as a floating cherub, which is why the "Life of St. Clare" plaque, depicting scenes throughout her life, meant so much to me. She exists now in her entirety, in her fullness, as infant, child, and woman. This, Vanauken and Lewis both write, is the condition of eternity. Clare's heavenly life is timeless; she is timeless. She has escaped the bounds of time and so of course she can be with us now, and also in heaven. And what is especially wonderful to me is that she is with us in all her fullness, not in her earthly form.

I am sure I have not done the concept justice here, but it still has managed to take my breath away. I feel that your daughter has given me a vision of heaven, or at least a glimpse. I know that others, such as Sister Barbara, have told you of their prayers to Clare. And I hope it is a comfort to hear it and not simply a presumption on our part that it should be a comfort.

Surely, it's not always this way. As I said, I did not feel the reality of my own mother when she died. It seemed she had died long before. I had only the emptiness of the second death, the grieving for grief itself, the longing to miss her. But I have no reality except in my dream life, when I see her in detail, in flesh and bone and freckle. And though so many of my dreams seem like the warblings of an overtired brain, these dreams always seem so clear and vivid and real; maybe they, too, are a gift from God. Why shouldn't he know my dreams, too?

Now I am remembering my father in his grief, and how much greater his grief must have been, as her spouse, her love, and not simply her child. My father endured her death in the way Van endured Davy's—unfailingly. He would have taken it on himself—I know he would have—and it makes me love him intensely to think so.

In the days after Davy's death, Van embarks on a project he calls "The Illumination of the Past"—he assembles all the pictures of Davy, letters they wrote, music they loved, perfumes she wore, and so on, from every period of her life; he even collects letters she wrote to others. He then holes up in their home and pores over all of it, reliving, in a sense, her life, so as to make the reality of her more vivid. This may seem crazy to some, or morbid, or even merely romantic, but to me it seems like the ultimate act of love. This complete engagement of grief is more than just psychology—it is a mystical act, an act of faith. For he knows that Davy has come into her fullness, and if he is to imagine a heavenly, perfected Davy, he must behold that fullness as well as he can. He cannot just imagine the Davy of their younger days or the Davy who was ill. He must see her as one sees a character in a novel after the novel is finished—in her entirety.

I do believe that my dad went through a similar process when my mother died. He was committed to mourning her entirely, although he wouldn't have articulated it in such a mystical way. I remember coming home from a high school football game and seeing the flickerings of our Super 8 projector through the window; he was watching our home movies, listening to Neil Diamond, drinking her favorite beer. He spent so many nights in this way during that autumn. Perhaps this was when her reality was still with him. And six months later, maybe this was the time of the second death, the time of the emptiness, and this is when he met Angel, and knew he could, should, move on.

But I haven't yet gotten to the second point that struck me, which was something Vanauken took from the Charles Williams book *Descent into Hell.* He and Davy chose to believe in what Williams calls the doctrine of substitution—that as Christians we are called to and able to carry one another's burdens, literally, and therefore, Van decided to take on Davy's fear of death. He engaged it fully, imagining it in every possible variation, so that she would not have to. And this seems to have worked for them and provided her with comfort.

If there is a way for me to take on some of your fear for John and provide you with comfort, I hope it will be done. I hope that it has been done, over the past several nights, as I have prayed for your peace and John's health.

I feel energized by writing to you (as if I'm finally *doing* something) and by imagining the fullness of Clare, and by thinking of my dad engaged in the "Illumination of the Past," which gives him nobility in my eyes.

Love,
Jess

May 24, 2007

Dear Jess,
I feel as if I've been granted a small respite. I woke up this morning and felt inexplicably peaceful, so I am seizing the opportunity to write a letter. Also, I couldn't let your last letter go by without a response.

I've never read *A Severe Mercy*, but even the title makes it seem right up my alley.

The connection between Davy and Van after her death, and between your father and mother, made me think about something in *Eschatology*, which I am still reading. (And by the way, I completely agree: it's a barn burner. I'd be farther along, but it's so good, I read every page twice.) I'm not sure exactly how Benedict put it, and I am too pregnant and too comfortable in this chair right now to get up and find the reference, but he said something like this: My own being is not closed off but is related to others through love or hate and so has its colonies within them. I love that idea of us colonizing one another's souls.

I've always disliked the sympathy-card platitude "Your loved one will live on in memory," because it seems like such a poor substitute for immortality. But if we really do live partially within and through others, then when we die our life really isn't over. Our life has not yet been fulfilled. It is a little hard for me to think of this with respect to Clare. Her whole body was a colony within mine, but I didn't know her soul. Is it still within me? Sometimes I fear that through this pregnancy I have let her slip away. When I think of her, I think of a baby who didn't make it, and I turn my thoughts to John so rapidly that most times I stop myself short. But even now I wear the locket with her name around my neck. Suddenly it seems so clear to me that this is one of the primary functions of prayer, to tend the colonies of others within our own souls. Praying for someone you love who has died is so painful, yet it might be less so if we really believed that we were helping them to live on, helping the part of us which is them flourish.

I have been thinking a lot recently of the beginning of our friendship. Maybe it is because John is coming and you are leaving; so much is drawing to a close. It really does seem like the end of an era.

What I think about most often is the night we found ourselves on the roof of a building in New York City. You told me a story about your mother's death that has stayed with me. You said that you were so young and so frightened by the decay of her body, her shorn gray hair and bony arms, that you knowingly stayed away and ever since have been unable to shake the guilt of avoiding her. You started crying when you told me the next part. You said one afternoon your sister thought to bring her a slushy. You imagine now how much this must have meant to your mother, to see one of her daughters braving the sight of her, hesitantly cracking the door and coming into the darkened room and bringing such a common little gift. "I never did anything," you said. "Not even a fucking slushy." I can't remember how I responded, or if I said anything at all. And another time, maybe right after your wedding or Charlotte's birth, when you were intensely missing your mother, you said, "My mother died a horrible, painful, terrifying death; how I am supposed to live with that? Where can I ever find redemption in that?" Again, I don't know if I said anything. What I wish I had said, what I wish I understood so that I could have said it then, is that your mother is not entirely dead. She lives in you—really lives, as her own true self, in your being—and that through your life you are helping to fulfill hers.

Benedict takes it even further, imagining that all of human history and all souls dead or alive are in a state of apprehension, waiting until the end of everything for satisfaction. This makes the Buddhist doctrine of the bodhisattva seem so true, that each of us must wait for all other souls to enter nirvana before we, ourselves, can be enlightened. I imagine it working something like this: I live in you, you live in Dave, and so by extension a little of me is in Dave, and on and on. Benedict suggests that one of the ways we take residence in one another is through grace or guilt. So even my guilt over losing Clare and your guilt over being afraid of your mother place living parts of them within our care and living parts of us within them—all of us awaiting forgiveness. To think that our chance to fulfill our love and theirs is not yet over, that we can still redeem one another's lives through prayer and faith and just plain living, makes me feel so fiercely hopeful.

Benedict beautifully imagines this same idea in the story of the last supper (and this part I can get right because there's a Bible on the end table). Christ says, "Amen, I say to you, I will not drink from the fruit of this vine until I drink it with you in the Kingdom," and then he offers the wine and bread, his very body, to his disciples. Even God must wait till the end for completion. Even God is parceled out, colonizing all souls. This seems to make sense of so much. A God in process, providence worked out in flesh and bone and freckle, and prayer that really matters. My mother, Siobhan, you praying for me, and by doing that truly succeeding in sheltering part of my being, part of Clare's. I think I will start praying for your mother, for Carolyn.

Love,
Amy

May 25, 2007

Dear Jess,

I don't know how I will make it through the next month.

We got a call a few hours ago from Mark's brother. Their first child was just born, which makes her the first living grandchild on either side of our family, born in May no less.

Mark's parents are visiting us right now, but they will leave next week to see her. They will meet her before they meet John. I've hidden out in my garden all day, pointlessly wrapping more twine around the makeshift tripods we had no idea how to erect. I can't bear to see the happiness in everyone's face. I know it is wretched and ungrateful and wrong to feel like this, but it just makes me ache for Clare and makes it so hard to believe John is really coming.

And on top of everything, John has been practically motionless all day. I keep running back inside to check his heart. I just can't stop imagining it, what it must be like for them right now, still in the hospital, doctors and nurses bustling in and out, endlessly congratulating. Even when I imagine those tacky, silver balloons—"It's a girl! It's a girl!"—which are no doubt bobbing in the corner of their room, they seem to me like the most glorious things, like I would be just as moved by their bubble-lettered, glittery faces as by an angel beaming its shining countenance down. The day after Clare was born, a resident came in to check on me and must have missed the purple flower on the door. The hospital posts those flowers to let everyone who comes in know there is only a mother inside, no baby. The resident checked me and then smiled, a little hesitantly, as if she were perplexed by how bleak I seemed. "Well, congratulations!" she said and quickly left the room. It took me a good ten minutes to figure out what must have happened.

Oh, Jess, sometimes it seems that I am right back there, that I haven't come any distance at all. I wrote such a different letter yesterday. Don't stop praying.

—Amy

May 25, 2007

Dear Amy,

On the phone earlier, you sounded terrible. I've been rereading Lewis's *A Grief Observed*. You're right—there is a passage in which he thinks of life after death as "pure intelligence." I admit that it sounds awful at first, but I'm convinced it wasn't at all awful to him. His vision of his wife's soul is better understood if we think of how he felt about his wife when she was alive.

> "The impression of her mind momentarily facing my own . . . the reverse of what is called soulful . . . not at all the rapturous reunion of lovers, much more like getting a telephone call or wire from her about some practical arrangement."

This seems right to me; what I crave of my mother is just that sort of practical meeting, nothing rapturous like her glowing in white with an angel's wings. Just as I imagine you would rather have Clare in diapers at your knee than some angelic form of Clare. (There is no real comfort in well-intentioned people saying that you now have an angel in heaven when all you want is your child on earth). I imagine what Lewis would say is that Clare in heaven is authentically human, only perfected, and it's the perfected part we can't fathom. In his encounter with Joy Gresham after her death, he experiences the fact of Joy Gresham, not the romanticized, imagined Joy Gresham. This is how he characterized her as a living person, too—intellectual, businesslike, brisk, no nonsense. If she'd come to him "soulful" and "rapturous," he certainly would have mistrusted the vision, or the experience, whatever it was.

"Yet there was an extreme and cheerful intimacy . . ."

Which, I imagine, is exactly what they shared in life.

And then he remembers that we must believe also in the resurrection of the body, and he seems to throw in the towel on trying to understand. He wonders again if, to God, our questions about eternity don't sound something like, "Is yellow square or round?" A few pages earlier, he interpreted God's silence not as a locked door but as a compassionate gaze; God shaking his head and waiving questions away, as if to say, "Please child, you don't understand."

Sometimes that would infuriate me, but today, it gives me some peace. I am thinking of God the compassionate father, not the vet or the vivisector. The Father, who knows all and asks us only to trust him.

I am praying for you all night.

—Jess

May 26, 2007

Dear Amy,

Whenever I talk to you and you are having a bad night, as you were tonight, I feel compelled to do something, but I never know what. I've lit candles; I've prayed. But whatever comfort these offer seems to happen in a vacuum. Tonight I wanted something more concrete. I had the urge to go for help.

Your letter on *Eschatology* sent me back to that book. The pope prefaces his whole exploration with a meditation on the Litany of the Saints, one of the most ancient prayers of the Christian church.

He writes that "the person who is thus set about by dangers in time and eternity finds a shelter in the communion of saints[,] . . . finds safety under their mantle[,] . . . in them the Christian promise has already proven its worth. They count for something not as the past but as the present of the Lord's power to save."

Reading this, I thought that I could go for help, after all. I know how much you love the litany. I remember it was the only prayer you requested for Clare's funeral. So I've written out a litany for you and John.

There are some rules about the order: Jesus, Mary, Joseph, first, then the apostles, the doctors of the church, and so on. But I read that you can personalize the litany in special circumstances. I spent some time looking for all the patrons who have an interest in your life—the patrons saints of you and Mark, patrons of childbirth, mothers, sons, children, even midwives and OBs. I made two copies, one for each of us, and I prayed it all night.

I love calling upon these people, these names that have become so dear to us: Teresa of Ávila, Michael and Raphael, Mary, Elizabeth, and John, Francis and Clare, Ruth and Naomi.

As I prayed, a picture formed in my mind of leading each of them by the hand to your beside, where you lay monitoring John's movements in the night. I made a circle of saints around you, all of us entreating God on your behalf. The combined force of their prayers in my vision is deafening.

—Jess

Litany for John Isaac

Lord Jesus, pray for us.
Mary, Mother of God, pray for us.
St. Joseph, pray for us.
Sts. Raphael and Michael, pray for us.
St. Teresa of Ávila, pray for us.
St. Paul, pray for us.
St. Anthony, pray for us.
Sts. Clare and Francis of Assisi, pray for us.
St. Anne, pray for us.
St. Monica, pray for us.
St. Gerard Majella, pray for us.
St. Rita, pray for us.
St. Catherine of Sweden, pray for us.
St. Margaret of Antioch, pray for us.
St. Erasmus, pray for us.
St. Raymond Nonnatus, pray for us.
St. Leonard, pray for us.
St. Nicholas of Myra, pray for us.
St. Felicity, pray for us.

Ruth and Naomi, pray for us.

All Holy Innocents, pray for us.

June 4, 2007

Dear Amy,

I can't believe it—a June dateline. The long-awaited month is finally, finally here. Your tortoise has prevailed again.

Today we interviewed a candidate for my job. She asked me if, given the choice, I would do it again—meaning take this job and move to South Bend. This totally floored me. I'd of course been going on and on about how we moved to South Bend and why we were leaving, and unfortunately, everyone in the room except this new woman knows all too well how happy I am to go. I felt almost as if God had spoken through her. If I had the chance to reset the clock, turn down the job, stay in Pittsburgh in the duplex on Kirtland Street—would I do it again?

Nobody was more surprised than I was when I practically shouted out "Yes!" in response. I didn't hesitate for a second. How could I? For the chance for Dave to do the work he was born to do? Of course I'd do it again. For the chance to know Clare and John in your womb, and to mourn Clare by your side? Yes. I'd do it a thousand times over.

I'm thinking of you and praying vigilantly.

Devotedly,

Jess

June 15, 2007

Dear Amy,

Time is dragging endlessly. Every day seems like a week. If John's lungs are developed, there will be seven more days until you are in labor. Seven more days of knitting and monitoring. I almost wrote seven more days of ceaseless prayer, but of course, my praying won't cease once you're in the hospital, or even when John is in your arms at home on Berwyn Avenue.

Last night I read the pope's interpretation of the parable of the Good Samaritan. He reads the parable on two levels: first is the love-thy-neighbor level—advice for living in this world. The second is the christological level, or what the parable tells us about Jesus as Lord. He writes, "in all the parables . . . the Lord really does want to invite us to faith in the Kingdom of God, which he himself is." So, he reads the Good Samaritan as the church fathers did: "Is not the man who lies half dead and stripped on the roadside an image of Adam, of man in general, who truly fell among robbers? Has not man been alienated, battered, and misused throughout his history?" He goes on to describe how the text says that the victim of the assault was stripped (*spoliatus*) and beaten half dead (*vulneratis*); the Scholastics took this as referring to the two dimensions of man's alienation—stripped of supernatural grace and wounded in nature. Thus, the half-dead man lying by the side of the road is an image of humanity, and earthly help alone—priests and Levites in the story—offers no healing. The Samaritan is God himself in Jesus, "no longer foreign and distant," and it is God who truly cares for the wounded man, pouring oil and wine (the sacraments) into our wounds. I thought it was remarkable that the text here uses the same words used to describe a mother caring for an infant, which shows us the magnificent tenderness of God's love for us, the tenderness we are called to emulate when caring for one another.

After I read this short section of the book, I closed it and lay down and thought of you going to Mass in the mornings, finding comfort and strength in the sacraments—the Samaritan coming to you each morning at St. Gregory's and nursing your wounds, sustaining you. I prayed (really prayed!) for a long time, thinking of God meeting you on the road and caring for you as a mother would.

I wrote to you a couple of weeks ago about how C. S. Lewis said that we must be asking the wrong questions of God—that to God it must sound like, "Is yellow round or square?" Benedict doesn't ask why God allows us to suffer; rather, he reveals a portrait of a God who loves us so deeply that he entered the world as a man. And he's still with us, every day, the Good Samaritan, still healing us in the Mass, in the bread and wine.

Ceaselessly praying,
Jess

June 26, 2007

Dearest Jess,

Well, the day is set. No more tests, no more waiting to see if his lungs are ready. John will be born two days from now, a Thursday, four days after the feast of John the Baptist. I love that passage in Luke when Elizabeth speaks out of turn in the temple. "He is to be called John!" she says. It sounds so historically definitive, so thunderous. But that is how we hear it now. Back then, John was just another baby. Well, that is not quite right. To Elizabeth he was a miracle. On Friday, when John comes, I think I will want to stand on mountaintops and call out as she did, "His name shall be John!"

A great calm has come over me. Today I folded up my knitting, a last unfinished sweater, and stashed it back in the closet with the left-over, balled-up ends from all the other projects. I know I will never finish that sweater, and it doesn't seem like a dark omen or even the least bit sad. I feel so certain John is coming now, and I'll no longer have time for knitting.

This morning I went to Mass, and as I was kneeling I was suddenly overcome with gratitude for you. These words came to me, "Thank you for your servant Jess." I kept saying it to myself over and over. Then I came home and gathered up the pile of your letters on my nightstand and put them back in the box with all the others from the past three years. And as I was stuffing them in (there must be hundreds of letters in there now), I came across that little pocket edition of the book of Ruth, the one we read together on the rooftop in New York. I sat down and read it from cover to cover.

When we read it back then, I think I was so in love with the poetry of the central line, "whither thou goest I will go," that nothing else really registered. For example, I hadn't remembered or really thought about how Ruth is cut off from her family, her husband dead, her parents far away, and Naomi, also widowed, has lost her children. They come together in their loss, two hearts sick with the same bruise. And I had forgotten that the story ends with a birth.

Ruth has remarried into Naomi's family, so when she gives birth, her son Obed is related by blood to both of them. Obed will eventually become the father of Jesse, who is the father of King David. But I don't think it would have mattered that much to Ruth and Naomi if they had been able to know the future. It might have given them a thrill and some vicarious pride, but it couldn't have matched the overwhelming vision of Obed lying fresh and real in their arms. If we really were able to lift up somehow and see the outline of the story, how it will all unfold, it still couldn't possibly have the power our daily lives have to move us. How could knowing a few plot points, a few resolutions, matter to us the way the human faces of our loved ones do?

It is Naomi who takes Obed out to see the townswomen. The neighbors cheer and say grand things. "May he be a restorer of thy life and a nourisher of thine old age!" "May his name be famous in Israel!" But they don't know the future either; these are just joyous things to say to try to heap more joy on the moment, mount it up into something that would have that feel of historical weight and not be as easily forgotten as other days. It is not so much providence but eternity they are reaching for.

The last significant line of the story is "And Naomi took the child and laid it in her bosom and became nurse unto it." In some ways it's an odd line, because she is treating the child as if he were her own. But it makes me think of your last letter—the Samaritan tending the man in the street, you tending me with letters and prayer, and God tending all of us through the hands of friends and family members. Also that last line feels so intimate that when I read it I imagine Naomi finally walking away from the crowd of women, returning on the path to her home where Ruth lies recovering. She walks slowly, holding Obed in the privacy of her embrace, studying the curves and creases of his skin, the sun shining down on both of them.

There is a beautiful passage by Walter Benjamin in which he imagines a chronicler recounting every detail of human history, making no distinction between the great and the small. Benjamin says that by including everything and giving everything equal weight the chronicler thereby accounts for the truth. And then he imagines the resurrection of humanity. "Each of its lived moments," he says, "becomes a citation *a l'ordre du jour*," in the order of the day. The day he is talking about is the day of God, the last day that includes all days.

The order of the day would not be a mere time line or illustrated storybook but the whole story complete with every minute detail, every touch of every hand. All our time would return at once, as you imagined, all the losses, the loves, the common task, and the daily round. Our letters would also have to be there—lived moments, smaller chronicles within the great chronicle, the birth of Obed, our births, and the births of Charlotte, Clare, and John. Right alongside my mother sitting by my bed, your mother stroking the inside of your arm. Alongside Elizabeth in the temple, Naomi walking out into the sun.

"All joy wants eternity," wrote Nietzsche, of all people. "Deep, deep eternity."

In joy,
Amy

V

Coda

I wonder if Eve could write letters in Paradise! But, poor Eve, she had no one to write to—no one to whom to tell what Eden was.

—Catharine Sedgwick

Ordinary Time 2007

Perfect joy could not be joy alone but must be a joy that somehow contains our past grief and sadness and longing.

—Jess, October 29

• • • • • • •

When I think back on that afternoon, it seems that we just couldn't take the glory of that place for more than a few minutes. We turned our backs and walked out. We didn't talk at all, but I could just feel the breathlessness between us. . . . We are right to be stunned by death and ask how it can take us. We are right to be amazed.

—Amy, November 23

October 29, 2007

Dear Amy,

Since John's birth, I think I've been paralyzed by the almost painful joy of his arrival. What has there been to say apart from thank you, endless thank you, for the coming of that long-awaited summer? And I know you've been enduring a joy more intense and consuming, a wrenching combination of happiness and grief. Chesterton has something to say about it in *Orthodoxy*:

> The perfect happiness of men on the earth will not be a flat and solid thing, like the satisfaction of animals. It will be an exact and perilous balance, like that of a desperate romance.

Perfect joy could not be joy alone but must be a joy that somehow contains our past grief and sadness and longing.

Tonight we went to the Browns for a beer, and as we stood in the meadow behind their house, which is a breathtaking vista even in the grips of a drought, flocks of birds banked left and right above our heads, shifting patterns in huge numbers. Their clicking and cooing and flapping was so loud at first, I couldn't imagine what it was. It sounded like some machine until it occurred to me that it was exactly the same noise that John Gregory Browne described in the opening passages to *Audubon's Watch*.

"This is exactly where it came from," he said. We watched together in silence, and his wife, Carrie, held Charlotte in the distant sunset, Charlotte pointing to the birds and trees and naming them with her little French-sounding words, and my happy little heart fluttered behind my ribs. Happiness is so heartbreaking sometimes, so easy as to seem pathetic. But there you have it. In that moment I was so happy my ears were burning.

This weekend I knelt before Charlotte and drew whiskers around her little nose, and when she saw her reflection in the mirror, she screamed with delight. At the Halloween party at the Boat House, there was a fire, and the air was cold and smelled like wood smoke. Dave was smoking a pipe as part of his costume, and I could smell the tobacco in his pocket as we danced. Charlotte danced around us in circles. Later I stood out on the deck, alone, straining to see the outlines of the trees over Sweet Briar Lake, feeling uncontrollably happy.

Again and again, I thank God and his inscrutable providence for bringing us here, to this place that instantly felt like home.

Last night, we walked through the oldest buildings on campus, the original plantation home, and heard stories about the founder, Indiana Fletcher Williams, and her daughter, Daisy, who died when she was sixteen. The little campus museum displays Indiana's Victorian mourning garb on mannequins. This is oddly macabre in the middle of Sweet Briar's ocean of pink and green, its giggling students who seem so much younger than the college students I've known before—or am I just older? The gowns are bombazine, so black they suck the light out of the room. They don't make fabric like that anymore. Black seems muted now, neutral. But this black takes everything into it. It was a black you couldn't ignore.

There was so much ceremony to mourning in those days. People respected the practice, and with that respect they honored the lives of those who died and the grief of those who loved them. Indiana Fletcher wore black for six months and had her calling cards edged in black so that people understood why she would not accept visitors. She covered her mirrors with black lace and stopped all the clocks at the hour of Daisy's death.

It seems wonderful to me, all of it. I thought of the wretchedness of life groaning forward after my mother died, and after Clare died. The utter insult of the sun rising. How right it would have been to have six months shrouded in black, to have the outside match what was within.

In the next room, Daisy's childhood is behind glass: her striped silk dresses, her dolls, her books, her tiny rocking chair. Now there is a towering statue of Daisy on Sweet Briar's Monument Hill, where she is buried. She looks regal and Roman, or like the Statue of Liberty, her arm extended into the air in a gesture of victory, so I had not thought of her as a baby until I saw these displays.

The ghost stories the students told were all of Daisy's pranks. People see her in mirrors, or behind the curtains of the house where she lived with her mother, or dancing in the dust motes under the chandelier. They say her statue screams in the night wind. Once, a collection of her books appeared in the library's rare-book room, which had been locked, and nobody knew where they came from. They had never been cataloged. None of the librarians had seen them before. There were little prayer cards, a book of psalms. They were all in perfect condition. They say these were the books she held in her hands as she died.

This was all supposed to scare us, but somehow this too made me strangely happy. I don't mean to be flip; in fact, I think it's awful to turn their story into a ghost story, their home into a haunted house. This mother's grief was so imaginable to me as I passed through the rooms where Daisy, living, had danced and played, and where Indiana had mourned her in that shockingly black dress. This campus was Daisy's home. Her mother left every penny of her estate and every acre of her land, all her worldly possessions, as a memorial for her lost daughter. This world, which I now live in, was created entirely out of love for a little girl.

With all this in mind it seems almost mystically wonderful to watch Charlotte play on these lawns.

I just took a long walk in the dark. I feel I could walk into blackness here and fear nothing (except the rumors of a coyote). The seasons are changing; no more acorns dropping in the night. Instead, we have John Gregory's magnificent birds zigzagging across the sky at dusk. As I walked by a big stand of bamboo I could hear them hiding out in there, thwacking around. I stood for a moment on the edge of a large dell and just admired the blackness. At night it seems the world ends at this dell, a giant, sloping, bowl of earth on the edge of campus.

Before I came inside, I kicked the soccer ball from our yard up onto the porch—Dave and Charlotte must have been playing while I was out. It was an afterthought, but when I planted my left foot and kicked with my right instep, the ball sailed through the air in a perfect arc and landed right on the porch. All at once, with the feeling of my foot connecting with the ball, memories flooded in—of endless hours of soccer practice in the Louisiana heat and gnats, of kicking the ball into our chain-link fence on Meadowmoss Drive, the chink and clank of the fence when the ball thrust into it. I spent hours in our front yard, kicking that ball, hoping someone would notice how strong my leg was. I was never a soccer star, but in these little practice sessions, I would narrate like a sports announcer, commenting on my stunning natural ability.

Those were times of loneliness, but it wasn't a sad memory. It was lovely to remember the way it felt to kick a ball in the grass of our front yard, to connect across time with a younger self. I thought of your tortoise, sitting in some playground in State College, Pennsylvania, quietly marking the time since you left, waiting patiently to bring your memories to you again, to transport you, in an instant, to a place that would have remained locked and forgotten, but still existing, all the same.

Love,

Jess

November 23, 2007

Dear Jess,

Your letters convince me that Sweet Briar is much closer to heaven than most places I know. I, too, have been meaning to write to you about birds. But there is something else I must tell you before I get into the bird stories. I got in touch recently with an old friend and found out that she's living with her ailing, ninety-year-old mother. She cares for her mother with unfailing love and never complains, but there is something about the situation that disturbs me. In college she always talked about pragmatism, and now she tries to put this aweless philosophy into practice. We die, she says, and that's that. We must let the dying die and then move on.

Of course, she is trying to cope with an immensely difficult thing, but on the face of it there is something so terrible to me about her approach, much more terrible than all-out grief. It makes me think of a short poem by David Ferry that I've been reading and rereading lately. Here it is:

> The old lady's face.
> Who knows whose it was?
> The bus slid by me.
> Who in the world knows me?
>
> She was amazed, amazed.
> Can death really take me?

The bus went away.
It took the old lady away.

That amazement before death is what seems totally lacking in my friend's current approach to death, or at least the part she shares with me.

I can't remember if I told you about visiting Clare's grave this summer. My mother bought a wild rose for her grave and put together a perfect array of tools and supplies so that we could plant the rose as a family. In the back of her car there was an empty bucket for the unearthed soil, a shovel, a container of good, rich soil, several scoops of rose food, a gallon or two of water, and a watering can. We drove the forty-five minutes out to Graysville Cemetery. Mark's parents were with us, and John, of course, was also there. His infant hair was soft and coppery in the sun. I held him as I looked at her grave—the little flowers and cross at the top, "Clare Elizabeth Alznauer, May 12, 2006, daughter of Mark and Amy." There I was with both of my children, John and Clare. I wish I could think of her without any sense of guilt, but the guilt lingers. I still feel that I failed her somehow. I know it is irrational, and you will hear this and want to protest, but there is no need really. I imagine that guilt is a natural reaction to losing anyone. You feel guilty about your mother. All those gestures of love we hoped we could make—all the ways I would have cared for Clare—are prevented by death.

Anyway, then Mark's mother took John from me, and my mother, father, and I got to work on the rose. My father dug a hole just beside her grave, lifting the soil and setting it aside. I couldn't help thinking about watching the soil dumped into the small hole for her coffin, and the sound of the backside of the shovel tamping the soil down. Just then, as I was preparing to plant the rose, two enormous birds sailed into the clearing above the graves. Cathy held John tightly and turned her body protectively away from the birds—they were that big. But my mother stared, open mouthed at the sky. "I can't believe it," she said. "Bald eagles." The entire time we worked, they circled out and back like guardians. It wouldn't have been the same if they had been the standard, brown field hawks that hover over dead mice and rabbits. These eagles were too high up, too beautiful, too strange in this part of Pennsylvania to be there to scavenge. I signaled to Cathy, and she came slowly back up the hill with John. We all stood there together then, before Clare's headstone, staring up at the sky.

It's odd, but I realize that the second story I have to tell you about birds also takes place in a graveyard. About a month or so ago I was trying to find a place to walk, and I happened onto Rosehill Cemetery. I've driven by it hundreds of times on different roads, the many borders of its grounds. I later found out that it's the largest graveyard in Chicago, some 350 acres, and that its antiquated deed specifies that none of its land can ever be sold off for any other purpose than to bury the dead. So there it sits in the middle of Chicago with its ancient groves of trees and five lakes and huge tracts of unused land waiting for more people to die. Since that first day I walked there, Mark and I have tried to go there at least several times a week. We always pick a direction based on whether or not we want sun or shade, and then we strike out and follow the curving paths around the old stones.

The strange thing is that no one else goes there. No one except the geese. The geese pace around the graves, in and out of plots of sunshine, their black necks and heads held at a slant, as if weighed down by grief. Like silent, stunned mourners, they wander aimlessly through the grounds. Sometimes Mark and I follow their lead and step off the paths onto the uncomfortably uneven earth that covers the graves, the old plots slightly sunken, the newer ones slightly raised. And like the bewildered geese, we begin to pace from stone to stone. "How can death take us," we all seem to be saying.

Often, groups of graves congregate around a central, family monument, and then each individual plot is marked with a low block of stone, engraved across the top with the simple designation of "Mother," "Father," "Sister," "Brother," or "Baby." Some families have two baby markers, and some have more than one mother listed. I guess that could mean several things—two wives, maybe the first having died in childbirth. Or maybe the second mother is also a daughter. For if I were buried in such a way in my family plot, wouldn't I be marked as mother rather than daughter or sister? My mother and I would lie side by side: "Mother," "Mother."

We stop at certain graves to read the inscriptions. Some give a little history or make a statement about how much the person who had died was or is loved. Some declare with a famous quotation or biblical passage that death is not the end. Even in the Jewish section there are bold denials of death's permanence. But the grave I always pause before when I again happen onto it is for Lulu E. Fellows. Lulu Elizabeth, I imagine. From a distance, the grave is a statue of a seated girl encased, like a museum piece, in a glass box. When you get closer, you can see how pretty she is, her hair swept up, a book open on her lap, her expression feminine and studious. The glass casing is broken on one side, and various tokens have been shoved inside. A spray of fake flowers lies on top of the book on her lap, and around her feet a bunch of bright, penguin toys lie scattered, toppled onto their heads or sideways, staring with their silly beaks through the glass. It is the inscription at the base of the monument, however, that keeps me coming back. "Lulu E. Fellows," it reads. "Died November 23, 1883. Aged sixteen." No mention of her birthday, just the day she died, and then, as if for brutal emphasis, the age she was when she died. And finally, beneath this, a single line in small script: "Many hopes lie buried here." The grave stands, not as a memorial, but as a rebuke: *How can death take us?*

I always stare at the grave for several minutes, memorizing the inscription again, and wonder who visits Lulu nowadays. I stop by every once in a while, and obviously someone thought to bring toy penguins. But aside from these visits from strangers, I imagine only the geese regularly pay respects.

Her grave is what I picture when I think of the cemetery. Her grave and also the secret lake. Early on in our graveyard expeditions, Mark and I asked for a map at the cemetery office so we could find the resting places of famous people. But we soon tired of that and decided instead to visit all five lakes. We quickly found four, but the fifth remained a mystery. So one day we headed out toward where it should have been and found in its place a path, with no-trespassing signs all over it, heading into a forest. John was still small enough to be snuggled up asleep against Mark in the sling, so we paused for a moment, trying to decide if we should involve him in a criminal act. We looked around for the gardener, who had driven by on a tractor minutes ago. He was nowhere to be seen, and the graveyard lay empty and silent around us, so we ducked into the trees and walked quickly out of open view. Soon we were on what could be a path through any North American forest: underbrush, rustling trees, solitude. We walked along, whispering our disbelief that something like this actually existed in the middle of Chicago. Around one turn a huge, rusted water tower rose up out of the forest. "Rosehill," it said in big block letters around its tank. We kept walking, and around the next bend we saw what appeared to be a clearing.

We tiptoed up for fear the gardener and his tractor were back there at some sort of grounds-crew station or that we were at the foot of some private drive. But we couldn't see or hear anything, so we walked around the turn, and there before us, shining in the sun, lay the fifth lake. Unlike the other four, which have manicured banks and fountains, this lake was wild. The forest grew right up to its edge. Immediately on our arrival, a flock of sparrows flew out of the forest and then back in. Several geese swooped down, their webbed feet bracing the air, and glided out on the water. A group of ducks swam quickly away from them, and then two heron lifted out of the brush, flew to a dead tree at the center of the lake, and flapped together in some sort of joyous dance on its bare branch. Mark and I stood there in silent awe. It is not that it was necessarily the most beautiful lake we had ever seen, it's just that it came out of nowhere: that this little bit of wilderness, teeming with life, with great, dancing herons no less, existed in the middle of a graveyard in the middle of Chicago, and that we discovered it, and that no one else knew.

We didn't stay long. I can't remember why, probably John started to squirm. But when I think back on that afternoon, it seems that we just couldn't take the glory of that place for more than a few minutes. We turned our backs and walked out. We didn't talk at all, but I could just feel the breathlessness between us. And then we were back in the graveyard, walking on the paved path. Here and there groups of geese were still pacing from grave to grave, but now instead of mourners, they seemed like emissaries from the hidden lake. They weren't paying respects, but walking from grave to grave to bring the good news. I saw Lulu's glass hood in the distance and thought of her mother and Daisy's mother and myself, and I thought of the graves of our daughters. We are right to be stunned by death and ask how it can take us. We are right to be amazed. If we were not, we might, like my friend, begin to believe in death and accept it. It is far better to carve our sorrow and disbelief in stone (she was sixteen, can you believe it? November 23, she died, she looked like this, a reader, her name was Lulu, can you believe it?). So instead of believing in death, I think of John Gregory's birds, and the Graysville eagles, and the Rosehill geese, and have hope that behind the obvious markers of death, life lies hidden and waiting.

Love,
Amy

Bibliography

Aristotle. *The Nicomachean Ethics.* Cambridge: Harvard University Press, 1994.

Berger, Peter. *A Rumor of Angels: Modern Society and the Rediscovery of the Supernatural.* New York: Doubleday, 1969.

Benjamin, Walter. *Illuminations.* Translated by Harry Zone. New York: Schocken Books, 1969.

Benson, Monsignor Robert Hugh. *The Friendship of Christ.* New York: Longmans, Green, and Co., 1912.

Berry, Wendell. *Life Is a Miracle: An Essay Against Modern Superstition.* Washington, D.C.: Counterpoint, 2000.

Brown, John Gregory. *Audubon's Watch.* Boston: Houghton Mifflin, 2001.

Cave, Nick. "Into My Arms." In *The Boatman's Call.* Burbank: Reprise Records, 1997.

Chapman, Graham, John Cleese, and others. *Life of Brian.* New York: Criterion Collection, 1999, 1979.

Chardin, Teilhard de. *Hymn of the Universe.* New York: Harper & Row, 1965.

Chesterton, G. K. *Heretics / Orthodoxy.* Nashville: Thomas Nelson Publishers, 2000.

Coetzee, J. M. *Elizabeth Costello.* New York: Viking, 2003.

Collins, Billy. "Days." In *Sailing Alone Around the Room.* New York: Random House, 2002.

Coppola, Francis Ford. *Peggy Sue Got Married.* Michigan: CBS/Fox Video, 1987.

Cortazar, Julio. *Hopscotch.* Translated by Gregory Rabassa. New York: Pantheon, 1987.

Day, Dorothy. *The Long Loneliness.* San Francisco: Harper & Row, 1981, 1952.

Dillard, Annie. *Pilgrim at Tinker Creek.* New York: Harper Perennial, 1987.

Dillard, Annie. *Teaching a Stone to Talk.* New York: Harper Perennial, 1982.

Dinesen, Isak. *Out of Africa and Shadows on the Grass.* New York: Knopf Doubleday Publishing Group, 1989.

Dubay, Thomas. *The Fire Within.* San Francisco: Ignatius, 1989.

Duras, Marguerite. *The Lover.* New York: Pantheon Books, 1985.

Eliot, George. *Middlemarch.* New York: Modern Library, 1994.

Ferry, David. "At the Bus Stop; Eurydice." In *Of No Country I Know.* Chicago: University of Chicago Press, 1999.

Flogging Molly. "Rebels of the Sacred Heart," in *Drunken Lullabies*. Side One Dummy Records, 2007.

Ford, Ford Madox. "On Heaven." In *Selected Poems*. Manchester: Carcanet, 1997.

Funk, Mary Margaret. *Tools Matter for Practicing the Spiritual Life*. New York: Continuum, 2004.

Goldman, James. *The Lion in Winter*. DVD. Directed by Anthony Harvey. Los Angeles: MGM, 2001.

Greene, Graham. *The Power and the Glory*. New York, Viking Press, 1946, 1940.

Hamilton, J. Wallace. *Horns and Halos in Human NatureI*. Grand Rapids: Fleming H. Revell, 1954.

Hearne, Vicki. *Adam's Task: Calling Animals by Name*. New York: Knofp, 1986.

Hegel, Georg Wilhelm Friedrich. *Hegel's Phenomenology of Spirit*. Translated by A. V. Miller. Oxford: Oxford University Press, 1977.

Hegel, Georg Wilhelm Friedrich. *Lectures on the Philosophy of World History: Introduction*. Translated by H. B. Nisbet. Cambridge: Cambridge University Press, 1975.

Indigo Girls. "World Falls." In *Nomads, Indians, Saints*. New York: Epic, 2000.

Jarrell, Randall. "Sick Child." In *The Complete Poems*. New York: Farrar, Straus and Giroux, 1969.

Joyce, James. *Stephen Hero*. Norfolk: New Directions, 1963.

Kelty, Matthew. *Gethsemani Homilies*. Quincy, Ill. : Franciscan Press, 2001.

Kundera, Milan. *The Unbearable Lightness of Being*. New York: Harper & Row, 1984.

L'Engle, Madeleine. *A Circle of Quiet*. New York, Farrar, Straus and Giroux 1972.

Lewis, C. S. *A Grief Observed*. San Francisco: HarperSanFrancisco, 2001, 1961.

Lewis, C. S. *Surprised by Joy: The Shape of My Early Life*. London: Geoffrey Bles, 1955.

Lobel, Arnold. *Frog and Toad Are Friends*. New York: Harper & Row, 1970.

Malamud, Bernard. *The Natural*. DVD. Directed by Barry Levinson. Los Angeles: TriStar Pictures, 1984.

Melville, Herman. *Moby Dick, or, the Whale*. New York: Modern Library, 1992, 1930.

Merton, Thomas. *No Man Is an Island*. New York: Harcourt, 1983.

Merton, Thomas. *The Seven Storey Mountain*. New York: Harcourt, Brace, 1948.

Montaigne, Michel de. *The Complete Essays*. Translated by Donald M. Frame. Stanford: Stanford University Press, 1965.

Monty Python. "Spam." In *The Complete Monty Python's Flying Circus*. DVD. Los Angeles: A&E Home Video, 2000.

Nietzsche, Friedrich. *Thus Spoke Zarathustra*. Translated by Walter Kaufman. New York: Viking, 1954.

Norwich, Julian. *Revelations of Divine Love*. London: Penguin, 1998.

O'Connor, Flannery. *The Habit of Being: Letters*. New York: Farrar, Straus and Giroux, 1979.

O'Connor, Flannery. *Collected Works*. New York : Literary Classics of the United States: Distributed by Penguin Books, 1988.

Pascal, Blaise. *Pascal's Pensées*. London: Penguin, 1966.

Plath, Sylvia. "Black Rook in Rainy Weather." In *Collected Poems*. Cutchogue: Buccaneer Books, 1998.

Plath, Sylvia. "Mirror." In *Collected Poems*. Cutchogue: Buccaneer Books, 1998.

Pope Benedict XVI. *God Is Love: Deus Caritas Est*. Boston: Pauline Books & Media, 2006.

Pope Benedict XVI. *Jesus of Nazareth: From the Baptism in the Jordan to the Transfiguration*. New York: Random House, 2007.

Rahner, Hugo. *Man at Play*. London: Burns and Oates, 1965.

Ratzinger, Joseph Cardinal. *Eschatology: Death and Eternal Life.* Washington, D.C.: Catholic University of America Press, 1977.

Ratzinger, Joseph Cardinal. *Introduction to Christianity.* San Francisco: Ignatius Press, 2004.

Rilke, Rainer Maria. "Duino Elegies." In *Ahead of All Parting: The Selected Poetry and Prose of Rainer Maria Rilke.* New York: The Modern Library, 1995.

Robinson, Marilynne. *The Death of Adam: Essays on Modern Thought.* New York: Picador, 2005.

Robinson, Marilynne. *Gilead.* New York: Farrar, Straus and Giroux, 2004.

Robinson, Marilynne. *Housekeeping.* New York: Picador, 2004.

Saint Augustine. "Letter 130." In *Saint Augustine: Letters. Vol. 2 (83-130).* Washington, D.C.: Catholic University of America Press, 1966.

Saint-Exupéry, Antoine de. *The Little Prince.* New York: Harcourt, Brace & World, 1943.

Saint Teresa of Avila. *The Life of Teresa of Jesus: The Autobiography of Teresa of Avila.* New York: Doubleday, 1991.

Saint Teresa of Avila. *Interior Castles.* New York: Image Doubleday, 1989.

Tolkein, J. R. R. "On Fairy-Stories." In *Monsters and the Critics.* Boston: Houghton Mifflin, 1984.

Tolkien, J.R.R. *The Return of the King: Being the Third Part of the Lord of the Rings.* Boston: Houghton Mifflin Co., 1965.

Vanauken, Sheldon. *A Severe Mercy.* San Francisco: Harper & Row, 1980.

Waugh, Evelyn. *Brideshead Revisited.* New York: Little, Brown and Company, 1973.

Weil, Simone. *Waiting for God.* New York: G. P. Putnam's Sons, 1951.

Welch, Gillian. "I Had a Real Good Mother and Father." In *Soul Journey.* Nashville: Acony, 2003.

Yonge, Charlotte M. *The Daisy Chain, or, Aspirations: A Family Chronicle.* London: Virago, 1988, 1873.

About the Authors

Amy Andrews won the *Annie Dillard Award for Creative Nonfiction* in 2005 and teaches mathematics at Northwestern University. She lives in Evanston with her husband and two children.

Jessica Mesman Griffith's writing has appeared in many publications, including *Image* and *Elle*, and has been noted in *Best American Essays*. She lives in Sweet Briar, Virginia, with her husband and children.

Also Available

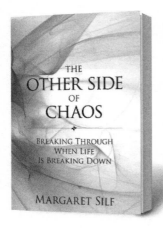

The Other Side of Chaos
Breaking Through When Life is Breaking Down
$13.95 • 3306-1 • Paperback

In *The Other Side of Chaos*, best-selling author Margaret Silf looks closely at the subject of chaos—and the intrinsic transition it brings—through the lens of Christian spirituality. Through Scripture stories and verses, personal accounts, and other anecdotes, Silf helps us develop an authentic "spirituality of transition" that leads us to live out life's changes constructively, creatively, and confidently.

Also Available

Thrift Store Saints
Meeting Jesus 25¢ at a Time
$13.95 • 3301-2 • Paperback

Thrift Store Saints is a collection of true stories based on Jane Knuth's experiences serving the poor at a St. Vincent de Paul thrift store in the inner city of Kalamazoo, Michigan. At the outset of the book, Knuth is a reluctant new volunteer at the store, sharing that her middle-class, suburban, church-going background has not prepared her well for this kind of work. By the end of the book, Knuth has undergone a transformation of sorts, and neither she nor we can ever view the poor in the same way again.

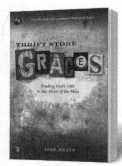

Thrift Store Graces
Finding God's Gifts in the Midst of the Mess
$13.95 • 3692-1 • Paperback

In *Thrift Store Graces*, Knuth introduces us to some far more challenging personal situations that emerge as a result of her volunteer work—where she learns that when we help the poor, they end up helping us. Additionally, she invites us to join her as she hesitantly embarks on a pilgrimage to Medjugorje in war-torn Bosnia. Through it all, her delightful sense of humor keeps her going, along with her conviction that some of God's greatest gifts come disguised as difficulties.

To order, call 800-621-1008, visit www.loyolapress.com, or visit your local bookseller.

LOYOLA PRESS.
A JESUIT MINISTRY

Continue the Conversation

If you enjoyed this book, then connect with Loyola Press to continue the conversation, engage with other readers, and find out about new and upcoming books from your favorite spiritual writers.

Visit us at **www.LoyolaPress.com** to create an account and register for our newsletters.

Or you can just click on the code to the right with your smartphone to sign up.

Connect with us on the following:

Facebook   **Twitter**   **You Tube**
facebook.com/loyolapress twitter.com/loyolapress youtube.com/loyolapress